Sure-Thing Options Trading

Other Books by George Angell

WINNING IN THE COMMODITIES MARKET
COMPUTER-PROVEN COMMODITY SPREADS

GEORGE ANGELL

Sure-Thing
Options Trading

A MONEY-MAKING GUIDE
TO THE NEW LISTED STOCK
AND COMMODITY OPTIONS
MARKETS

DOUBLEDAY & COMPANY, INC.
GARDEN CITY, NEW YORK
1983

Library of Congress Cataloging in Publication Data

Angell, George.
  Sure-thing options trading.

  Includes index.
  1. Put and call transactions. I. Title.
HG6042.A5 1983   332.64'52
ISBN 0-385-18080-2
Library of Congress Catalog Card Number 82-45281

For Jana

Acknowledgments

Since so many of the trading strategies discussed here are new, especially those covering stock index futures and options on futures, I've relied on information provided by a number of leading futures exchanges. Among them, I'd like to thank the Chicago Board of Trade, for information concerning its new Treasury bond option contract; the New York Commodity Exchange, for details of its gold options; and the Coffee, Sugar & Cocoa Exchange, for information on its sugar options. Since the regulatory issues are still in flux concerning the new options, I'm alone to blame for any inaccuracies. Every exchange was careful to explain that the new futures options program was still tentative.

For the section on stock index futures, I'm indebted to the marketing department of the Kansas City Board of Trade and the Chicago Mercantile Exchange.

For providing information or leading me to sources of information that made this book possible, I'd like to express a special note of thanks to Dr. Fredric Goodman, publisher of the *EVM Marketweek* advisory service in Los Angeles, who was instrumental in generating my interest in options; Gail Osten, of the Chicago Mercantile Exchange, for suggesting a number of valuable sources; and Alex Reik, for sharing his trading strategies with me.

Contents

Introduction

There's money to be made in the new options and index markets. And plenty of it. What's so amazing about the success of the new markets is that ten years ago—and in the case of index futures, just one year ago—they didn't exist. The innovative, fresh, and fancy financial products being served up on Wall Street these days have whetted the appetite of even those skeptics who thought there would never be an improvement on the common share. Stock is still king, but now there's a new wrinkle in the investment game— highly leveraged, fast-paced, versatile options and index futures, complementary financial instruments to the common share. Wall Street is only beginning to gear up for these new financial products of the eighties; their full potential is yet to be tapped. Regardless of whether you include yourself among the ranks of small investors or large institutional managers, there's an options strategy that's right for you. Exploring those strategies, many of which actually *lower* the risk of investing in common stocks, is what this book's all about.

While options trading in one form or another has existed for hundreds of years, the new options market got off the ground in 1973. Starting with just 16 call options traded on just one exchange, the options business has mushroomed to the point where listed put and call options are traded in New York, Philadelphia, Chicago, and San Francisco. So eager are the exchanges to sign up new stocks for options trading that a lottery has to be held to equalize the opportunity to trade the most popular stocks. During 1981 more than 100 million option contracts changed hands, a number representing only 16 per cent fewer shares than were traded on the New York Stock Exchange that year.

What's behind the options boom? Certainly, an opportunity to make big money. Investor enthusiasm is always fueled by the story of the "big killing" made on the Street. In recent months the corporate takeover has been popular. Headlines such as "Calls on Take-Over Stocks Soar," which appeared in *Barron's* during October 1981, related the huge profits being made by those playing the takeover game, culminating in the now notorious Santa Fe International incident. It seems that just prior to the announcement that Santa Fe International was being acquired by Kuwait Petroleum Corporation, near-worthless call options, some trading for as little as a sixteenth or an eighth, were bought up in huge quantities. Upon announcement of the news, the near-worthless calls soared in value and millions of dollars changed hands as a result. Naturally, the Securities and Exchange Commission, sensing insider manipulation of the stock, stepped in and staged an investigation. Someone knew the takeover was in the offing.

The Santa Fe affair, coming as it did on the heels of a number of takeover bids—St. Joe Minerals, Kennecott, Amax, and Pennzoil had all been previous targets—hardly seemed startling. Investors had grown to accept the occasional windfall profit that resulted in sheer bonanzas for those armed with the necessary knowledge, nerve, and money to play the takeover game. Among recent winners in the takeover ranks were St. Joe Minerals, which gained $15 a share the day after Seagram made a $2.5 billion bid, offering $45 a share. For the buyer of St. Joe call options, the news was welcome indeed. Call options trading for $1,875 per 100 shares of stock the day before the news hit were bringing $15,500 the day after. No sooner did the St. Joe story hit the financial pages than Standard Oil of Ohio began bidding for Kennecott Corporation. Standard Oil bid $62 a share for Kennecott, whose shares were currently trading at $27. Once again, the high-leveraged call options provided the big winnings. A $1,250 investment in Kennecott calls was worth $19,000 the following day. When Dean Witter became a takeover target, its call options soared in value from $\frac{3}{8}$ point to $13 a share, or $1,300 on the $37.50 investment.

Unfortunately, these success stories are relatively few in number among option buyers. A full 25 per cent of all listed options expire worthless—not worth even a dime. But to the sophisticated option investor, who more often than not writes, spreads, strad-dles, or otherwise hedges his risks in a variety of trading strategies, options provide a more certain avenue to profit. While the big-money deals capture the headlines, the real insiders make their money quietly, yet consistently, on high-percentage trades that favor one or another option strategy. Learning to use these lesser known professional trading strategies is what this book is about.

Wall Street has not sat idly by in the past 10 years while the op-tions boom has been growing. On the contrary, the initial success of the Chicago Board Options Exchange soon captured the atten-tion and then the imitation of those Street watchers in New York, Philadelphia, and San Francisco—all cities that maintain options exchanges today. Just as Chicago provided the leadership in intro-ducing listed stock options trading during the early seventies, it's also the first to trade options on financial futures, an innovative new product introduced by the Chicago Board of Trade in the mid-seventies. While the success of the commodity options idea is still to be proven, the viability of the next generation spin-off from the listed stock option, the stock index futures contract, is already assured. For years, stock market pundits spoke in theoretical terms of buying this average or that. Now, with the new stock index futures, you *can* buy the averages. Stock index futures are currently being traded in New York, Chicago, and Kansas City with additional contract proposals in the works, including plans to trade group averages on drug, computer, air transport and petro-leum stocks, among others.

For the stock market investor who enjoys the flexibility of being able to choose among high- and low-risk strategies, the opportu-nities on Wall Street have never been better. And this is true whether the market rallies or declines in the months ahead. The intelligent investor has always been able to make money in bull markets and bear markets alike. Only now, thanks to increasing sophistication of stock options and index futures, the task is ea-sier. Harnessing the proper strategies to one's expectations of what the market will do is the key to success.

And that brings us to the subject of risk. Intelligent risk taking is what generates profit in the market. Without risk, after all, there would be no profit. Obviously, trading options is a risky business. Buyers of puts and calls can lose their entire investment if they aren't careful—and many do. Option sellers, who are often known as *writers,* expose themselves to unlimited risk unless corrective action is taken. Yet despite these risks, the number of participants in the options market continues to grow.

Why?

First, options trading *can* be risky but it is not inherently so. Indeed, pension fund managers and large institutional investors are finding that *not* to rely on the sophisticated strategies available to today's investor can be riskier than simply holding large portfolios of stocks. The options market enables such investors to hedge their risk, making options a conservative market tactic. Second, investors have learned that an active approach is required to make it in the market today. The notion that you buy stock and hold it indefinitely, despite the periodic recessions which have occurred in recent years, is one that simply doesn't work anymore. Today's stock market investor wants and needs an investment tool that will enable him to change with changing economic times and conditions. Options permit such flexibility. Third, today's investor is more sophisticated. Options provide a suitable challenge for those who want to be master of their own economic destiny. Uniquely suited to a diversified approach to the securities markets, options *complement* stock ownership, making it not only safer, but also more profitable—an ideal combination by any standard.

THE ADVANTAGES OF OPTIONS

While options trading *can* be risky, it can prove profitable to a number of investors seeking different goals. Let's outline a few of the more notable advantages of options trading:

1. Predetermined Risk. When you purchase a put or call option, your total liability is limited to the cost of the option, known as the *premium.* The premium payment constitutes your total risk as an option buyer. After you purchase an option, you can make many, many times the cost of the option. But you can never lose more than the entire premium cost. This is the primary attraction of option buying—the risk is limited, but the profit potential is unlimited. Let's say you purchase a stock for $45 a share. Your investment on a round lot amounts to $4,500 plus transaction costs.

Should the stock decline to $30 a share, the entire $15-a-share loss is sustained by you, the stock owner. But let's say you purchase a call option on the same $45 stock for, say, a $5 premium. Now, if the stock declines to $30, your loss is just $5 a share, or $500. You simply abandon the call—*and limit your loss to the cost of the option premium, $500.* Thus, the risk in *purchasing* listed options is always predetermined and limited to the cost of the premium.

2. Leverage. Leverage means a small amount of money controls an asset worth a lot more. When you normally purchase common stock, your leverage is limited since you must put up at least 50 per cent of the value of the shares you are purchasing. When you purchase an option, however, you are paying for the right to buy or sell shares at an agreed-upon price. Should the option prove profitable, you will participate in the full move of the underlying shares—often for a fraction of the cost of buying the shares outright. Even a small movement in the underlying shares can translate into a huge percentage gain on the option. This is the magic of leverage.

3. Price Protection. Owners of stock can achieve price protection by *writing,* or *selling,* call options against their stock position. For example, if you own a stock valued at $25 a share, you might write or sell a call option for a premium of, say, $2 a share. This would ensure that your stock will bring in at least $25 a share as long as the market price held *above* $23 a share. Since you *received* $2 a share for writing the call option, you pick up $2-per-share price protection from your writing activities. Thus, call writing can protect you from a modest stock decline.

4. Versatility. Few investment vehicles offer the versatility of options. You can buy or sell them covered or uncovered—that is, with or without a related stock position. In addition, you can utilize sophisticated trading strategies such as spreading, straddling, or combining—all designed to carefully hedge your risks and provide you with an easily identifiable profit zone. By using one or more of the many option strategies, you can create an options trading program virtually tailor-made for your own investment needs.

5. Liquid Secondary Market. The option secondary, or resale, market is simply a marketplace for the disposal of previously bought or sold options. Prior to the establishment of the Chicago Board Options Exchange in 1973, no liquid secondary market for standardized options existed. Because a continuous auction market exists today, you can take profits or cut your losses at any time prior to the expiration date of an option. As a result, you are free to enter and exit the options market as you wish and are never locked in to a position you don't want. Since option contracts are standardized, their interchangeability makes them a liquid commodity readily converted to cash.

INVESTORS AND SPECULATORS

Options trading appeals to a broad spectrum of the investment community. Since the motivations behind an option trade can be quite different, it is difficult to say with precision who gains and loses. Benefits can accrue to both buyers and sellers of options, depending upon their reason for entering the options market. Take an investor who purchases put options to protect his stock portfolio. He may view his option investment as cheap insurance. The peace of mind he achieves by owning puts outweighs their cost— even if he abandons the options and sustains a 100 per cent loss. Indeed, both parties to an option trade can "win," if not in profits, at least in realizing certain objectives.

No doubt you've heard that options trading *can* be risky. It is true. The buyer of a put or call can easily lose 100 per cent of his investment within a short period of time. But for those who enjoy speculating in puts and calls, the rewards can be worth the risks. Typically, for a small investment, which usually ranges about 10 per cent or less of the cost of the underlying stock, the call buyer gains the opportunity to participate in the full price rise of the security—just as if he owned the stock. For many risk-oriented traders, such opportunities are often difficult to pass up *despite* the high odds against them.

For the investment-oriented—and here we have to include a growing number of pension funds, insurance firms, and large institutional investors as well as individual stock market participants— options provide a meaningful way to *hedge* risks associated with stock ownership. Such conservative investors might write or sell options on their stock holdings—a strategy known as *covered writing*—in order to generate income on a steady basis. They do so knowing that the risk they incur is primarily one of lost opportunity—the profit they *might* have made if the stock is *called away*.

For those whose market stance falls somewhere in between the outright speculative and the downright conservative, you may rest assured that options trading has something to offer you as well. As in every investment, risk is commensurate with reward. They haven't invented the investment yet that is completely free of risk yet offers high profit potential. But options trading comes as close as you're likely to get to that elusive "sure-thing" investment.

If you're going to win as an option trader, you're going to need knowledge. The odds of making a success out of *any* investment venture are not good unless you know what you're doing. In options trading, where the pace is accelerated and the leverage enhanced, the necessity of knowing precisely what you are doing becomes an imperative.

If you are new to these markets, the pages that follow will provide you with a sound background in the mechanics of buying and selling options. And if you are a seasoned trader, you may find some of the more sophisticated strategies to your liking. Since options trading offers such a wide range of investment opportunity, surely there's something here for everyone, whether their investment attitude is conservative or speculative. Making money in *any* investment is never easy, but to those who are willing to do their homework, to learn the best way to trade, the opportunities in the options and index markets are worthy of the challenge. With time you will find that sure-thing trades *are* possible. Considering the rewards, hopefully you'll find they are worth the effort required to find them as well.

PART ONE

Understanding the Basics of Listed Stock Options Trading

1

What Are Put and Call Options?

In listed stock options trading, puts and calls are contracts which you purchase and sell. They are the mirror image of one another: the *call option* provides its holder with the right, but not the obligation, to *purchase* 100 shares of a given security at a specified price, known as the *striking price,* within a specified period of time; the *put option* provides its holder with the right to *sell* 100 shares, again at a specified price within a specified period of time. The stock in question is known as the *underlying security*.

Prior to April 1973, when the Chicago Board Options Exchange first opened its doors for *listed* options trading, puts and calls had been traded in a more informal manner in the over-the-counter market. In the OTC market, if an investor wanted to purchase a call option, he'd go to a stockbroker or options specialist who, in turn, would find someone owning the shares of the underlying stocks he wanted to purchase the option on. The broker would then act as middleman—for a fee—between option buyer and seller. The seller, who already owned the stock, would agree to sell, or *write,* a call option binding him to deliver 100 shares of his stock at a fixed price within the required amount of time—*if* the option were later *exercised* by the call buyer. To see how this might work, let's assume a buyer purchases a three-month call on XYZ stock for a premium of 5. Under the terms of the call contract, the buyer has the right to purchase 100 shares of XYZ common stock at a price of 60. If, during the life of the option, the price of XYZ rises above 60, the call will become profitable and the call buyer can "call away" the seller's shares. Should XYZ rise to 70, the call buyer will call in his shares at the striking price of 60 and immediately resell the shares at the prevailing market price of 70. His profit of 10, the difference between the purchase price of 60 and the resale price of 70, will be offset, in part, by the cost of the call option, which was 5. The call seller, of course, would retain the full premium of 5, or $500 for the 100-share contract. The call buyer was rewarded with a profit of 100 per cent on his initial $500 investment because his market judgment proved correct. By purchasing the option, the call buyer assumed the risk that his option might have expired worthless had the shares underlying the option not risen above $60.

The drawback of the over-the-counter market is that it relies on a one-to-one relationship between buyer and seller. First, the buyer—or his broker acting as his agent—has to locate someone who not only has the shares of stock he wishes to purchase the option on, but who also is willing to write an option on the stock. When it comes time to exercise the option, the buyer receives the seller's stock which he, in turn, then has to sell in the stock market —a procedure involving a number of commissions. Once the buyer purchases the option, he has only two alternatives. He must either exercise the option or allow it to expire worthless. Should he change his mind about the option and decide to sell it, he is unable to do so. He is committed to holding the option.

The advent of listed options trading changed the market in significant ways. Most importantly, it established liquidity. Liquidity means you can easily convert an asset to cash. By creating a continuous, centralized marketplace for listed stock options, the Chicago Board Options Exchange ensured liquidity. No longer would investors who wanted to buy and sell stock options have to shop around among a number of OTC option dealers for an option contract with the best terms. Instead, the CBOE offered *standardized* contracts. To standardize contracts, the founders of the Chicago Board Options Exchange borrowed a concept from the commodity futures markets. They standardized the key specifications in stock options—striking prices, expiration dates, number of shares to be purchased or delivered—immediately creating a liquidity that provided a strong *secondary market,* a market in which the options could be purchased or sold anytime prior to expiration. By limiting the number of stocks, strike prices, expiration dates, and concentrating on just 16 calls on actively traded stocks at first, the CBOE created a financial product that was to win wide acceptance. With standardization, the call options could then be traded just like any stock or futures contract. The reaction was immediate.

AN AUCTION MARKET

What was the impact of an organized auction market for stock options? For one thing, no longer would an individual buyer and seller be bound to one another. This had been the case with the over-the-counter options. With the advent of listed options trading, a buyer could purchase a call option from one seller and turn around and sell the option to yet another buyer. Not only wouldn't he be bound to hold the option for three months or six months or whatever the duration of the option called for, but he could dispose of the option in the secondary market the very same day, or within minutes, even seconds, after having purchased the option. The options market had finally become liquid. For another thing, it had become continuous, operating during the same hours of trading as the major equity markets. Other benefits of the organized auction market include the consolidation of market price and volume data, and a centralized clearing system for processing all trades. By reducing the number of variables associated with options trading and making available pertinent price data to many investors at the same time, the organized market greatly enhanced liquidity—the prime requisite for a successful market.

The auction market concept provides the most equitable means of establishing prices. Buyers and sellers meet in a centralized marketplace where competitive forces of supply and demand keep the quoted bid and asked prices close together. At any moment in time, an option will have both a *bid* and an *asked* price. *The bid is the price buyers are willing to pay for the option; the asked price or offer is the price at which the sellers are willing to sell.* For a trade to be consummated, both buyer and seller must agree on a single price. This may be either the bid or asked, or a compromise price which is somewhere in between. The difference in price between the bid and asked is known as the *spread*.[1] Typically, the more active options have the most narrow spreads. A narrow spread between bid and asked prices reflects a competitive, liquid market in which there are a number of buyers and sellers vying for the same options. In *illiquid,* or *thin,* markets, the spread is apt to widen since competition will be less and sellers will insist on higher prices while buyers insist on lower prices to take an option trade.

Understanding how option prices are established is important. Since the market price, at any moment in time, can be the bid, asked, or some price in between, it is important that you realize when placing a so-called *market order* that you will generally be filled at the *higher asked price when buying* and at the *lower bid price when selling*. Typically, the other side of your order (the selling side if you are buying, and vice versa) will be taken by a *market maker*—sometimes called a *local*—who trades for his own account. On market orders, when buyers *hit the offer* or sellers *hit the bid* (agreeing to trade at those prices), they are said to be *giving up the edge*—the small difference that separates the bid and offer prices. As a rule, the market makers are reluctant to give the edge to public traders, since they make their living buying and selling for tiny profits—often as little as an eighth or a sixteenth.

Options trading is a highly competitive game. This is reflected in buyers vying for the lowest price obtainable and sellers desiring the highest prices. What determines the bid and asked? The most recent highest bid and lowest offer. Thus, once buyers establish a bid level (the price at which they are willing to buy), the bids of other buyers unwilling to meet or exceed that price are no longer acceptable—at least not in the immediate time frame in which the bids are being made. It is for this reason that a limit order will often go unfilled and will be sent back to your account executive with the word "Unable" marked on the order. If you limited your broker to buying an option for, say, 18⅛ or better and the lowest bid was 18¼, the trade becomes "Unable" and is sent back

[1] Don't confuse the spread between the bid and asked with spread trading, which is something different altogether. Spread trading will be discussed in Chapter 5.

option, the seller c
position and thus b
the strike price. If
seller will be requir
received for selling

Options are ofte
option series is just
class. Exxon calls,
Exxon April 35 ca
calls would be yet
another. And so on

In learning the n
every option has a
at which the buyer
and the price at w
shares. Typically, t
price. Striking pric
selling at or under
up to $200 a shar
$200 a share.[3] Th
security prices fluc
with 45 and 50 st
security rises or fa
accounts for why
strike prices and a
trading at six or se

INTRINSIC VALUE

Options are fre
on-the-money, or
call purchaser with
a call is in-the-m
security is *above*
market price of th

[3] The intervals ma
Slow-moving, nonvol
known to have optio
above $50 a share.

unfilled. On the selling side, the reverse is true. The floor broker may *offer down* your offer (go lower than the previous asked price), but not offer *above* the prevailing offer. Let's assume an option contract has a relatively wide spread: the buyers are bidding 1⅝ and the sellers are asking 2. Now, as long as both buyers and sellers hold their ground, no trading takes place. Both traders must agree on a *single* price. In the absence of that agreement, no trading can take place. For trading to commence, therefore, the sellers must offer down their selling prices or the buyers must "bid up" their buying price—or both—until a price level is reached that *both* buyer and seller agree on. Depending upon a host of factors, including the movement of the underlying stock price, the general direction of the market, and the types of market orders the floor brokers hold in their trading decks, prices will move higher or lower.

In our hypothetical example, let's say one of the sellers breaks ranks with the others and offers the contract at 1⅞, down an eighth from 2. The other sellers must now meet this offer or go lower. Now the buyers may agree to meet the seller halfway. They may bid an eighth higher at 1¾. The spread has narrowed to ⅛ point. Anticipating still lower prices, a seller may be willing to take the option at the bid of 1¾.

"Sold!" he'll shout out, in a voice loud enough for all the market makers in the immediate vicinity to hear. And the trade will be consummated.

Now contrast this highly organized and centralized marketplace with the OTC market, where there might be just one seller offering to write an option on the shares you want. He makes an offer and that's it. In such an illiquid market, there are not ten or twenty other sellers all eager to give you the most competitive price possible. The importance of liquidity cannot be overestimated.

THE OPTION CONTRACT

Put and call options are promises—promises to meet the terms of the legally binding contractual agreement between buyer and seller. Since the specifications are standardized, the features of the contracts are few and simple to understand. Let's say you purchase a Syntex December 55 call option at 5. What have you

bought? And w
contract? You h
tex common st
purchase and th
the third week
cise the option.
unilateral contr
any time. Nor
tion. Because a
call anytime pri
is 5 or $5 pe
shares.

The seller o
binding legal a
agreed to deliv
share at any tim
expiration. In
option premiun
of whether the

The seller m
If he does own
writer. If he do
he is taking a s
soar in value,
Whether or no
written is unim
quired to post
marked to the
each day to d
account requir
diately.² Shoul
you exercise th
the shares in t
to you. The se
the call buyer,
tion, neither i

² Please note t
cash and a cove
cised.

On-the-money (also known as *at-the-money*) calls are those whose strike prices are identical with the prevailing market price of the stock. Since puts are the mirror image of calls, their designations are reversed. For a put to be in-the-money, the price of the stock must be *below* the strike price. Remember, the put gives you the right to *sell* the security; thus, a put with a 35 strike will be profitable when the underlying security is at 30, but not when the security is at 40.

Focusing on calls, let's say XYZ stock is trading at 45. There are three calls available for trading on this stock: those with striking prices at 40, 45, and 50. The 40 call will be in-the-money by 5 points; the 45 call will be on-the-money; and the 50 call will be out-of-the-money. Naturally, the in-the-money 40 calls will fetch higher prices than the out-of-the-money 50 calls. With XYZ trading at $45 a share, the 40 calls have $5 of what is known as *intrinsic* or *cash value,* the value represented by the difference between the price at which you could purchase shares ($40) and the market price at which you could immediately sell those shares ($45). In addition to intrinsic value, options have what is known as *time value*—the value represented by the amount of time left prior to expiration. In this case the XYZ 40 calls would have both intrinsic value ($5) and time value, or the amount of additional value the market gave the option beyond its intrinsic value. With XYZ at $45 a share, the XYZ 40 call might be selling for $6, or $5 for intrinsic value and another $1 for time value. Both the XYZ 45 and 50 call options, however, would be valued according to their time value alone since, with XYZ common stock trading at $45, the on-the-money 45 and out-of-the-money 50 have no intrinsic value at all. At expiration, time value ceases to exist and options are valued according to their cash value alone. In this instance, should XYZ still be trading at $45 a share at expiration, the 40 call will have a value of $5, and the 45 and 50 calls will expire worthless.

The notion of wasting time value is an important one for the option trader to understand. Since time value is often a significant component of an option's premium (the full component in the case of out-of-the-money options), the option trader must be aware that options are *wasting assets.* That is, with the passage of each day, their time value grows less, until, at maturity, the time value ceases to exist and becomes zero. At expiration the option will be valued at whatever intrinsic value it has achieved.

As a rule, options become more speculative as the time value decreases; thus, as an option's expiration date draws closer, its trading volume tends to increase in a flurry of speculative activity. This heightened activity in a soon-to-be-expired option reflects the uncertainty of the stock's chances for appreciation. Since the right to acquire a stock for a given price between now and some future date is almost always worth a certain amount of money, buyers and sellers eagerly match wits over these speculative options, hoping to get the competitive edge.

STANDARDIZED EXPIRATION DATES

At any moment in time, three option expiration months will be trading. These expiration dates, which are standardized, are set at three-month intervals. Thus, the longest-term option will never exceed nine months. As the near month expires, the most distant option nine months out commences trading, enabling traders to *roll over* their option positions, or move into a more distant month.

Precisely what months you trade will depend on the stock's option cycle and your own judgment of whether a near month or far month suits your trading strategy. There are three fixed option cycles. One cycle consists of expiration in the months of January, April, July, and October. Another cycle consists of expiration dates in February, May, August, and November. And a third trades in expiration dates of March, June, September, and December. Since only three option expiration months trade at a time, one month of each cycle will be inactive while the other three are trading. For instance, while February, May, and August options are trading, November will not be trading. But once February ceases to trade, the cycle will consist of May, August, and November. At the end of May, the distant February contract will again trade. And so on.

All options expire at 5:00 P.M. Eastern time on the Saturday immediately following the third Friday of the named month. You, of course, will want to exercise your option, if it is profitable to do so, *before* expiration. As an alternative to exercising an option, you can always *offset* your position by selling any options you previously purchased and buying any options you previously sold.

The expiration dates are important to you for at least two reasons. First, if you are a buyer, you'll want to keep your eye on the expiration date as the most distant time when you'll be able to trade or exercise your option. Sellers, of course, who *receive* the premium money when they first write the option, want the option to expire worthless (be out-of-the-money) at expiration. In order for the seller to profit, the premium price must decline by expiration. Second, the remaining time to expiration will influence what trading strategy you'll employ.

WHAT INFLUENCES OPTION PRICES?

The option premium, which is simply the cost of an option or the amount of money the buyer pays to the seller, is determined by open outcry in the auction market on the floor of one of the options exchanges. The premium is payable at purchase of the option, and it is *not* a downpayment and is *not* applicable to the purchase price of the stock should the option be exercised. There are three key factors that influence option levels:

1. The current market price of the underlying stock relative to the strike price of the option. Since a call option provides you with the right to purchase shares at the strike price, it is only understandable that as the price of the underlying security moves above the strike price, the option becomes more valuable. In fact, for a call option, the increase in value above the strike price is point for point with the security price. Thus, if you gain a point in the value of a $50 stock, you likewise gain a point in the value of a $5 call option *above* the strike. A point, remember, represents one dollar per share, or $100 for an option contract. Below the strike, of course, the call option will not make a point-for-point gain, since the option is still out-of-the-money. Being out-of-the-money, the option has no intrinsic value, only time value, and that value is being eroded daily as you move toward expiration. For puts, the reverse is true. Puts become more valuable as prices *decline* since the option conveys the right to *sell* shares at the strike price. The relationship of stock price to strike price is vital to the valuation of an option. When Texas Instruments was selling for $132 per share, the in-the-money January 80 call was selling for $53½ —that's $52 in intrinsic value and $1½ in time value. At the same time, the out-of-the-money January 150 call was selling for $2¼ —the entire premium of which was time value. Upon expiration, had Texas Instruments stayed at $132 a share, the January 80 call would sell for its intrinsic value of $52 and the January 150, being still out-of-the-money, would expire worthless. As you can see, the stock price is far and away the most important influence on option prices. If the stock is far above or far below the striking price, the other factors will have little influence.

2. The length of time until expiration of the option. Out-of-the-money options, by definition, *only* have time value, not intrinsic value. Since an option is a wasting asset, whose value will diminish to zero should the option not be in-the-money at expiration, it is logical to assume that options with a longer time to expiration will fetch higher premium prices than shorter-term options on the same stock at the same strike. Since options of the same strike price convey the same right, the difference in premiums between, say, a Syntex March 50 and Syntex June 50 is time value alone. When Syntex was recently trading at $60¾, for example, the in-the-money March 50s were trading for $12¼ and the June 50s at $14¼. The $2 premium that June sold over March reflected traders' estimates that the time value was worth another $2 per share.

3. The volatility of the underlying stock. Volatility is vital in determining an option premium. Options on stocks that are apt to be more volatile will have higher premiums, since the sellers have to contend with the greater risk of having the options exercised. Buyers, of course, are willing to pay more for options on volatile stocks since the likelihood of such options becoming profitable to hold is greater as well. A convenient index to measure volatility is known as the *Beta rating.* Beta is a measure of a stock's sensitivity to the movement of the general market. A Beta of 1 is considered normal, or in line with established major averages. Beta ratings greater than 1 suggest that a stock has a greater volatility than stocks making up the major averages, and a Beta rating less than 1 suggests that a stock is less volatile than those comprising the averages. Other factors being equal—which, of course, they never are—high-Beta stocks will have relatively high premium values, low-Beta stocks will have relatively low premium values. Your broker can provide you with the Beta rating on any stock.

Other factors, such as interest rates and cash or stock dividends of the underlying stock, will, of course, have an influence on option premiums. But the interplay of forces can be complex and often uncertain. For example, you can purchase an out-of-the-money call and have the stock increase in price and still lose money on the option. This would occur if the declining time value had more of an impact on the option premium than the momentary rise in the price of the underlying security. As for dividends, option holders do not participate in cash or stock dividends, since they only have the right to purchase the security. Typically, large cash dividends translate into low option premiums. As a rule, an anticipated stock dividend will lower the price of the underlying security on the ex-divided date and this is reflected in a lower premium for the call as well.

RESTRICTED OPTIONS

Due to market action, some option contracts become *restricted* prior to expiration and are limited in who may trade them. A call option becomes restricted when its premium is less than ½ and when the underlying security price has fallen more than 5 points below the striking price. A *restricted option* means you cannot enter *opening* transactions in the options, only *closing* transactions. An opening transaction creates a new position, whereas a closing transaction closes out an existing position. When an option becomes restricted, therefore, you cannot enter into a new position in that option, only close out an existing one.

OPEN INTEREST

The number of open contracts outstanding at any moment in time is called the *open interest*. Every time you purchase or sell an option, the open interest increases by 1. When you close out your position, the open interest decreases by 1. The open interest statistics are important because they pinpoint the most liquid contracts. As a rule, the nearby expiration months with strike prices near the market price of the underlying security will have the greatest open interest. As expiration approaches, however, traders will roll over into more distant months and open interest will decline. At expiration, open interest will be zero.

READING THE NEWSPAPER REPORTS

While the *Wall Street Journal* offers the most comprehensive coverage of daily options quotations, you'll also find daily quotations published in a number of leading newspapers. For weekly coverage of options, you should read *Barron's,* not only for the statistics, but also for its informative and well-written "Striking Price" column that deals exclusively with options trading. In the *Wall Street Journal,* you'll find all the information you need to track options on the page marked "Listed Options Quotations." You should notice first that options quotes appear under the headings of one of the four options exchanges, the Chicago Board, American Exchange, Philadelphia Exchange, and Pacific Exchange. Next, the quotations are listed under one of the three expiration cycles with just the current trading months listed. Let's look at the actual numbers printed in the *Wall Street Journal* of November 2, 1981, for the trading results of Syntex options for the previous trading day, Friday, October 30, 1981 (Table 1).

Table 1

CHICAGO BOARD   October 30, 1981

Option & NY Close	Strike Price	Calls—Last			Puts—Last		
		Dec	Mar	Jun	Dec	Mar	Jun
Syntex	45	14⅜	r	r	r	r	r
59⅛	50	10½	r	r	½	1⅝	r
59⅛	55	6¼	9½	r	1⅛	2¼	r
59⅛	60	3⅜	6	r	3¼	4	r
59⅛	70	⅜	1⅞	s	11¾	r	s

r — Not traded. s — No option offered.
Last is premium (purchase price).

The above quotations provide you with the last, or closing prices, for Syntex options on the Chicago Board Options Exchange for Friday, October 30, 1981. Under "Option & NY Close," we find the name of the underlying security and option—in this case, Syntex—and the closing price of the underlying shares, 59⅛. Under "Strike Price" are listed the five different strike prices available for Syntex options. This is followed by three double columns listing the three exercise dates that are available. The closing prices of the respective puts and calls are then listed under the individual contract month. Note that only the three most current expiration months are trading. Once the December 1981 options expire, the September 1982 options will be listed. In Table 1 the nearby December 1981 option is listed first, followed by the more distant March 1982 and even more distant June 1982 options.

Let's assume you are interested in following the Syntex 50 December call. You read across the line where the 50 appears, and you see the December 50s are selling for 10½. The 10½ is the per-share cost; thus, a 10½ call will cost you 100 times as much, or $1,050 plus commissions, to purchase. As a potential seller, you would see the 10½ as meaning the $1,050 minus commissions that you'd *receive* for *selling* the call option. You'd also realize that the Syntex December 50 calls would almost certainly be exercised and the 10½ credit you'd received for writing the call would almost certainly be offset by a debit of comparable magnitude. Since the market price of the shares is 59⅛, you know that the December 50 is in-the-money and that a full 9⅛ points of the premium represents intrinsic value—with the balance of 1⅜ points representing time value. The "r" designations, as the footnote suggests, indicate options of that category did not trade that day. While the Syntex December 50 calls are relatively valuable, you'll note that the Syntex December 50 puts are dirt cheap at ¼, or $25 plus commission for the option. Since a December 50 put gives you the right to *sell* Syntex shares at 50, this option is almost worthless since it is so far out-of-the-money. The ¼-point premium represents time value alone, and that is rapidly wasting away since just over a month exists prior to expiration. For the December 50s to acquire value, the price of Syntex shares would have to plunge more than 9⅛ points prior to the third week in December. The March 50 puts have a somewhat greater time value, since they provide the put holder with a greater length of time prior to expiration. But still, the buyer of any 50 puts needs at least a 15 per cent loss in stock value to realize a profit.

THE ROLE OF THE CLEARING HOUSE

While there are always two parties to an option contract—buyer and seller (or writer)—you never trade directly with another individual but with what is known as the *clearing house*. The clearing house is a party to every trade. It ensures the integrity of every option contract by requiring sufficient margin to cover every open option position and by clearing the books daily—that is, paying winners and deducting losses from those whose positions have lost money during the day. Officially known as the Options Clearing Corporation, this agency becomes the purchaser from the option seller and seller to the option buyer immediately after sale and purchase orders are matched following the close of trading. The purpose of the clearing house, which is strictly a nonprofit organization, is to ensure the integrity of every contract by requiring strict margin standards.

By insisting that all parties to an option trade guarantee the performance of the contract, the clearing house serves a valuable role. Since buyers must pay cash for options purchased, the sellers are assured of receiving their funds immediately upon writing an option. The writers, in turn, are required to post margin lest an option they've written soars in price. Since all positions are marked to the market daily, an undermargined writer would be required to deposit additional funds with his brokerage house should his account not meet minimum standards.[4] As a result of these safeguards, you need not worry that the funds won't be available should your position prove a winner. Lastly, the clearing house insists that all accounts be kept strictly segregated. There-

---

[4] Since calls are purchased for cash, no margin is required. Covered writers, of course, are fully hedged by their long stock position. Naked writers, however, who are exposed to risk, are required to post 30 per cent of the market value of the underlying stock. This 30 per cent requirement is reduced by the amount of the premium collected. The margin is then increased or decreased by the amount the option is in- or out-of-the-money. A $250 minimum margin requirement applies to all naked writing positions.

fore, if the brokerage house you are dealing with makes some bad investments, your account will not be affected.[5]

STOCKS VERSUS OPTIONS

You should be familiar with the similarities and differences between stock ownership and options trading. As an investor in securities, you purchase a number of shares in a company which makes you part owner in that company. As a shareholder, therefore, you stand to gain, in the form of dividends or a capital gain, when the company prospers. And here's where the difference between stocks and options exists. Shareholders actually own a portion of a corporation; option holders, on the other hand, only own a promise, albeit one that will be kept, to purchase or sell shares. While shareholders participate in dividend income, option holders do not. For years, a profitable strategy on Wall Street was to buy shares in growth companies and put them away. This "buy 'em and forget 'em" philosophy doesn't work in the options market, however, because puts and calls have only a very limited life—nine months at the longest. As a result, you *have* to make decisions concerning your option trades. But the real difference between purchasing a security and purchasing an option rests with leverage. Both the positive and negative leverage in options trading is so much greater that the gains and losses are likewise magnified.

Let's compare the purchase of 100 shares of stock with the

[5] Should your brokerage house go bankrupt, however, your assets may be temporarily frozen. In short-lived investments such as options, this temporary freeze may prove disastrous, since you can neither buy back your short position nor sell your long position once an account has been frozen. The recent John Muir & Company bankruptcy resulted in huge losses to investors who were unable to take appropriate action during the time that all John Muir accounts were frozen. Because the New York Stock Exchange and the National Association of Securities Dealers stiffened their financial requirements and intensified their surveillance of member firms following a spate of brokerage collapses in the late sixties and early seventies, the chances that your broker will go broke are slimmer than ever. Nevertheless, during 1981 nine firms went under, bringing the total number of failures since 1971 to 152. Due to recent legislation aimed at protecting investors, a little-known agency, the Securities Investor Protection Corporation (SIPC), protects your investments against loss up to $500,000.

purchase of a call option on the same 100 shares. Assume you are bullish on the near-term prospects of a company called Super Home Products. Currently trading at 25, Super Home is about to introduce a new product that will likely revolutionize the home-building industry. Stock analysts are forecasting a 20 to 30 per cent increase in value in Super Home shares in coming months. As an investor, what are your alternatives?

If Super Home is a significantly large enough company to have listed options trading (the requirements for options listing are rigorous), you'll have a choice between purchasing Super Home securities or Super Home call options. Let's say you purchase 100 shares of Super Home at $25 a share. Should the price of the security rise to, say, $30 a share, you will enjoy a nice $5-per-share profit. This will translate into $500 on a $2,500 investment, or 20 per cent. (We'll ignore commissions for the sake of simplicity). Assuming the same move, let's say you also choose to purchase a call option on Super Home. At the time Super Home was trading for 25, December 25 calls were selling for 1½. Since the option was at-the-money, the 1½ premium reflected time value alone. It would be necessary for the underlying stock to rise for the option to have a value at expiration. Since you were bullish on Super Home, let's say you purchased a call option, paying just $150 plus commission for the right to buy Super Home at $25 a share prior to the December expiration. Again assuming the same move to $30 a share in the underlying share, the option would have a *far greater percentage rise* than the stock. At 30, the option would have a value of at least 5 and whatever time value the market felt the option still retained. So the option you purchased for 1½ will now bring 5 in the secondary market (actually more if there is considerable time left to expiration). You immediately sell the call for 5 and make a profit of 3½, or $350 in *profit* on an investment of just $150. That's 233 per cent!

As you can see, the leverage in the options transaction was far greater. For a relatively small amount of money, you were able to participate in the increase in value of an asset worth far more. Moreover, your entire risk in the venture was just $150 plus com-missions. Regardless of the subsequent movement of Super Home, you could have lost no more than $150 on the option transaction.

Unfortunately, this was not a risk-free investment. Far from

it. Had Super Home never risen above $25 a share and had you
held the call option until expiration, you would have sustained a
100 per cent loss in the option. The stock you'd purchased at 25,
however, would still be worth whatever the market was offering
for Super Home—25, 24, 20, or whatever. Almost certainly, the
stock price would have been significantly above zero, where it
would have had to fall to to equal the percentage loss in the option.
On the one hand, you had a somewhat more conservative investment and corresponding conservative gain in the stock transaction; on the other, a far more speculative investment and far more
speculative gain was made in the options investment. Because the
two approaches are so different, you have to think differently
when you use one or the other. Stock buyers tend to be investors
while option buyers *can* be investors but far more frequently
are actually speculators.

THE SPECULATIVE APPROACH

Speculation has been given a bad name in recent years. We
hear of speculators driving up the cost of housing and food products and causing currencies to be devalued. Fortunately, the
label is not deserved. Speculators simply *capitalize* on an existing
state of affairs, whether the demand for housing is about to outpace supply or whether a country has artificially maintained its
currency valuation at an unrealistic high level. The speculator spots
the imbalance between supply and demand and *risks* his capital
by trying to get in on a profit-making opportunity before the information becomes well known. For taking this risk, the speculator
is often well rewarded.

During periods of economic instability, speculation becomes
more profitable. The reason? Uncertainty breeds volatility in the
marketplace as prices seek a true balance between supply and
demand. During turbulent economic times, prices often overshoot
their level of balance between supply and demand and become
what is known as *overbought* or *oversold*. As a result of this
imbalance, the speculator attempts to profit by *anticipating* a price
move—whether it be in the price of real estate, food grains, or
securities. By buying up a product he anticipates will soon be in
short supply, or, conversely, selling short an overpriced product

that will soon be in abundance, he seeks to earn a profit. In a sense, the speculator, operating in his own behalf, provides a valuable economic function. He assumes risks others are unwilling to assume and brings prices in line with a realistic estimation of supply and demand.

The successful speculator knows there is a very strong psychological component determining prices. He knows that buyers and sellers, being human, are apt to overreact. His job is to see when and where this overreaction occurs and act on it. He is often willing to "take the other side" of a trade, recognizing that the majority is always wrong at the major reversal points in the market. By doing so, he proves himself a leader, not a follower. In the process, he hopes to earn a profit.

Being oriented to the short-term, a speculator realizes that change is inevitable. He knows that the old rules that applied yesterday will not necessarily apply today or tomorrow. As a result, he is *flexible* and never wed to one opinion for too long. He knows that his market vision is limited and that mistakes are inevitable. Being a realist, the speculator keeps an open mind and is able to change market strategies quickly in response to changing trends in the marketplace.

The successful speculator tries to make the most of his opportunities and seeks the highest level of reward commensurate with the risks. He searches for highly leveraged investments whenever possible, knowing that his dollars work the hardest for him when they are controlling ten and twenty their number in leveraged investments.

THE INVESTMENT APPROACH

An investor, unlike a speculator, is far more likely to take a long-term view of the market—indeed, some investors have been known to "marry" stocks, and even pass them down from generation to generation. But the fundamental difference between speculator and investor is that the investor seeks *income* or *growth* on his assets, whereas the speculator wants a substantial, rapid *capital gain*. It's true that the line separating investor and speculator is one of degree. But it is important to recognize your own temperamental leanings if you are going to participate in puts and calls.

Fortunately, there's a role for both speculator and investor in the options market. Just as an investor may write, or sell, a call option on shares he already owns, the speculator may take the other side of the trade in hopes of making a substantial capital gain. Whereas the investor is looking for income—say 1½ points for selling an at-the-money 50 call—the speculator may view the same trade as an opportunity to make a small killing by *buying* the same 50 call the investor writes. Both speculative and investment purposes are served by the transaction: the speculator hopes to use a small amount of money to make a large percentage gain, while the investor seeks to make a more modest percentage return on a relatively large investment. The difference between the two is one of attitude toward risk. The speculator stands to lose his entire premium; the investor, who is a covered writer, however, may have already made a profit on his shares, having purchased them 15 or 20 points lower, and he may be quite willing to have the shares called away at the strike price of 50. His profit is assured, barring a sharp break in the market. By writing a call, however, he knows in advance that his maximum profit will be just 1½, or $150 on 100 shares. But given the short period of time left to expiration and the risk, which is small, he is satisfied with the premium income.

BUYERS AND SELLERS—PUTTING IT ALL TOGETHER

We've seen that call option buyers and sellers may have different motivations for taking an option trade. Let's now look at the results of a hypothetical trade when both buyer and seller hold their contracts until the moment of expiration. We'll assume both potential buyer and seller are looking at Hilton options trading on the Pacific Stock Exchange. The buyer, looking for a highly leveraged speculative investment, is interested in purchasing low-priced, out-of-the-money calls. Why the out-of-the-moneys? Because these calls, having no intrinsic value, will be the cheapest. They'll also provide the greatest leverage (the ratio of money invested to money returned) *if* Hilton shares rise. Scanning the options quotations, the option buyer sees that Hilton shares are trading at $38, with call options available at three different strike prices—35, 40, and 45. The 35s, being below the market price of the stock, are in-the-money, whereas the 40s and 45s, being above the stock price, are out-of-the-money. The most speculative options—those with the lowest premiums—are the 45s. For the 45s to prove valuable at expiration, the price of Hilton shares would have to rise more than $7 a share from the current level of $38 a share. That's an increase of more than 15 per cent—a real long shot. Despite the high odds against this happening, the buyer is a risk taker and willing to invest a little money to make a lot. He sees that Hilton calls trade in the November, February, May cycle with the near-term November options scheduled to expire in just three weeks. The November 45 calls are going for ⅛ of a point, or just $12.50 for the 100-share option. The odds against Hilton moving $7 a share in three weeks are almost astronomical. Although such events do occur, let's assume the buyer wants more time. He notices that the February option doesn't expire for more than three months and its 45 call is trading at 1¼. Beyond the February call, the distant May 45 call is trading at 2¼. Which call does the buyer select? Having dismissed the November 45 as not having sufficient time, he ponders whether the time value between the May and February expiration warrants paying another point, or $100 on the call. He thinks not. So he calls his option broker and tells him to buy one Hilton February 45 call at 1¼. Assuming his order is filled, what has he purchased? The right to purchase Hilton shares at the strike price of $45 a share at any time prior to expiration of the option. He is under no obligation to continue holding the call if he changes his mind concerning Hilton's prospects. He may sell the call for whatever it will bring in the secondary market. If the option proves profitable, he has the choice of either selling it for a profit or exercising it and purchasing the stock at the strike price. If the option proves unprofitable, he will either sell the option at a loss or simply abandon it upon expiration. But since the option buyer anticipated a rise in Hilton shares, chances are he'll hold the call in anticipation of higher prices.

The option writer, on the other hand, may have a somewhat different viewpoint on the Hilton situation. He, too, may be bullish on Hilton over the long term but he may be looking to acquire Hilton below the current market price of $38 a share. To accomplish this goal, he decides to purchase Hilton at $38 a share, but he seeks to *lower* his cost by immediately writing a February

45 call for 1¼. His true cost is thus $36¾, since he paid $38 a share for the stock and received 1¼ points for writing the call ($38 − $1¼ = $36¾). By writing the 45 call, he offsets a portion of his cost in purchasing the common stock. He is now obligated to deliver the shares at $45 a share. But at that price he will have a profit of 8¼. The profit would result from a $7-a-share profit on the security *plus* the income he receives for writing the call. If the shares are not called away, he gets to keep the stock. His only risk is that the price of Hilton shares falls below $36¾ a share.

The risk/reward situation should now be clear for both buyer and writer. To earn a profit, the buyer needs an improvement in prices at least sufficient to overcome the shrinking time value in the call option. The seller is in good shape at any price above 36¾. Above 45, the seller may regret having written the call. But this is a risk he is willing to take. Even at 45, however, the call writer still has a substantial profit on his investment. The only thing he would miss out on should the price of shares rise above 45 is the *opportunity* to earn an even greater profit.

Let's assume the price of Hilton shares moves up to $44 a share, or one point below the strike price. Would the buyer of the February 45 call have a profit? It depends. If he held on to his call in anticipation of still higher prices just prior to expiration and it expired at 44, he'd have nothing but a worthless call. After all, who's going to buy stock at 45 if he can only sell it for 44 in the market? As Hilton moved up from 38, however, the call option, while still out-of-the-money, would be becoming more and more attractive because the *potential* of its becoming profitable would be so much greater. With two months left to expiration, should the February 45 call double in price to 2½, the call buyer could *sell* his call in the secondary market. By doing so, he would make a 100 per cent profit *despite* the call never rising over its 45 striking price. Although the option's intrinsic value may never rise above zero, the call buyer, as you can see, can still earn a profit.

The buyer, having purchased the call for 1¼, sells the call for 2½—a 100 per cent profit. What about the seller, who, you may remember, bought shares at 38 and immediately sold a February 45 call for 1¼? The seller has two alternatives. He can go into the secondary market and buy back his call—in this case, at a loss—or he can await events and see if the stock is called away from him, in which case he'd still have a profit since he bought the stock at a net price of 36¾. Please note that because the call premium has *increased*, the seller would have to pay more for a February 45 call than he originally received for selling it. He shorted the call at 1¼, and should he wish to buy it back, he'd have to pay twice as much, or 2½. Because he is indifferent as to whether the stock is called away, the seller decides to continue holding his short call option and, of course, to continue holding the stock. The stock's rise is halted at $44 a share, and the option is never exercised. As you can see, *both* buyer and seller made money. The buyer of the call made money because he had the good sense to sell his call when it increased in value—and *before* its value sank to zero on expiration. The seller, or call writer, being content with his position, also made money, because the stock rose in value and the call option expired worthless—meaning he kept the entire premium. Despite different motivations, both buyer and seller benefited.

If this "best of both worlds" scenario sounds promising, rest assured it could have proven a disaster for both buyer and seller had Hilton shares declined. The seller of the call would have a loss on his stock position below 36¾, because the small 1¼-point premium would not compensate for a loss below that price. Had Hilton shares declined, the call buyer also would have sustained a loss, since his call would have expired worthless.

THE CALL BUYER

The call buyer is often the most ambitious—and perhaps unrealistic—of all traders in the options market. His goal is to make a large percentage gain on his money by using the powerful leverage inherent in call buying. He buys a call option often for a fraction of the price of the underlying shares and then hopes for rising stock values to earn him a profit. The amount of the premium he pays is his gamble on price appreciation.

If you want to make the most with the least, call buying is certainly worth investigating. But be forewarned. The risks are commensurate with the rewards: only a small portion of calls are ever exercised; the rest expire worthless.

The most widespread use of calls is for the leveraged potential. Because the premium of a call is considerably less than the cost of the underlying security covered by the call, the call buyer can take a *substantially larger position* in call options for the same amount of money. For instance, on a recent trading day, shares of General Dynamics closed at 25 on the New York Stock Exchange. On the same day, a General Dynamics February 25 call (with more than three months left to expiration) was trading at 2½, just one tenth as much. Using the same $2,500 that would be required to purchase 100 shares, you could buy 10 February 25 General Dynamics calls. With the calls, you could potentially control 1,000 shares—ten times as many as the outright stock purchase. When the strike price and market price of the underlying shares are identical, as they are in this illustration, any rise in price in the shares will be matched point for point in the call.

But the call buyer must be correct about market direction. If he is wrong, he could lose his entire investment. Let's assume the General Dynamics shares do rise by 3 points to $28 a share. The 100 shares of General Dynamics common will now be worth an additional $300. At the same time, the calls, which were trading at 2½ when they were at-the-money, will also rise. By how much? Well, that depends on how much time value is retained in the options. But the cash value of the calls will be 3 when the stock is at $28. Assuming the calls retain an additional point in time value, they will be trading at 4, a 60 per cent increase in value. Since you have 10 call options, let's assume you immediately sell all 10 at the market and receive $4 per share on the calls covering 1,000 shares. You take in $4,000 on a $2,500 investment in the calls, for a profit of $1,500. This works out to five times as much money as you would have made had you simply purchased General Dynamics shares at 25 and sold at 28.

If the options play seems much more attractive than the traditional stock market investment, you have to remember that the price of the underlying shares moved up. Had this not occurred, the outcome would have been quite different. Had General Dynamics remained at 25, the option buyer's leverage would not have helped him. At best, he could have sold his options at a loss.

Had the buyer held the calls until expiration, the February 25 calls would have expired worthless and the entire premium would have been lost. This is in contrast to the stock buyer who would have retained all of his purchase price at 25.

That upside potential and downside risk are both enhanced by the high leverage associated with option buying should be kept firmly in mind. During 1980, one of the most profitable years in Wall Street history, stock option buyers were both rewarded and punished by the highly leveraged options markets. In the six-month period between March 27, 1980 and the record volume day, October 16, 1980, Homestake Mining shares rose from $27^{11}/_{16}$ to 82, a 196 per cent gain. The Homestake October 30 calls, during the same period, rose from $3^5/_{16}$ to $56\frac{1}{8}$, a 1,584 per cent gain. Fluor gained more than 33 points, rising from $26^5/_{16}$ in March to 60 in October. That 128 per cent gain in the stock was magnified eightfold in the Fluor October 30 calls, which rose from $2\frac{5}{8}$ in March to 30 in October, a 1,043 per cent gain. But there's a negative leverage at work in option buying as well, one that magnifies not profits but losses. Had you sunk $10,000 into Burroughs October 70s during the same six-month period during 1980, come October 16, 1980, your investment was worth about $100. During that time, Burroughs shares declined only 9 per cent. But the Burroughs October 70s lost 99 per cent of their value and ultimately expired worthless. McDonnell Douglas remained virtually the same, losing only an eighth of a point as it declined from $36\frac{3}{4}$ to $36\frac{5}{8}$. But the McDonnell Douglas November 40 calls declined by 87 per cent during the same period, falling to $1^3/_{16}$ from $6\frac{1}{4}$. Black & Decker stock actually *rose* 5 per cent, from $18\frac{3}{8}$ to $19\frac{1}{4}$. But the out-of-the-money Black & Decker November 20 calls managed to give up 76 per cent of their value. A similar performance was recorded by J. C. Penney shares that gained 7 per cent in value. The company's out-of-the-money calls lost 70 per cent in value.

You should remember that these results were obtained during a year when investors decided that stocks were an inflation *hedge*. Prior to the end of 1980, the average daily volume in the stock market was under 32 million shares a day—the 1979 record-setting volume. But the average volume during 1980 was almost 45 million shares. It is true you could have made some spectacular

profits speculating in calls, but you must not lose sight of the fact
that *even during good times* call buyers must be correct in their
market judgment.

THE PUT BUYER

The put buyer is a bear on a particular stock. Anticipating
lower prices, he purchases a put which enables him to *sell* 100
shares of the underlying stock at the exercise price. Should his
judgment prove correct, the put buyer will be able to put shares to
the seller at the striking price and buy them back lower at the prevailing market price. The difference will be his profit.

Like the call buyer, the put buyer pays a premium to purchase
the option. Also like the call buyer, the put buyer may sell his option prior to expiration or exercise the option by "putting" 100
shares to the put seller at the agreed-upon striking price. A third
alternative, of course, is to abandon the option if it proves unprofitable.

Being the mirror image of a call, the put works in *reverse* fashion. Whereas a call is in-the-money when the stock is *above* the
strike price, the put is in-the-money when the stock is *below* the
strike price. Thus, an April 90 put is in-the-money when the underlying stock is at 80. Conversely, an April 90 *call* would be out-
of-the-money when the stock was at 80. Were shares trading
above the strike price of the April 80 put, the option would be
out-of-the-money; the April 80 call, of course, would be profitable
with the stock trading above the strike price. The put gives you
the right to *sell* shares; you could only do this profitably if the
market price were *below* your potential selling price.

Put premiums tend to be lower than call premiums, although
exceptions will always exist. The reason? Investors tend to be
more bullish than bearish, and the premium rate reflects this inherent predisposition. In addition, a call option can theoretically
rise to infinity. A put option's potential profit, on the other hand,
is limited, since a stock can only fall to zero. A put option with a
striking price of, say, 20 can only gain 20 points in value, since
the stock can only decline to zero—granted, a highly unlikely
event. But a call option with a striking price of 20 can rise an

infinite amount, even hundreds of times its original premium value, although this, too, is unlikely.

The put buyer faces some of the same hurdles confronting the call buyer. Just as a call buyer must recoup his premium investment cost in the market, so must the put buyer. Thus, if you pay a 1½-point premium to purchase a put with a 20 strike price, the stock will have to trade at 18½ or lower at expiration for you to recoup your investment—if you hold it that long. Most option buyers dispose of them in the secondary market long before expiration. Fortunately, from the buyer's standpoint, put premiums tend to be a little lower than call premiums. The smaller premium means the buyer must overcome less adversity. Put buyers will find that the general trend of the overall market will affect premiums. In bear markets, when puts are apt to rise in value, put premiums will be higher; in bull markets, put premiums will decline.

Traditionally, stock market speculators sold stock short in anticipation of lower prices. While often profitable, this practice had its drawbacks—especially when the stock soared in value and the short sellers found themselves facing unlimited risks. With the advent of listed options trading, however, the erstwhile short sellers had an alternative strategy available to them. They could buy put options. For the first time, their risk became limited. The fear of being a short seller could now be handled and successfully managed. The put option was the answer.

So far, we've looked at a number of illustrations using calls. So let's look at one using puts. When Bally was trading at 28¼ not long ago, its November 30 put was available for 2⅛. The November 30 put gives the put holder the right to sell Bally shares at a price of $30. Since Bally is at 28¼, the put is in-the-money with an intrinsic value of 1¾. The remaining ⅜ of a point reflects time value which is rapidly decreasing, since the option only has three weeks left to expiration. Should Bally shares remain unchanged just prior to expiration of the November 30s, the put buyer would sustain a loss, since the option at expiration is only worth its intrinsic value, or the difference between the striking price and the stock's market value when, of course, it is in-the-money. Should Bally move up to 30 or higher, the put premium would rapidly lose value. At 30 the put would only be worth its time value. Therefore, the buyer who pays 2⅛ for a Bally put is counting on the underlying shares to decline in value. Assuming Bally does decline to 25 by expiration of the put, the put would be valued at 5, and the put holder would have a profit of 2⅞ points minus commissions, or $287 on his $212 investment—a return of more than 133 per cent.

We've seen how puts can be used as a speculative tool by an investor who is bearish on a stock, but what about the investor who's sitting on a nice paper profit in a stock and wants to protect that profit? Let's consider the investor who bought Bally at 20 and has ridden it to 28¼. He can take profits on his stock position, or he may wish to protect those profits by purchasing a Bally 30 put. Again, his premium cost will be 2⅛. If Bally continues higher, he will simply abandon his put, whose premium cost will be offset by the gain on the stock position. Should Bally decline, however, his put will ensure that he receives a price of $30 for his shares. From this profit he'll have to subtract the cost of the put, however. By using the put in this manner as a protective tool, you might consider it a cheap form of insurance.

Looking at the other side of the transaction, an investor who is bullish on Bally's prospects might have sold the November 30 put for 2⅛ points. The seller would have received that premium for writing the put, and had Bally indeed risen to 30 or above at expiration, he would have been able to retain the full premium. The seller's risk is that Bally's shares drop precipitously. Should this occur, the seller either must rapidly buy back the option he sold— at a loss—or be prepared to pay the put buyer for the full increase in the value of the put. Remember, below the striking price, the put *gains* in value identically with the decline in the stock's value. If, therefore, Bally falls to 10 in three weeks (granted, a highly unlikely event), the put writer would have to pay the difference between the strike at 30 and 10, the market price. This amounts to $2,000, a considerable loss considering the put writer was only given 2⅛ points for writing the put.

Unlike put and call *buying,* the selling or writing of puts and calls can result in virtually unlimited losses. Put and call buyers are *limited* in the amount of money they can lose on a trade to the cost of the premium. Put and call writers, however, are *unlimited* in their risk exposure, since they are responsible for the full movement away from the strike when they write an option. Despite put and call buying being limited to a fixed amount of liability and call selling being unlimited in its liability, a paradoxical situation exists: namely, put and call buying is considered highly risky, and put and call writing is considered a conservative option strategy under the *right* circumstances. It all depends, as we shall see, on how you manage your option strategies.

THE CALL WRITER

The investor who writes or sells a call option promises to deliver 100 shares of the underlying stock to the option buyer at the striking price. The seller may or may not own the underlying shares when he writes the call. Remember that if he does own the shares, he is a covered writer; if he doesn't own the shares, he is an uncovered or naked writer.

Naked writing is far more risky than covered writing. If you write a call and the value of the underlying stock soars in value, you are liable for the full amount of the move. To a covered writer, the stock rally only represents profit he *might have had* had he not written the call. The covered writer will deliver his shares to the buyer of the option, who will call them away at the lower strike price. But to the naked writer, who doesn't have the shares to deliver, the rally in the stock represents a loss, since he'll have to either buy back his short option at an inflated price or go into the stock market and purchase the underlying shares. He'll then have to deliver them to the call buyer at the agreed-upon strike price. Moreover, because a stock can rise to infinity, the potential loss to the naked writer is unlimited. Strangely enough, the naked writer takes this risk knowing that his potential profit is limited to the initial premium he receives when writing the call.

Obviously, covered writing is the most conservative approach. A number of institutions, including large insurance companies, pension funds, and banking firms routinely engage in covered writing programs. The drawback with covered writing is that it takes a lot of cash. The premiums you'll receive relative to the size of investment in the stock market are apt to seem small. The naked writer, on the other hand, makes more sizable gains on the money he deposits in the form of margin. But his risk can be greater if he isn't paying close attention to the market.

The basic stance of a call writer, whether covered or uncovered, is neutral to bearish or perhaps even slightly bullish, depending on the kind of options he's writing. The call writer always has the premium working for him. In writing a call, the seller knows the stock must advance by more than the amount of the premium before he'll lose money. This is a decided advantage over the call buyer, who must first *overcome* the premium he pays before he'll be in a profitable position. An out-of-the-money call will still generate income for its writer even if the stock rises. The reason? As long as the stock doesn't close above the striking price at expiration, the option will expire worthless and the option writer will receive the entire premium income. Unfortunately, out-of-the-money options are apt to have low premiums. The option writer has to determine if it is really worth it to write an option with a premium of a quarter, an eighth, or even a sixteenth. For now, it is only important to know what an option writer does—not why or how he selects a specific option to sell.

Having written an option, the writer or seller is always concerned with the movement of the underlying stock. The intelligent option seller will always determine his break-even point in advance when he writes an option. And when break-even is threatened, he'll promptly buy back his option for whatever it will bring and look for other writing opportunities.

For example, when McDonnell Douglas is trading at $31½ a share, a call writer may decide to sell an out-of-the-money May 40 call for a premium of 1½. Although the May expiration date may still be six months away, he reasons that the underlying shares will probably not gain 8½ points during that time and that the call will most likely expire worthless. For writing the call, he receives the $1½ premium. By adding the $1½ premium income to the striking price of 40, he establishes his break-even point at 41½; above that level he'll sustain a loss on the trade. Between 40 and 41½ he'll retain a portion of his premium, since the option will certainly be exercised above the striking price. Below 40, of course, the option will only have time value—which, upon expiration, will be zero, enabling the writer to retain the full premium of 1½.

In slow-moving markets or bear markets, call writing is a profitable strategy. But in explosive markets or markets characterized by takeover bids, the naked writer can find himself in serious trouble if he isn't careful. In the illustration above, if McDonnell Douglas rose to even 43, the naked writer would lose twice what he gained on the transaction. Above the striking price the losses to the naked writer mount steadily. The covered writer, however, is in a much more enviable position, since his losses on the short call are offset by corresponding gains on the stock he holds.

There's another aspect of risk that applies only to covered writing. If the price of the underlying stock declines, the covered writer may lose more on his stock position than he gains in writing income. This is a very real risk and one that covered writers must be aware of. Using the McDonnell Douglas example just discussed, let's say the covered writer buys 100 shares at 31½ and simultaneously writes a May 40 call for 1½. Where does he actually begin to lose money? Below 30—the point at which he actually purchased the shares, since his 31½ purchase price was offset by 1½ in writing income.

There are defensive strategies the covered writer can use, however. Once prices fell to 30, the writer could have written more calls. This tactic would serve to generate more income and lower his overall net cost on the 100 shares. On the other hand, it does, of course, make him more vulnerable should the stock stage a rally. Since out-of-the-money calls are apt to have small premiums, however, additional writing may have limited appeal. Should McDonnell Douglas shares continue to decline, the writer may begin to wish he'd purchased a put or sold the stock short. Lastly, the covered writer could always opt for selling his stock and becoming a naked writer. But this would require the posting of margin for his short option position and would involve all the risks associated with a naked option position. For many large institutions, which are limited to covered writing, this strategy would neither be prudent nor practical.

THE PUT WRITER

The put writer is neutral to bullish on the stock's prospects, since he is willing to have shares "put" to him at the striking price. Typically, put writers aren't covered when they sell put options, but they may take on a covered position by selling short shares of the stock they write the put on. Remember, the put gives its holder the right to sell shares at the strike price. Thus, if prices fall *below* the strike (the mirror image of the call), the put proves profitable and the seller or writer must be willing to buy back shares above the prevailing market price.

The naked put writer, therefore, sustains a loss below the strike price. In part, this loss will be offset by the premium received for writing the put. But if prices declined sharply, the premium received will be insufficient to offset the loss. On the other hand, if prices stay around the put's striking price, the premium will be the put writer's to keep, since the put certainly won't be exercised. You may be somewhat bearish on a stock's prospects and still write puts. Consider a situation in which you've sold short stock which has made a substantial decline. You now have a profit on your short stock position. But you write a put because you anticipate a modest rally *prior* to a resumption of the decline. Should the rally indeed occur, your short stock position will have temporary paper losses which can in whole or part be offset by the put premium. Once you think the rally has carried far enough, you then buy back your short put and allow the short stock position to again resume a profitable direction. Obviously, for this strategy to work, you must have excellent timing. But it does illustrate how put writing can capitalize on even temporary rallies in the market.

Let's look at an example of put writing. When Syntex shares were recently trading at 57⅞, Syntex March 50 puts with three months left to expiration were quoted at 2. As a writer, you may have welcomed the opportunity to pick up $2 per share by instructing your broker to sell a Syntex March 50 put. Three weeks later, however, Syntex had declined to 55 and the March 50 put had *increased* in value to 2⅜. At this point you would have had a paper loss on the position, although you may have had good reason to hold on to the short March 50 put in anticipation of stabilizing or higher prices. Remember, the jury is out on any option you write until the option expires worthless. In the interim, however, your broker will insist on a fully margined position at all times. While the margin requirements won't be listed here, it is important to understand that you, as the writer, are responsible to your broker and, in turn, the clearing house for your position at all times. This responsibility includes the posting of sufficient "good-faith" margin to demonstrate your financial integrity in the transaction. In the illustration above, should Syntex shares plunge below $50 a share, you must match the decline below 50 dollar for dollar or buy back your put in the secondary market. This will relieve you of the responsibility to continue posting margin on the position.

The put writer knows there is money to be made writing puts on stocks that remain stable. Assuming stabilized prices, decreasing time value will work in the put writer's favor. Let's look at an example in which Teledyne shares were stable and actually traded at identical prices more than three months apart. In the period under discussion, Teledyne shares held steady at 147¾. First, we'll look at the in-the-money January 160 puts. Remember, for a put to be in-the-money, the market price of the underlying shares must be *below* the striking price. When Teledyne is at 147¾, the 160 puts have 12¼ points of intrinsic value. That is, if the options were to expire today, their worth would be 12¼ points based on the difference between where the stock could be sold at the striking price and where you could buy the underlying shares in the market.

Looking at the options table, let's assume that three months ago you could have sold the Teledyne January 160 puts at 14½. Today, with about two months left to expiration and the underlying shares trading at the same price, the January 160 puts still bring 14. The time value has decreased by ½ (the difference between 14½ and 14), while the intrinsic value has remained the same. The inference to be made is that in-the-money puts give up their time value slowly. But if we look at an out-of-the-money put on the same stock, we'll see a dramatic difference. As the chances of the out-of-the-moneys ever proving profitable become less and less, the premium drops faster and faster. During the same period of time, with Teledyne shares still quoted at 147¾, the January out-of-the-money 130 puts declined in price from 2⅝ to 1⅝, or a whole point. On a percentage basis, that's a 100 per cent better return. If you are going to write puts, therefore, write them on out-of-the-money options, where the percentage gains are apt to be more rapid. The trade-off, of course, between risk and opportunity in writing puts—or any other option, for that matter—will always be there. The puts with little chance of proving profitable will have low premiums. Thus, your income in writing these puts will be strictly limited. On the other hand, you must consider the possibility, no matter how remote, that the stock will plummet in price—and you'll sustain a huge loss in terms of the premium income you received.

WRITING PUTS TO ACQUIRE STOCK

Another strategy is to write puts in hopes of acquiring stock. Remember, as a put writer you'll have the stock put to you if it *declines* below the strike. Let's say you are looking to acquire General Foods stock, but you'd prefer to pay a little less than its present market value of 30. You might write a General Foods 30 put for 1¾ in anticipation of the option being exercised. Should General Foods fall below 30, the put will prove profitable to the put buyer and you will be asked to buy the stock at 30. Since you received 1¾ for writing the put, your actual cost of acquiring the stock is 28¼ (30 − 1¾ = 28¼). At 28¼, General Foods may be attractive to you. Should the stock stay above 30, you may prefer to stand aside—in which case you will have still earned the 1¾ points for writing the put. Obviously, only an in-the-money put will be exercised. Your eagerness to acquire the stock, therefore, will have some bearing on which particular option you write. Put writing is not a sure thing when it comes to acquiring stock. There is no guarantee the stock price will fall below the strike price and be put to you. On the other hand, you may find yourself acquiring stock that is declining rapidly. In such an instance you may seriously regret buying a stock that was put to you when its market value was so much lower. Yet perhaps the worst scenario is to write a put in anticipation of picking up stock at a "bargain" only to have the stock skyrocket out of sight without your having the opportunity to buy it. In such a case you will have your premium profit in hand, but the upward move of the underlying stock (which you were *right* about) may be quite large in comparison. You would have missed the move. Having insisted on buying a dollar or two lower, you would have given up many times that amount in profit.

As you can see, there are a variety of strategies you can employ in using the listed stock options markets. Some are conservative, some speculative. The more popular strategies will be explored in detail in subsequent chapters. But for now, let's cover some of a few of the preliminary necessities of trading before deciding on a specific approach to the options market.

2

Getting Started in the Options Market

Having familiarized yourself with the information in Chapter 1, you may be eager to get started trading puts and calls. You may even have already taken the plunge into the options market. Regardless of your results in the past, however, it is time to rethink your investment strategy, to step back for a moment to work out an approach to the market that is right for you. Since no two investors have the same temperamental makeup, it is important that your investment decisions reflect your unique attitudes toward risk. After all, it will be your money at risk, and you'll be the one who'll have to bear the losses for any mistakes. With that in mind, let's mention a few of the considerations you'll want to make *before* you start trading options.

START SLOWLY

In the options markets, as in life itself, experience is often the best teacher. Although a book such as this one can prove helpful in providing information and recommending specific strategies, the real learning experience comes from actually trading. Advocates of "paper trading," those who suggest you follow a particular option on paper rather than committing funds, are apt to disagree with this suggestion, but there is no substitute for putting your money on the table and experiencing the emotional ups and downs that follow. Paradoxically, perhaps the worst thing that can happen to an option investor is to make money right at the outset. Such success is often short-lived, and the hapless investor is apt to turn cynical when his initial good fortune isn't repeated. Seasoned traders will tell you that if you want to make a success of your efforts in the options market, you must get your mistakes behind you and, at the very least, learn to stop making the less intelligent ones, since the intelligent mistakes will stay with you throughout your trading career.

Since making mistakes and sustaining losses are a part of options trading, you must cultivate an attitude toward them that will enable you to take them in stride as part of the investment game. Losses to the option trader are as much a part of the day-to-day buying and selling as taking a punch is to a prizefighter or striking out is to a home run hitter. They are inevitable setbacks. On the other hand, you want to always maintain a defensive attitude. Just as the fighter doesn't want to be knocked out in the first round, you don't want to be knocked out of the market either. Hence, a simple rule: always remember that your financial survival is paramount. If you plunge recklessly today, you may not be around to make profits tomorrow. This rule should be obvious, but it is remarkable how many investors come and go in the options game trying to make big profits at the outset *before* they have an opportunity to learn how the game is really played.

By starting small you'll give yourself the opportunity to gain invaluable experience at low cost. Most certainly, if you trade options for long, you'll have some losses. By keeping these losses to a minimum, you'll be able to gain a feel for how the market operates. You'll also gain the confidence required to trade aggressively when the time comes.

OPTIONS ARE NOT STOCKS

Most investors come to the options market with a background in the stock market. This is poor training for the high-risk, high-gain game of options trading. If you are going to speculate in puts and calls, you are far better off trying your hand in the commodity futures markets than the stock market. The approach to stock

market investing is totally different than the approach required of
the option trader. If they were indeed comparable, there would
be no good reason to purchase stocks at all. But options trading is
an entirely different investment game, and you'd give yourself an
advantage by conveniently forgetting all the "conventional wis-
dom" that applies to the stock market.

One such time-honored practice in the stock market is known
as *averaging*. Using this approach, if you think Dean Witter stock
is a good buy at 50, you'll likewise reason that it is an even better
bargain at a lower price. Should Dean Witter common, therefore,
begin to decline, you simply begin to accumulate more and more
stock as it falls, thereby averaging a progressively lower cost. In
time the investor who averages expects the stock to rally. But in
the options market, the time is strictly limited, and the option
trader who averages is apt to end up with worthless call options
and nothing else. Thus, the option buyer must rid himself of any
notion that time is on his side. If anything, option buyers are giving up time value every day that they hold an option. The option
trader must think in terms of speed and excellent timing. The idea
is to spot an opportunity and jump quickly or not at all. Today's
good trade probably won't be available tomorrow.

DECLINING TIME VALUE

When you buy a stock, you own something that has a given
market value. True, the value may fall tomorrow, but the stock
buyer has the luxury of time on his side; he may hold his stock position indefinitely. When you purchase an option, however, you
buy a promise that has a specific time limit. Moreover, the premium you pay for the option must be overcome in the underlying
stock before you'll have a profit. Thus, if you pay 5 per cent of a
stock's value for an at-the-money call and the stock doesn't move
upward by that amount, the option will stay at-the-money and will
expire worthless. If you buy a stock and the price of the stock
doesn't move up, you can still sell the stock for what you paid for
it. Moreover, even if the stock does move up, the call buyer is not
guaranteed a profit. In fact, he may still sustain a 100 per cent
loss. How? Well, let's say you buy an out-of-the-money call and
you pay just 5 per cent of the total value of the stock. This would

be just 2½ on a $50 stock. Having done so, you may find that although the stock may move up 5 per cent by expiration, the option may still expire worthless if it remains out-of-the-money at the maturity date. The investor who purchased the stock, on the other hand, retains the security, and the 5 per cent gain will be reflected in the enhanced value of the market price of the stock.

Taken a step further, if the stock investor makes his purchase on 50 per cent margin, his 5 per cent gain translates into a 10 per cent profit on his invested funds. This compares with zero per cent for the option holder. Having lost your call premium, you may purchase another call, paying the identical premium. But there is no guarantee that what didn't work out before will work in the future. In fact, you may view this tactic as throwing good money after bad. All things being equal, a security trading at 40 today is just as likely to be trading at 40 tomorrow, and the day after, and so on. For the call buyer facing a limited number of tomorrows prior to expiration, the likelihood of unchanged prices isn't a pleasant one.

All this is not meant to dissuade you from options trading. Indeed, given the high leverage of options trading, a comparable amount of dollars invested in listed call options would be magnified many times in profit potential in the options investment *if* the price of the underlying security makes a move upward prior to expiration. The point is, options and stocks are quite different. This necessitates a different approach on the part of the investor.

BE FLEXIBLE

If there's a sure way to lose money in the options market, it is to have an opinion about the direction of prices which you are determined to stand by through thick and thin. Inflexible people make bad option traders. Inflexibility suggests that a trader thinks he knows more than the market. This, of course, is nonsense. The market is always right. And the best traders know this.

It is helpful to have an opinion about the direction of prices and act accordingly. But as an option trader, either buying or writing puts and calls, you must be quick to change your mind and to cut losses whenever possible. Let's say you are bearish on the prospects of Hilton shares and you buy 10 in-the-money Hilton

February 45 puts at 5½ each when Hilton is trading at 40. Your cost is $550 per option plus commission, or $5,500 plus commissions for the 10 puts. This constitutes your total risk, since as a put buyer you can never lose more than the total premium. But let's say Hilton shares begin to move up closer to the strike price. Naturally, the value of the options will decline, since the intrinsic value is decreased by 1 every time the stock moves up a dollar. At this point, your judgment on the direction of Hilton shares appears to be wrong and the put premium falls to 4. You now have a 1½-point loss on your 10 puts, or a total of $1,500. The sensible thing to do is to *take the loss immediately* rather than await a downward trend in prices. Once proven wrong, your chances of exiting this trade a winner decrease dramatically. Yet this approach requires flexibility and discipline. Not to do so will only invite losses.

USE TECHNICAL ANALYSIS

There are two primary approaches to the study of market behavior, the fundamental and the technical. Fundamental analysis relies upon important supply and demand information: a company's earnings, the dividend rate, new product development, the state of the economy, consumer demand for the company's products, corporate borrowings and debt, interest rates, potential takeover bids, and so on. While it pays to know the fundamentals of the stock, for day-to-day trading decisions you'll have to rely on the technical indicators. Ultimately, the total mix of the company's fundamentals *will* determine share value. The drawback with being a fundamentalist, however, is that no one knows precisely *when* the market will value the shares higher or lower. Moreover, people with different viewpoints—differences which, after all, make the market—may interpret a given set of fundamentals differently. The technical approach, on the other hand, relies on the notion that every factor affecting the stock will be reflected in price. By concentrating primarily on price patterns, the technician believes he'll be better prepared to anticipate future price movements. The fundamentals only tend to cloud the issue for the technician. The technical analyst wants to make future price predictions based on what the stock is doing today. Because so many investors follow price patterns, there is also the school of thought that maintains that technical analysis is simply a self-fulfilling prophecy. Whether or not technical analysis has *intrinsic* value, the option trader should learn to pay attention to chart patterns and other technical tools. Why a particular trading tool works is not as important as the fact that it does work. Technical analysis is far too widely subscribed to by stock market traders not to be used by anyone seeking to get in on the beginning of a move. Typically, in the absence of fundamental news, a given market move will be attributed to *technical* factors. It is knowing how to read these technical trading signals that will generate profits in the long run. Since options are so much more volatile than their underlying stocks, their technical moves, at least on a percentage basis, are even more important.

How do you get started in technical analysis? By learning the most familiar chart patterns and either subscribing to a chart service or keeping up your own daily charts. Technicians rely on two basic kinds of charts: the *bar chart,* in which the daily range and settlement is recorded every day in the form of a vertical line connecting the high and low and a small horizontal line for the close; or the *point-and-figure chart,* in which small *x*'s and *o*'s measure highs and lows and meaningful price reversals.

Technical analysts place a great deal of importance on the concept of *support* and *resistance.* Put simply, support is that price area where prices tend to stop declining and begin to stabilize and rally; resistance is that price area where prices tend to stop advancing and begin to stabilize and decline. As you begin to use some of the tools outlined in this book, pinpointing support and resistance zones will become second nature. For now, just remember that support and resistance areas are significant psychological areas on the chart where technical analysts "expect" additional buying and selling. Often, the expectation alone is sufficient to move prices in one direction or another.

SPECIALIZE IN ONE OR TWO STRATEGIES

Options offer such a wide variety of trading strategies that it is easy to get carried away with the numerous profit possibilities and overextend your trading capabilities. It is true that options are versatile. And it is true that you must be flexible to win on a consistent basis. But as a general rule, it pays to be a specialist. One such strategy is to write only covered out-of-the-money calls. Another might be to concentrate on writing naked calls. Other investors might feel more comfortable just buying calls. A sophisticated spread trading program might appeal to other option investors. The point is, you have to play your own game, the one with which you are most knowledgeable and most at ease. By concentrating on the strategy you do best, you'll have the edge on those who switch from buying to writing to spreading without a firm grasp on any one technique. While call buying strategies will no doubt prove more profitable in bull markets than call writing strategies, knowing your specific strategy will stand you in good stead from the first to the last. As for which strategies lend themselves to specific market situations, we'll cover them in subsequent chapters. But you must make the decision to use a strategy that best fits your own temperament and trading objectives.

PAY ATTENTION TO COMMISSION COSTS

Before you get started on an options trading program, you should shop around for the most favorable commissions and keep a few important points in mind. Because the brokerage business has become much more competitive in recent years, the customers are getting a much more favorable deal. This is primarily due to the arrival of the discount brokerage firms, which offer stock option executions minus the fancy window dressing we've all come to expect of a full-line brokerage firm. While the discounters specialize in fast and reliable service, they *don't* provide advice, research, or function in a hand-holding capacity. Nor do they take you out to lunch. They do keep their opinions strictly to themselves. Thus, you won't find a discounter second-guessing your trading decisions. For many stock market investors who are used to hearing their brokers saying, "I wouldn't do that if I were you," or some similar comment, this lack of editorial advice should be welcome. What services do discounters provide? They take orders; provide fast, efficient executions; read fills back to you; and provide all the paperwork the full-line houses do. They'll also provide you with quotes on request, of course, all via toll-free telephone numbers.

There are two schools of thought on discounters. Advocates of the full-line, high-price "wire" houses will claim you need all the help you can get in the market—and who's closer to the market than a capable stock and options broker? In addition, brokerage houses frequently encourage their clients to spend time in their comfortable offices watching the ticker. A capable broker can indeed provide a variety of services: keeping you aware of recent research, watching your position, putting orders through to the floor, and the like. But a lot depends on your individual broker. The level of broker competency ranges from the superlative to the abysmally poor. Then, too, so much depends on your personal relationship with your broker that it is hard to make a judgment concerning whether a discounter or full-line house is best for you.

SELECTING A BROKER

How to select a broker? One characteristic that many investors look for in a broker is a willingness to risk his own funds in the market. Although some brokerage firms won't permit their account executives to trade their own accounts, many will. After all, do you want someone reluctant to risk his own money in the market advising you to risk yours? Moreover, why would a truly skillful trader not want to trade his own account? If a broker doesn't have the temperament for trading, fine—applaud him for his honesty and find someone who does trade the market. And this leads us to another important consideration: insist on opening your account with an *options specialist*. Just as you wouldn't select a general practitioner to do brain surgery, you don't want a stock broker who dabbles in options to assist you in complicated options strategies. Going a step further, you want an options specialist who specializes in your specific strategy—naked writing, spreading, call buying, or whatever. The closer you can bring your interests in line with the interests of your broker, the better relationship you'll have. After all, this specialized service from an expert is what you're paying for when you do business with a retail broker. If you aren't getting the service you're paying for, perhaps you should investigate the discount route.

DISCOUNT BROKERAGE FIRMS

As we've mentioned, a discount brokerage firm does not provide trading advice. The discounter makes his money *not* directly from the commissions paid, but from the *float*—the interest he earns on excess margin in your account that is not committed in the market or invested in securities in your name. Having less overhead in the form of expensive office space, advertising, and commissioned sales people, the discounter can pass his savings along to you in the form of reduced commissions. Over time, you can expect to make considerable savings by using the services of a discount brokerage firm. Certainly, if the entrance of a number of new discount houses into the brokerage business is any indication, the trend is in the direction of discounting. It is important that the firm you select will safeguard your funds. Ask for financial references prior to opening an account. Find out if a prospective discounter is a clearing member on any of the options exchanges— and if not, who they clear through. You may then want to contact the clearing member concerning the discounter's financial reputation. Since firms which engage in less-than-ethical practices in the financial community rapidly attain notoriety, ask around for word-of-mouth recommendations. And shy away from any firm with less than a sterling reputation.

Discounters tend to be located in the major cities, although some are now opening regional offices. But most provide toll-free telephone services for orders and quotes. Location is not as important as service. Pay attention to how quickly and professionally your orders are handled. The brokerage house can't be held responsible if you make mistakes in forecasting the market, but it *can* be held accountable if the orders are not filled properly. Always *insist* that your limit orders are filled according to the limits you specify. *Never* take a trade that a broker tries to give you that doesn't fit the order you gave him. The broker knows that he will have to take a trade refused by his customer. As a result, he will try not to make any mistakes. A good broker, of course, will sustain a loss rather than insist a customer take a trade that resulted from a miswritten order. It pays to tape-record phone conversations to your broker when giving orders. Also, ask your broker to read back any order you give him. Most brokerage firms already tape-record phone conversations to avoid misunderstandings —but this is to protect *their* interests in the event of a litigation. Recorded phone orders will prove valuable in the event a misunderstanding arises.

Since commission costs can range as high as 50 per cent of the price of the option at some firms, it pays to shop around. Make sure you understand the commission fees clearly before you open an account. Most firms have $25 minimum commissions on any order involving more than $100. This translates into a 25 per cent commission cost for trading a $1 option. Percentagewise, the costs for buying or selling an option whose price is less than 1 can be even greater. As a rule, the lower the cost of the option, the greater the commission will cost on a percentage basis. To minimize commission costs there are some steps you can take, however. First, never trade a single option. Always trade at least two options at a time. The reason for this is to overcome the minimum commission most firms impose. Brokerage houses reason, with some justification, that it takes as much work on their part to execute one trade involving a single option as it does a trade involving ten options—hence the minimum fee. But on a per-unit basis, the cost drops drastically when you trade multiple contracts. As a general rule, it usually makes sense to trade heavier but less frequently. That is, it is better to trade five options at a time than one option five times. The lower commissions on a per-share basis will translate into a higher net return on a successful 500- or 1,000-share position than with a 100- or 200-share position. Not only does this encourage you to be more selective, but it cuts down on the commission cost. Moreover, with your money on the line in a more concentrated manner, you are far more likely to watch the market closely and less likely to get sloppy in your trading techniques. Second, from a commission standpoint you can get more for your money by concentrating on the higher-priced options—Teledyne, Syntex, Getty Oil, and IBM all come to mind. Since public companies like to encourage shareholder participation, stocks are frequently being split, on the theory that there are many more investors willing to buy a $30 stock than a $60 stock. Nevertheless, the higher-priced stocks and options offer the better deal on the commissions. Lastly, try to keep it simple.

When we get into some of the more sophisticated strategies, such as spread trading, combinations, straddles, and the like, you'll see that the more complex strategies require additional commissions. Frequently, the strategy's risk/reward ratio will be well worth the additional expense, but you should be aware that this is not always the case. Try to watch commission costs. Often, you'll find there is an easier, more efficient way to achieve the same investment goal without using as many options—and, of course, paying as many commissions.

LIMIT LOSSES

Much is written about the opportunity for profits in options trading, but relatively little about the potential for loss. Understandably, this is a subject many investors would want to avoid. But unless you have a firm grasp of the risks involved in trading options, chances are you won't be around long enough to reap the potential rewards. And that leads us to a paradox concerning options: to avoid losing a lot of money trading options, you must be willing to lose a little. Put another way, you absolutely must keep your losses small. Learning to take a loss quickly and without regret when you are wrong in the market is the mark of a good trader. The amateur, on the other hand, will resist taking a loss in hopes of the market reversing and perhaps extricating him from his losing position. Rarely does this work, however. Bad trades tend to get worse.

The need to take losses quickly is especially important when you write naked options. The buyer of an option, you may recall, knows his ultimate risk at the outset—100 per cent of his invested funds, the entire cost of the premium. But the writer who is naked risks an unlimited amount of money. For example, consider the plight of those unfortunate naked writers who sold calls on any one of a number of takeover bid stocks in the past few years. Santa Fe, Kennecott, Pennzoil, Marathon Oil—all returned huge percentage profits to call buyers and comparable huge losses to call writers. Unfortunately, most of the writers never had a chance to avoid ruin, since the news frequently hit when the market was closed. Writers who had received as little as $18.75 for writing a call contract on St. Joe Minerals a few months ago found themselves paying as much as $1,550 per call just three days later. While this is an extreme case, it illustrates the point that even knowledgeable traders occasionally get caught on the wrong side of the market and that losses must be kept to a minimum.

When you write soon-to-expire, out-of-the-money calls, as did a number of market makers in the St. Joe Minerals example above, you must always remember that the remote chance exists that the option will prove profitable for the call buyer. Options selling for as little as $\frac{1}{16}$, or $6.25 for 100 shares, have been known to soar in price when news hits the market. Above the strike, remember, the call option will move point for point with the stock.[1] So if you write a 40 call for $\frac{1}{16}$ just weeks before expiration and the stock is at 32, you'll be in serious trouble should the stock soar in value and close above 40. When the stock is at 41, you'll owe $1 for every 6¼ cents you received for writing the option. By the time the stock reaches 45, the losses on the short call position will amount to $5 for every 6¼ cents you realized in writing income. Fortunately for naked writers, such occurrences are rare.

To prevent such losses, however, you must monitor your position. Unlike the stock and commodity markets, the options markets don't allow *stop-loss orders*. Stop-loss orders are orders to liquidate or offset an open position once a specific price is reached —in this case, an adverse price, since you literally want to stop the losses when the stop price is touched. Since stops are not allowed, you or your broker should make an effort to monitor your position. Having set a specific limit on your losses when entering a trade, you should automatically take the loss once your stop-loss price is hit. To establish your stop-loss price, you may want to use daily settlement prices only, the prices which are published in the *Wall Street Journal* and in the financial pages of your newspaper. During a trading session, prices may be quite volatile. Thus, to use a mental stop on an intraday fluctuation may get you out on only

---

[1] Actually, call premiums only move point for point with the underlying stock when the option is at *parity*. Parity exists when the exercise price plus the premium equals the market price of the stock. (For example, parity exists when there is an exercise price of 35, a premium of 5, and the market price is 40.) Premiums tend to move less than point for point prior to reaching parity.

a temporary technical movement. Precisely where you should place your mental stops should be decided after you consider a number of factors. These may include the underlying stock's Beta rating, which will reflect volatility; the amount of profit or loss you feel comfortable with; your analysis of overall market trends; the prospects for your particular stock; technical and fundamental information affecting your stock; and time left to expiration, among other factors.

Under no circumstances should you allow a wounded ego to get in the way of taking a loss. Not to take action when losses are small will ensure that you may be forced to take action later on when the losses have become intolerable. This is especially true for naked put and call writers whose risk is unlimited the entire time they hold a short position.

MAINTAIN ACCURATE RECORDS

Before you start trading puts and calls, invest in a couple of notebooks to track your options positions. Your brokerage house will send you profit and loss statements, of course, but you'll want to have your own record of transactions (as well as recorded tapes made when giving orders) to avoid any mistakes. It is especially important in trading options to know exactly where you stand every day, since, due to the high leverage, a forgotten position can impair your equity position in a hurry. Never leave the status of any position to memory, but rather record in writing every order you give your broker as well as where the order was actually executed, the strike price, expiration month, underlying stock, and mental stop-loss order. You'll also want to keep track of the recent trading history of any option you are following even if you don't have a current position in that option. This written price history will provide you with accurate information concerning how the option trades (the magnitude of its rallies and declines), the support and resistance, contract highs and lows, and other valuable information that will enable you to make intelligent decisions before you take an option position. As a rule, it helps to follow twice as many options as you normally trade. Hence, if you normally have a position in five options, you may want to follow at least ten options full time. Your own style of trading, of course, will determine how you track options.

You should keep at least two sets of notebooks. One for recording the information on positions you've actually taken, and one for tracking the price action of options you follow. The former will prove invaluable at tax time, and will immediately alert you if a discrepancy exists between your records and the statements that will be mailed to you by your brokerage house. Despite efforts to keep them at a minimum, mistakes are common in the brokerage business. The mere dropping of a decimal point can result in thousands of dollars of losses showing in your trading account. Be diligent in checking over brokerage house statements and insist immediately on correcting errors. As a last resort, change brokers or brokerage houses if the mistakes become too common. It is hard enough trying to beat the market without having to worry about the brokerage house making mistakes in your account.

It is important that you know how to read your entries and can make sense out of the data you've recorded. You'll want to keep separate entries for puts and calls, including all the pertinent data for each trade. You'll want to know the date of each trade; whether you bought or sold (remember, the order is not as significant as knowing whether you closed out each trade); the name, number, expiration, and strike of every option; and the price you paid for buying the option or the price you received for selling the option. One sample recording method for call trades appears in Table 2.

Table 2

CALLS

Date	Bought/Sold	Quantity/Name/Expiration/Strike	Price
11/02	Sold	1 American Express Jan 40	6⅜
12/30	Bought	1 American Express Jan 40	4⅛
11/02	Bought	10 USAir	Mar 10	3¾
12/30	Sold	10 USAir	Mar 10	2⅝
12/29	Bought	3 Marathon Oil	Jun 80	8
12/30	Sold	3 Marathon Oil	Jun 80	5¾
12/29	Bought	7 AMF	Feb 25	3⅜

In your second notebook you'll keep a daily record of the option and underlying stock prices. In Table 2 you can see that you completed (both bought and sold) three trades and are still long 7 AMF February 25 calls. The purchase of both the USAir and Marathon Oil calls resulted in losses. The writing of the American Express January 40 call, however, resulted in profits, since you received 6⅜ for writing the call and only paid 4⅛ for buying it back. The difference, of course, minus the commission proved to be your profit. Note that the highly speculative Marathon Oil calls, which were out-of-the-money, lost a substantial percentage of their value in a single day's trading. The loss was quickly taken.

It is important that the quantities, options, expirations, and strikes match every time you wish to offset or close out a trade. It is also important that you sell each time you buy or vice versa. If you *bought* an additional 10 USAir March 10s after your initial purchase, you would be long 20 USAir March 10s, albeit at different prices. Moreover, if having purchased the initial 10 USAir March 10s, you forgot how many you were long and later sold 5, you would still be long 5. Since there are different strike prices and delivery months, it is vital that you correctly specify the option, quantity, expiration, and strike to your broker. If you were to sell 7 AMF February 20 calls against your long February 25s, you would be both long and short, or spread AMF calls. Since it is vitally important that all the relevant information match when you wish to close out trades, a written record of where you stand in the market is very valuable.

TRADE BOTH SIDES OF THE MARKET

When most investors think about the stock market, they think about buying stocks. This is unfortunate. Stocks, like interest rates, real estate, and practically every other investment vehicle, both rise and fall. For years some of the most sophisticated stock investors were short sellers: those traders who sold shares they didn't own in anticipation of price declines. Once the market declined, they stepped in and bought back the shares they'd previously sold and profited by the difference.

It should come as no surprise that the smart money is still active on the short side of the market, since we've had a number of sustained market declines in recent years. Yet probably not one trader in twenty seriously thinks about the downside potential when he thinks about stocks. One of the reasons for this, no doubt, has to do with the typical investor's attitude toward risk. The investor who buys a stock can only see it fall to zero. But a short seller could get "squeezed" and see the stock rise—theoretically, at least—a hundredfold. Put another way, the stock can only fall to zero (hence the short seller's profit is limited), but there is no such limit to what the stock buyer can make, since the stock can rise to infinity. In the options market the trader can benefit from down moves in the market in a number of ways. But the most popular method of capitalizing on declining markets is to buy puts and write calls. Remember, the put buyer wants the market to decline so that he can put his stock to the put writer— or, more likely, simply sell his put at a profit. The call writer, of course, wants the market to stay below the strike price, enabling him to keep the full premium he received for writing the call.

Psychologically, it is hard for many investors to think about, let alone trade, downside moves. Most investors are natural optimists. But successful trading demands that you be neither an optimist nor a pessimist, but a *realist*. It is realistic to think that a market that goes up will decline—if only for a short period of time. In the absence of market-moving events, it is realistic to think that a stock will stay pretty much the same. As a result, many traders in the options market make money by simply going against the trend. These contrarian thinkers buy market declines and sell market rallies. They know that bullish enthusiasm is always greatest at a market top and bearish pessimism is always greatest at a market bottom. They capitalize on this tendency by selling when the majority is still buying and buying when the majority is still selling. They are percentage players, and very often they are correct.

If you take the attitude that most of the time the market doesn't do much of anything, you'll be surprised how often you can make money by simply trading the small but persistent cycles that tend to bring every move "back into line." By this is meant most moves return toward the middle. Traders know this and are quick to sell into rallies, anticipating subsequent declines, and buy into dips, anticipating rallies.

Because of the low cost and high leverage associated with options trading, options lend themselves to active trading. But to be successful at trading, you must allow yourself to trade the downside as well as the upside. Which is the best side of the market to be on? That depends on the temporary direction of prices. You can be sure there will be ample opportunities on both sides if you are alert enough to changing market trends and are not afraid to think of downturns as well as upturns.

MONITOR YOUR TRADING CYCLE

Since success in the market depends so much on your individual response to market conditions, it will pay you to go with the trend when you have a series of winning trades and pull back when you are incurring losses. In part this is only normal, since you will understandably be reluctant to plunge following a loss. But some traders insist on recouping losses immediately and take bigger positions following a loss. In general, this is a mistake. Trading success tends to run in cycles. There will be times when you may not expect a loss ever again. But rest assured this will pass with time and you'll run into a cycle where it may seem that you'll never have a winner again. This, too, will pass.

It is important that you know when to be bold and when to shy away from the market. Most successful traders intuitively understand that the time to be bold is when you're winning and the time to be reluctant to take additional positions is following a series of losses.

You must rid yourself of the idea that you have to be in the market all the time. When you don't take a trade, you also reduce the probability of a loss to zero—a nice probability considering how risky some trades can be. Often, the best response to a series of losses is to take a trading break. Simply remove yourself from the market for a while. Hopefully, when you return, you'll be in a better state of mind to begin trading successfully again.

Some traders actually chart their trading equity. You can easily chart your equity level, plotting it as it rises and falls. Then you apply technical analysis to the chart pattern. For instance, you may find that every time your equity rises to, say, the $20,000 mark, you sustain a series of losses back to $15,000. You may find you have a double top at the $20,000 mark. A breakout above this area may indeed signal a move to higher ground—in your equity—in precisely the same way that a stock or option might break out above a resistance level.

This somewhat novel way of looking at your own trading record can prove beneficial *if* you are honest with yourself. Has your account been in a downtrend equitywise since you started trading options? If so, you may want to rethink your strategies. Perhaps you've insisted on buying speculative calls in a bear market. Or perhaps you wrote puts in a bear market. You may want to try writing calls and buying puts. A close monitoring of your equity position should provide you with an early warning signal. You may find you're generating profits on a steady basis and will want to continue with your present strategy, or that you're doing something wrong and remedial action is needed quickly lest you lose all your trading capital.

How you decide to cope with your own trading record will vary from individual to individual. There are naked option writers who consider buying options strictly a sucker's game. On the other side, there are buyers who wouldn't consider ever writing options. And, of course, there are both buyers and sellers, covered writers, and traders who engage in a host of complex options strategies, such as spreads, straddles, combinations, hedges, variable-ratio writes, and other market techniques. Most of them swear by their particular market technique. But that doesn't mean another strategy is not better for you. By monitoring your individual record, you'll find which strategy works best for you.

KNOW THE FUNDAMENTALS FOR THE UNDERLYING STOCK

Knowing the fundamentals won't necessarily improve your market timing—that must come from technical indicators—but it will help make the selection process easier. Here again, specialization helps. It would be impossible to know something about the hundreds of stocks that have listed options trading on the major exchanges. But you should know virtually everything about the handful of stocks you follow. Most importantly, you'll want to know the overall trend of the underlying stock, the major highs and lows of both the stock and option, the cycle in which the option trades, the open interest in the option, and the stock's Beta rating and volatility. These fall under the category of technical information. The fundamentals governing a stock include the company's main products, research and development activities, likely takeover suitors, the prospects for both the industry and the particular company's products over the near and long term, and whether market analysts think the company's stock is priced too high or too low. You might write for the annual report and ask to be put on the company's mailing list for future interim financial reports. You'll want to know the earnings, debt structure, dividend rates and general health of the balance sheet as well. Since every public company must file an annual 10-K with the SEC, you should also try to obtain a copy of this document, by writing to the SEC in Washington, D.C. Pertinent data concerning the company which may not appear in the annual report will appear in the 10-K. You'd be surprised at the wealth of information that is readily available about public companies in 10-K reports. Often, this is information which is required by the SEC. Financial public relations departments frequently leave out much of this information when they write the glossy annual reports, which are apt to be much more encouraging about a company's prospects. As an investor you'll be in a better position to spot potential opportunity and trouble when armed with these reports.

While having a working knowledge of a company's fundamental and technical condition won't make you an insider, it will help you make intelligent investment decisions. Moreover, by concentrating on just a handful of stocks and options to follow, you'll have an advantage over those who haven't limited their scope and aren't aware of some market-moving developments about to be announced. In short, the more you know, the better your chances of investment success—whether in stocks, options, or any other investment. There's no substitute for knowledge.

What to look for? The real story is in the numbers—and the relationship the numbers seem to generate over time. A company's management can talk all they want, but unless their optimism is reflected in the bottom line, the stock is going nowhere. One indicator that most investors swear by is known as the *price/earnings ratio,* which is obtained by dividing the market price of a stock by its earning per share. Thus, if XYZ common shares sell at 80 and the company earns $8 per share, it has a price/earnings ratio of 10 ($80 divided by $8). Reported daily in the financial pages of most metropolitan newspapers, this ratio, which can also be calculated by the company's reported earnings, reflects investor confidence in a security. Suppose six months ago a stock's price/ earnings ratio was ten, but you check in the paper and see that the current ratio is six. This would suggest that investors are decidedly less bullish on the company's prospects—or perhaps simply that the market as a whole has fallen and the particular stock you're following was among them. In either case the lowered P/E ratio suggests investor confidence is down.

The decline in the price/earnings ratio might serve as a signal to investigate other factors about the company's operations. What is the trend in earnings compared to a year ago? Were market conditions similar then? Have operating costs risen over the past year? How about the margin of profit, obtained by dividing net income by net sales? Has this figure been rising or falling? And how does it compare with a year ago? You may also want to compare one company's profit margin with generally accepted margins in the industry.

Next, look at the company's balance sheet and compare current assets with current liabilities. What is the company's cash position —and how has it changed recently? You may be concerned if you notice the company's accounts receivable—the amount of money owed the company—have increased recently. At some future time these accounts receivable may turn into bad debts, with the predictable negative effect on the company's earnings—and ultimately, share prices. The level of inventories also deserves close scrutiny, since rising inventories may suggest the company has overproduced and may not be able to move merchandise without cutting prices in the future.

Security analysts, who, incidentally, are the people who are quite influential in moving stock prices higher, are quick to calculate the ratio between current assets and current liabilities. As a general rule, current assets should be at least twice as large as current liabilities, but the accepted ratio will vary from industry to industry. The company's net working capital, which is derived by subtracting current liabilities from current assets, represents, perhaps, the most important figure that analysts follow. This is the money that the company has available to grow on. A serious decline in net working capital deserves investor concern.

Investors, understandably, are concerned with a company's bottom line, and shareholders' equity or net worth on a per-share basis should provide them with a glimpse of what their shares are really worth in terms of actual assets and liabilities. During times of depressed market conditions, low price/earnings ratios and even shares priced below the company's book value (the value per share if the company were simply closed down and liquidated tomorrow) are often found. A stock selling below book value is not necessarily a bargain, but it can provide a good indication that in better economic times the company's shares will rise.

Lastly, a company likely to prosper must be rich in sound management—an often intangible factor that, though not easily measured, can be the most important of all. People make a company work—not money. Unless management is sound, all the other factors, no matter how good they look on paper, may be of little value in successfully analyzing a company's prospects for the future.

PART TWO

Listed Stock Options Trading Strategies

3

Buying Puts and Calls

Buying puts and calls is a lot like throwing dice in Las Vegas. Unless your numbers come up, you're going to walk away a loser. It also shares another characteristic with the Nevada pastime. The percentages are against you whenever you start to play, sometimes prohibitively so. This is not to say you can't make money buying puts and calls. You can. But unless you familiarize yourself with the good and bad bets to be made, your chances aren't very good of emerging a winner.

THE IMPORTANCE OF LEVERAGE

The put or call buyer seeks to use the enormous leverage in the options market to transform a relatively small amount of money into an important sum of money. He attempts to do this by buying low-priced calls on stocks he anticipates will rise in value and by buying low-priced puts on stocks he anticipates will decline in value.

The high leverage of options trading serves to magnify the return of the successful option buyer. With leverage, an option buyer controls a potential asset worth many times his initial investment. As a result, the option buyer stands to earn an enormous percentage gain on his invested funds with only a modest rise in the price of the underlying stock. The amount of risk in any unhedged option is 100 per cent of a buyer's invested funds. That is, he can and will lose up to 100 per cent of his premium money if the option is not profitable by expiration. Prior to expiration, even if the option stays out-of-the-money, it will retain some time value, however. Precisely where the stock must trade in relation to the strike price at expiration is known as soon as the option is purchased. The stock must trade sufficiently above the strike, in the case of a call, to return the premium the buyer paid for the option; in the case of a put, the stock must trade sufficiently below the strike of the put to return the premium paid by the put buyer. Above and below the respective strike prices, the call and put will retain *some* cash value, but, if recent history is any indication, the likelihood of any given option expiring profitable is not all that great. Looking at the stock market from a historical viewpoint, the long-term growth rate of equities is between 5 and 10 per cent per year. Compare this relatively modest overall gain against the typical option buyer's need for a 15 per cent move in five or six months' time and you'll see why buying options is risky.

The problem for the option buyer rests with 1) overcoming the cost of the premium, and 2) selecting the correct direction of the stock. If the option you buy contains a considerable time value, the stock must move sufficiently to overcome the cost of the premium—which in the case of an out-of-the-money option will fall to zero upon expiration. As for stock direction, in the short term it is extremely difficult to forecast stock prices, primarily because so-called technical factors are apt to influence their movement. Thus, if you purchase a put at a very favorable premium only to have the market rise, the put will expire worthless and you'll lose your entire investment. The reverse, of course, is true with respect to call options. But assuming you can make some valid judgment concerning futures stock movement, you are still faced with the problem of timing. For an option to prove profitable, the stock must make a favorable move *before* the expiration date. Many option buyers have purchased options only to have them expire before the stock had a chance to move—in the direction they anticipated. One suggestion is to purchase options with longer durations if this has been a problem. The longer-duration options hold their time value better than the options with only a few weeks left to

How to Profit From BUYING Options

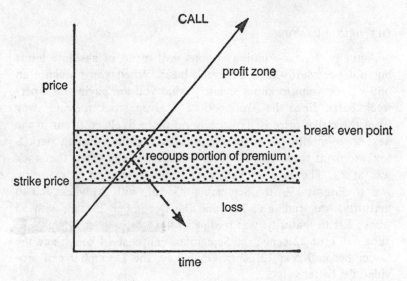

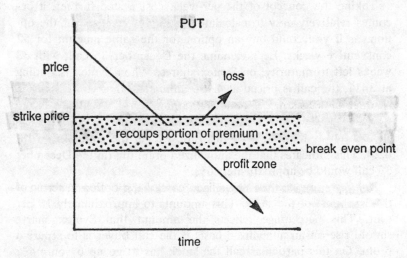

Figure 1.

expiration. The drawback, however, is that the longer-duration options cost more.

THE BEST DURATION

Actually, longer-duration options cost more in absolute terms but not necessarily on a per-week basis. When you purchase an option, you want to know precisely what you are paying on a per-week basis, since the likelihood of a given stock moving away from the strike price is statistically no more likely to occur in the next three-month period than the following three-month period. Let's look at three Hughes Tool Company calls when the stock was at 25. The June 25 call, with seven weeks left to maturity, was trading at 1½; the September 25 call, with 20 weeks left to maturity, was trading at 2⅞; and the December 25 call, with 33 weeks left to maturity, was trading at 4. On a per-week basis, the June call cost 22 cents; the September call cost 14 cents; and the December call cost 12 cents. Obviously, the December call provided the better value.

Taking the concept of the per-week cost a step further, it becomes relatively easy to calculate the *annualized* cost of the option, as if you could buy an option for the same amount for 52 consecutive weeks. Let's examine the December 35 call, with 33 weeks left to maturity, on Syntex shares. When Syntex is trading at 34¼, the call is priced at 4. To annualize, first you divide the number of weeks in the year by the number of weeks left in the option. Fifty-two divided by 33 weeks is equal to 1.57. Multiplying the premium of 4 by this rate, we get the annualized rate, 6.28. This indicates that the annualized premium on the December 35 call would be approximately 6¼.

Next, you express the annualized cost of the option in terms of the total cost of the stock. This amounts to approximately 18 per cent. This percentage reflects the amount that Syntex shares should rise on an annualized basis if the call buyer is to secure a profit. On this particular call the stock has to go up by only 4¾ points, or approximately 14 per cent, for the option buyer to earn a profit. But if you annualized this figure, you'd see that the stock would have to rise even faster for the option to prove profitable.

It is important to always annualize a premium and translate it into a percentage of the stock price *before* you decide to buy a particular option. These calculations provide you with a way of looking at an option investment that you may not have considered before. If you need a 20 per cent rise in the stock to break even on an option investment in a year's time, that amounts to 5 per cent on a three-month basis. How many stocks rise 5 per cent every three months? Moreover, what happens if you buy a call on a stock that doesn't move the required 5 per cent—indeed, what if it doesn't move at all? You may then want to recoup your invest-ment—100 per cent of which you've now lost—by buying another three-month call. The problem is, you now require a 10 per cent rise in three months, or 40 per cent on an annual basis, just to break even! Chances are you won't make a profit. You have to ask yourself continually: will this particular stock on which I've pur-chased an option move sufficiently away from the strike price prior to expiration for me to make a profit? Unless you are rea-sonably sure the market is about to turn bullish on your stock, you may be in for a surprise. In the absence of news, your stock will probably stay pretty much where it was on the day you pur-chased the call.

THE BEST STRIKE PRICE

Since any given stock might have options with a variety of strike prices, depending upon the stock's immediate past volatility, you may be confused as to which option presents the best oppor-tunity. Understandably, in-the-money options will have higher premiums than out-of-the-money options, since a portion of the premium represents cash value. But are the in-the-moneys better buys than the out-of-the-moneys? The answer depends on a vari-ety of factors, including the past volatility of the stock, how far the out-of-the-money option is away from the striking price, and the relative premium costs. But as a general rule, the deep-in-the-money options are bad investments. Let's consider a recent exam-ple in Burroughs Corporation calls. With 10 weeks left to matu-rity, Burroughs July calls were recently trading at the premiums shown in Table 3 when the stock was at 36⅝.

Table 3

Burroughs Corp.

CALLS

July 30	*July 35*	*July 40*
7	2 13/16	7/8

Both the July 30 and July 35 calls are in-the-money, with Burroughs trading at 36⅝. The lower-strike July 30 has 6⅝ points of cash value, whereas the July 35 has just 1⅝ points of cash value. The July 40, which is out-of-the-money, has no cash value. Assuming that Burroughs mounts a rally prior to expiration and rises a couple of points to close at 38⅝ upon expiration of the July options, the July 30 will have a value of 8⅝, for a 1⅝-point profit; the July 35 will have a value of 3⅝, for a profit of 13/16; and the July 40 will have no value, for a loss of ⅞-point. Since the largest profit was registered by the July 30 option, you might think that it presented the best value. But this is not the case. You must think of returns in light of how much money was required to generate the return. In this instance the 1-point gain in the July 30 call required a $7 commitment. That translates into a percentage profit of just 14 per cent. The July 35, on the other hand, generated a 13/16-point profit on an investment of just 2 13/16. As a percentage of invested funds, this comes to almost 29 per cent—making it twice as profitable. The July 40 call, of course, proves to be a 100 per cent loser. Whereas the July 40 gave you the most leverage, the likelihood of its being exercised at a profit is not nearly as great as it is with the other two calls. As a rule, you don't want to buy options that are deeply in-the-money or out-of-the-money. The in-the-moneys tend to be too expensive; the out-of-the-moneys tend to have too little chance to turn profitable. The options that are slightly in-the-money or out-of-the-money tend to be the best buys.

In the Table 3 example, the stock would have had to make a sharp market rise prior to expiration in order for the July 40 to become profitable at expiration. Only a 5 per cent rise in the underlying stock, however, from 36⅝ to 38⅝, would have generated a 29 per cent profit on the July 35, which was slightly in-the-money. Since stocks don't tend to soar out of sight within any given short period of time, it is unlikely that the inexpensive higher-strike call would prove a good investment. The option that is too deeply in-the-money, on the other hand, represents too expensive an investment for the risk involved and defeats the high-leverage advantage of option buying.

To illustrate this point, let's say you had $700 to invest in Burroughs calls. That amount of money would buy one 30-strike call option at $7 per share (cost: $700), two 35-strike call options at $2.81¼ per share (cost: $562), and eight 40-strike calls at $.87½ per share (cost: $700). The risk is thus fixed at a maximum of $700 for the 30- and 40-strike calls and $562 for the 35 call. A listing of the results of each investment at different stock price levels is shown in Table 4.

Table 4

PROFIT/(LOSS)

Burroughs Corp.

CALLS

Price of Stock at Expiration	One Call at 30 Strike Price	Two Calls at 35 Strike Price	Eight Calls at 40 Strike Price
$30 or under	($700)	($562)	($700)
$35	($200)	($562)	($700)
$40	$300	$438	($700)
$45	$800	$1,438	$3,300
$50	$1,300	$2,438	$7,300
$55	$1,800	$3,438	$11,300
$60	$2,300	$4,438	$15,300
$65	$2,800	$5,438	$19,300
$70	$3,300	$6,438	$23,300

In the event of a big move to the upside, the out-of-the-money 40 call will clearly emerge the winner. But the chances of Burroughs shares rising from a little over 36 to 45 or higher prior to expiration are quite slim. In fact, there is a 50 per cent chance the stock will *decline* from its present 36⅝ price.

The deep-in-the-money 30 call has only limited upside profit potential because so much of the premium consists of cash value of the stock. The 30-strike call has 6⅝ points of cash value when the stock is at 36⅝ and the call is selling for 7. In terms of leverage, therefore, the out-of-the-money call offers a much more attractive investment. When Burroughs is trading at $45 a share, the 30-strike call will return 114 per cent of the initial $700 investment; at $45 the same $700 investment in the out-of-the-money 40-strike calls will return 471 per cent.

The deep-in-the-money 30 call will provide only a slight advantage over the in-the-money 35 call in a very narrow range around the 35 strike price. When Burroughs is above 40, the two 35-strike calls gain $2 for every dollar gain in the single 30-strike call. As Burroughs rises just above 40, the eight 40-strike calls magnify profits enormously as the stock rises. In fact, the 40-strike calls return $8 for every single point rise in the stock above 40. This compares with just a $1-per-point rise for the single 30-strike call and a $2-per-point rise for the 35-strike call.

Anytime you are purchasing options, you have to ask yourself whether you are paying for a portion of the cash value of the stock or for time value in the option. In terms of obtaining leverage, buying cash value of a stock doesn't make sense. The advantage of option buying is to purchase, for very little cost, the *potential* of a stock move. Thus, in the case of the 30-strike call selling for 7 on the 36⅝-priced Burroughs stock, approximately 95 per cent of the cost of the call goes for the cash value of the stock and only 5 per cent toward the option. The 35 call, however, selling for $2^{13}\!/_{16}$, has only 42 per cent of its value tied up in cash value; and the out-of-the-money 40 call has no cash value. The drawback with the out-of-the-money 40 call, however, is that the stock must make a substantial move prior to expiration before it will turn profitable.

If the 30 call has any advantage at all, in our example, it is that the pure option value is the lowest of the three options. But its high cost negates any advantage, as does the distance that the stock must travel to become profitable in the case of the 40-strike call. In fact, the pure option value of the slightly in-the-money 35 call is highest among the three calls. But the reasonableness of its premium cost relative to the likelihood of its yielding a profit makes it the most attractive.

As a general rule, the absolute dollar value of an option should *not* be the deciding factor whether you purchase the option. Where the stock stands in terms of the strike prices *is* important.

Generally, the options which are trading slightly in- or out-of-the-money offer the best opportunity to the option buyer.

COMPARING PUTS AND CALLS

If you have any doubts concerning the difficulties involved in making money by buying listed stock options, you might look at Tables 5 and 6. For the identical four-month period, from January to May 1982, a random list of 20 stocks with their respective put and call options were selected. Both puts and calls had the same strike price. The price of each put and call was compared, assuming the option was purchased on the close of trading on January 7, 1982, and liquidated on the close of trading on May 7, 1982. The results proved interesting. During the period under study, the market was in a general downtrend. It is not surprising, therefore, that the put buyers might have fared better than the call buyers. The interesting aspect of the comparison, however, is that *neither put or call buyer would have made a profit over the four-month interval.* One would assume that if the call buyers couldn't make money because the market was declining, perhaps the put buyers profited. But this was not the case. In fact, both put and call *writers* made money. Of course, there are individual options that proved profitable. Among the 20 calls, 25 per cent returned a profit; among the puts, 30 per cent were profitable. The point gain was only slightly better for the put options than for the calls. But the net point loss for the calls exceeded the loss on the puts by about 45 per cent.

Among the individual options, the biggest point gainer was the Lockheed June 40 call that rose from 8 to 15⅛ during the four-month period, on a stock rise from 44⅜ to 54½. In this instance, Lockheed, a major defense contractor, proved an excellent options play for the call buyer who wanted to cash in on a hot defense stock at a time when defense expenditures promised to be on the rise but the economy overall was in the doldrums. Percentagewise, the puts proved the winners, with E. F. Hutton, one of the major brokerage houses, providing a profit to the put buyer. During the period under study, the E. F. Hutton July 35 puts rose from 2¹³⁄₁₆ to 5¾ on a stock decline from 36¾ to 30¼. Asarco Inc., a metals producer, likewise experienced difficulty during the period, falling from 25⅜ to 20⅜. As a result, the Asarco June 30 puts rose from 4⅞ to 9¾, a gain of 100 per cent.

The move in the Disney options provided an enlightening view of the problems encountered by option buyers. The Disney July 55 calls remained unchanged for the four-month period, while the Disney July 55 puts lost 87 per cent of their value. During the pe-

Table 5

CALLS

4-month Period
January 7, 1982—May 7, 1982

Stock	Option/Strike	CLOSING PRICES		Net % Gain/Loss
		January 7	May 7	
Allis-Chalmers	July 15	3	1¹⁄₁₆	−65%
American Home Products	July 35	2⅞	3½	+22%
Atlantic Richfield	July 45	3½	1⅛	−68%
Asarco Inc.	June 30	1¹³⁄₁₆	⅛	−93%
Baxter Travenol	May 35	2⅛	1⅜	−35%
Boeing	May 20	3½	½	−86%
Burlington Northern	July 50	7	3¾	−46%
Digital Equipment	July 80	11¼	5¼	−53%
Disney	July 55	4	4	unchanged
Gillette Co.	June 35	1½	1⅞	+25%
Hospital Corp. of America	July 35	3⅜	1¹⁄₁₆	−68%
E. F. Hutton	July 35	5⅞	1⁷⁄₁₆	−75%
Lockheed	June 40	8	15⅛	+89%
Manville Corp.	August 15	1⁹⁄₁₆	⅝	−60%
Marathon Oil	June 80	1¾	2⁷⁄₁₆	+39%
Mesa Petroleum	July 20	2⅞	¾	−74%
Mobil Corp.	August 20	4⅝	4⅞	+ 4%
Natomas	June 20	4⅝	⅝	−86%
Sears	September 15	3¼	5⅛	+58%
U. S. Home	June 15	1½	⅜	−75%

Point gain = 10¹¹⁄₁₆
Point loss = 34³⁄₁₆
Net   = −22½

riod, Disney shares rose from 52 to 56¼. The buyer of the stock would have made 4¼ points, yet the same investor who purchased out-of-the-money calls on Disney stock would have only managed to break even. The put buyer, of course, whose judgment on the direction of Disney was wrong, saw most of his investment evaporate during the four-month period.

Table 6

PUTS

4-month Period
January 7, 1982–May 7, 1982

Stock	Option/Strike	CLOSING PRICES January 7	May 7	Net % Gain/Loss
Allis-Chalmers	July 15	1⅜	¾	−45%
American Home Products	July 35	1⅝	⅜	−77%
Atlantic Richfield	July 45	3½	9⁄16	−84%
Asarco Inc.	June 30	4⅞	9¾	+100%
Baxter Travenol	May 35	3½	5⁄16	−91%
Boeing	May 20	3¼	9⁄16	−83%
Burlington Northern	July 50	4⅛	1⅞	−54%
Digital Equipment	July 80	3½	4	+21%
Disney	July 55	5⅜	11⁄16	−87%
Gillette Co.	June 35	3½	¾	−78%
Hospital Corp. of America	July 35	3½	3	−14%
E. F. Hutton	July 35	2¹³⁄16	5¾	+104%
Lockheed	June 40	2	¹⁄16	−97%
Manville Corp.	August 15	1½	2	+50%
Marathon Oil	June 80	5⅝	9⁄16	−90%
Mesa Petroleum	July 20	2⅜	3⅜	+42%
Mobil Corp.	August 20	1½	¼	−83%
Natomas	June 20	⅞	1½	+71%
Sears	September 15	11⁄16	³⁄16	−73%
U. S. Home	June 15	2¾	2	−27%

Point gain = 10¹⁵⁄16
Point loss = 26⅜
Net = −15⁷⁄16

Among the oil stocks, Mesa Petroleum returned a profit on its July 20 put, which gained a point in value, while Marathon Oil and Mobil returned profits on their respective calls and losses on their respective puts. For the buyer of both a put and a call on Mesa Petroleum—a strategy known as a *straddle*—the results would have been unsatisfactory, however, since the 1-point gain on the put would have been offset by more than a 2-point loss on the call.

In almost every instance, the loss on either the put or call was not offset by the gain on the other option. The Manville calls lost almost a point, while the Manville puts gained only ½ point. A 22 per cent gain in the American Home Products July 35 calls was offset by a 77 per cent loss in the same company's July 35 puts. A 6-point loss in Digital Equipment calls was countered by only a ¾-point gain in the Digital Equipment puts. To make matters worse, you might have purchased puts and calls on Allis-Chalmers and experienced a loss on both options. For the period, Allis-Chalmers stock declined slightly from 15⅝ to 14⅞. This is the kind of move that makes money for put and call writers, but is extremely frustrating to put and call buyers.

Since the options selected were always the closest strike to the market price of the stock, the deterioration of the options' time value resulted in the bulk of the losses suffered by put and call buyers. Whenever you buy an out-of-the-money option, you are paying for time value alone. When that value decreases and the stock does not move favorably, the option buyer must have a loss.

TIMING

Correct timing, as you can see from Tables 5 and 6, our sample list of puts and calls, is vital to a successful option buyer's strategy. One's degree of certainty concerning a possible price move will influence one's choice of maturity dates, other factors aside. For instance, let's say you are bullish on a stock trading at 47 and you are looking to purchase call options on the stock. There might be a 50-strike call with four weeks to maturity available for a premium of ½ and another 50-strike call with four months to maturity available for 1⅜. Which one do you choose? If you have reason to believe the stock will take off within the next few days or weeks, the shorter-duration call available for ½ point would be the better choice. Because the call is so inexpensive, the leverage is much higher than the longer-duration call; in fact, for the same amount of money, you can buy almost three times as many of the shorter-duration calls. But if the timing is uncertain, you're better off paying more for the calls and selecting the longer duration.

In this case your analysis of the risk/reward factor plays a role. If you think a takeover bid is imminent, you'll want to throw caution to the wind. But if you do so, you must be willing to sustain a 100 per cent loss should your judgment prove faulty. If you are confident that some market-moving news is imminent yet you'd prefer to hedge your bet, you're probably better off with the longer-duration call. The impact of the news may only be slow to assert itself, and the longer-term call will give the stock time to rally.

You must be quick to act once you've taken your position. The general rule is to "buy the rumor, sell the news." But this is not always easy to do. In fact, most investors, looking for certainty in the investment markets, hold off buying until the news has been released and the stock has already shown evidence of its bullishness by moving up in value. They then become buyers. Unfortunately, it is usually too late to begin buying at that stage of the rally. By then more sophisticated investors, who accumulated shares on the initial rumor, are selling and taking profits. Learn to take quickly any windfall profits you make as a result of option buying. And forget buying options on stocks that have already made their move. While there are instances of stocks that have held Wall Street's interest for years and years, most highfliers have their moment in the spotlight and fade away. If you are lucky enough to get in on a stock that takes off, take your profit quickly —and move on to other option-buying opportunities.

OPTION HEDGES

One reason why listed options trading has become so popular is that puts and calls are so versatile. Just as you can use options for speculative purposes, betting on the price direction of stocks, you can also use them to lower risks. One popular method of hedging using listed options is known as the *protected short sale* or *syn-*

thetic put. This technique involves purchasing a call option to limit the risk on a short position in the underlying stock. By owning a call the investor who has sold stock short is potentially long the stock at the strike price. Since the risk is theoretically unlimited anytime you sell stock short, the purchase of the call eliminates the risk, and hence the reluctance, associated with short selling.

Let's say you are fundamentally bearish on a stock's prospects, and you wish to sell the stock short but are concerned lest the stock rally after you've put on your short position. We'll assume the stock is trading at 10 and you can buy a three-month call option for 1½. By selling the stock short at 10 and buying the 10-strike call for 1½, you will be fully hedged. Your cost is the price of the call, or 1½. Now, no matter how far the stock rallies, you will be fully protected. Since your cost is 1½ points, however, the stock will have to fall below 8½ for your profit on the stock to outpace the cost of the call. If the stock rallies, however, you simply exercise the call option and take delivery of the shares at $10 a share. You then use these shares to "cover" the shares you initially borrowed in putting on your short stock position. The total cost will be the premium you paid on the call plus any commissions involved in the transaction. As a rule, it is best to purchase a call which is at-the-money or only slightly out-of-the-money when you are seeking protection for the short sale. Out-of-the-money calls will be cheaper, but their protection will likewise be less in the event of a stock rally. You might think of these out-of-the-money calls in terms of deductible insurance. When you purchase an out-of-the-money call as insurance against a short position, you are saying you are willing to give up, say, the first 5 points in loss if your judgment proves wrong. But beyond 5 points you want safety. An illustration of this principle would be to short stock at 10 and purchase a 15-strike call. Should the stock rally against you, the call won't begin to provide protection until the stock reaches 15. Thus, the first 5 points of adverse movement must be borne by the short seller.

Another type of hedge involving the purchase of calls against short stock is known as the *reverse hedge* or *simulated straddle*. Using this strategy, you purchase calls on more shares than you sell short. While you don't need to utilize this strategy with stocks that have listed put options—a straddle, or purchase of a put and call together, serves the same purpose—you'd use a reverse hedge if you wanted to profit from a volatile stock. The maximum loss of the reverse hedge will be at the strike price of the calls. For instance, let's say you short 100 shares of XYZ common stock at 46½ and purchase two September 50 calls for $3 each. You now have a $6 investment in the two calls, and if the stock is trading at 50 or lower upon expiration, you lose the entire $6. At 50 not only will you lose $6 on your calls, but you will lose $3½ on your short stock position. Above or below the price of 50, your position will improve. At 42, for instance, you will have a profit of $4½ on your stock. This will be offset by a $6 loss on the two calls, for a net loss of just $1½. As the stock falls below 40½, however, the short stock position will outpace the loss on the long calls. On the upside the fact that you have two calls working for you will quickly generate profits in excess of your loss on the short stock. At 59, for instance, you will have a total of $18 in profits on your calls. The loss on the short stock will be $12½ at that price, and the balance—$5½—will be profit. At 69 the long 50 calls will have $38 in profit ($19 × 2 = $38), and the short stock will have a loss of $22½ ($69 − $46½ = $22½). The net profit before transaction costs, therefore, will be $15½ per share. If you attempt this strategy, be sure to use a volatile stock. Not only must the stock move significantly higher or lower, but volatile stocks have the advantage of being low-dividend payers. This is an advantage because short sellers are required to pay dividends on stocks they sell short.

Once the reverse hedge is in place, you need not take any preventative action to avoid loss. The loss will occur near where the position was placed, with the maximum loss occurring at the strike price of the calls. The strategy requires patience, because you want the price to move significantly below where the stock was shorted or significantly above the strike price of the calls. As you may have already noted, the number of calls will influence the results. The more calls you have, the greater the profits if the stock makes a significant move upward. The greater the number of calls, the more distance you need to the downside in order to return a profit on the short sale of the stock.

To modify the reverse hedge, you may use calls at different

strikes. You may have one at-the-money call and another out-of-the-money call. Or two out-of-the-moneys. The number of variations are many. With stock at 17, for instance, you may purchase one in-the-money 15-strike call and one out-of-the-money 20-strike call. The average cost of the two premiums will determine precisely where the reverse hedge will be profitable to the upside or downside.

The reverse hedge is primarily a proxy for a straddle position (which will be explained in a subsequent chapter). It will prove profitable if the underlying stock rises or falls far enough during the life of the calls. You would use it, therefore, for a stock on which puts are not trading and for stock that appears to be volatile in nature. The reverse hedge is relatively simple to use. You short a quantity of stock and buy calls for more stock than you are short. If the market price of the stock rises, the calls will provide your profits; if the market price declines, your short stock position will increase in value. In either instance, you win.

HIGH-VOLATILITY STOCKS

High-volatility stocks are important not only to the user of a reverse hedge, but to the option buyer in general. Option buyers need stocks that move in order to generate profits on their puts and calls. Although options on volatile stocks cost more than options on more conservative stocks, they are generally worth the extra expense. One way to identify a volatile stock is by its Beta rating. As a measurement of a stock's tendency to move relative to the averages, Beta pinpoints stocks that are likely to prove volatile in the future, although past volatility or performance is no guarantee of future volatility or performance.

Another simple way to identify a volatile stock is to glance in the financial pages of your newspaper and look at the stock's past 52-week high and low. Once you know the 52-week range, calculate the percentage of this range that you'll need to make a profit on the purchase of a put or a call. Let's say a stock has had a 10-point range over the past year and you're looking at an option with a premium of 1½. You'll need a 15 per cent move in the entire year's range just to break even on the option. You may consider this percentage move reasonable. But if you need a 5-point move in the same stock over the next three months, the likelihood of earning a profit is considerably less.

While stocks change character from time to time, chances are stocks with a history of volatility will continue to show volatility in the future. The same is true of the conservative blue-chip issues that rarely exhibit volatile price behavior. Be willing to pay a little more and buy options on volatile stocks. The reason these stocks are volatile is that investors are quick to buy and sell them in anticipation of news that may or may not prove significant. As an option buyer you stand to profit from the stock's gyrations. Remember, if your judgment proves correct, the high leverage of put and call options will magnify your profits considerably. That's why you buy options in the first place.

VOLUME

Increased volume in a stock is a sign that investors are eagerly buying or selling shares. If you want a simple rule signifying which stocks are possible significant price candidates, look to the most active column. Increased volume nearly always accompanies a genuine stock price move. Stocks that move on low volume are often suspect. Large volume also suggests that a stock or option has sufficient liquidity.

THE TRADER'S INDEX

Since most stocks tend to follow the direction of the broad market averages, it often pays to have a method for determining when the market has switched direction from bearish to bullish, and vice versa. One popular indicator is known as the *Trader's Index,* which measures the ratio of advancing stock market issues to declining issues, and factors in the ratio of advances and declines with volume. The information to compile the daily Trader's Index is published every business day on the inside back page of the *Wall Street Journal* under the headings "Market Diary" and "Trading Activity." These statistical columns appear to the right of the "Abreast of the Market" column.

The Trader's Index is calculated by dividing the number of advancing issues by the number of declining issues. Thus, on a recent market day when 927 issues advanced and 505 issues declined, the ratio of advances to declines would be 1.84 (927/505 = 1.84). The advance/decline ratio is then *divided* by the ratio of the *advancing volume* divided by the *declining volume* on the New York Stock Exchange. Because the volume of advancing and declining issues is generally in the millions, it helps to delete the last three digits and simply divide the first five digits of the volume of advancing stocks by declining stocks. Thus, recent advancing volume of 36,957,500 was rounded to 36,958 and recent declining volume of 10,540,000 was rounded to 10,540. Dividing advancing volume by declining volume, therefore, yielded a ratio of 3.51 (36,958/10,540 = 3.51). You now have two ratios: the ratio of number of advances to number of declines, and the ratio of the volume of advancing issues to the volume of declines. The first ratio is divided by the second, and yet a third ratio is generated. For the numbers given, the calculations would appear as shown in Table 7.

Table 7

Trader's Index = $\dfrac{\text{advances}}{\text{declines}}$ divided by $\dfrac{\text{advancing volume}}{\text{declining volume}}$

Assuming: advances = 927   advancing volume = 36,958
declines = 505   declining volume = 10,540

Thus: $\dfrac{927}{505} = 1.84$ $\dfrac{36,958}{19,540} = 3.51$

$\dfrac{1.84 \text{ ratio of advances/declines}}{3.51 \text{ ratio of adv. volume/decl. volume}} = .52 = \text{TI}$

The Trader's Index of .52 (in the example used for Table 7) is bullish on the market as a whole, and perhaps on the stock you are following. A ratio of 1.00 is considered neutral. A ratio of less than 1.00 indicates a strong market, with a ratio of 0.40 considered very strong and 2.00 considered very weak. *Smaller numbers are considered bullish and larger numbers are considered bearish.* As a buyer of options, you'll want to *purchase calls when the Trader's Index remains under 1.00* and *purchase puts when the Trader's Index moves over 1.00.* Persistent readings at an extremely high or low number, however, may mean the market has temporarily become overbought or oversold and you may want to use this indicator as a *contrary sentiment* measurement. For example, if the Trader's Index suggests that stocks are very bullish by moving to a relatively low number and staying there, you may want to *buy puts* in anticipation of the extreme bullishness temporarily subsiding and the market moving in the other direction. In the event of extreme bearishness, of course, you'll likewise want to *buy calls* in anticipation of the reverse happening. It is a well-documented fact that the majority of traders are invariably wrong at the major reversal points in the market. By trading contrary to the prevailing trend at the major turns, you can often get in the market ahead of the crowd.

TAKING PROFITS

At every point throughout an option trade, the investor must have a contingency plan for taking action. The plan may call for cutting short a loss or other defensive action or it may call for taking a profit. Torn between fear and greed, the option trader often is confused about the correct form of action. Let's consider a hypothetical example.

We'll assume a call buyer has purchased a 45-strike call on XYZ stock for a premium of $5 a share when the stock is at 49. His judgment proves correct as the stock rallies to 57, and the 45 call rises in value to $14. The call buyer now has a $9 profit in the call.

What should he do?

Chances are, he'll be torn between taking the profit and using some other strategy to protect himself in the event the stock falls. We'll assume sufficient time exists in the option, allowing him a variety of choices. First and foremost, he should consider taking the $9 profit.[1] The odds are against call buyers making any sort of

---

[1] As a rule, you should always sell a call rather than exercising the option. When you exercise a call and take delivery of the stock, you must pay additional commissions. First, you must pay a commission when you buy the stock at the striking price. Second, you must pay a commission when you sell the stock. Since option commissions are smaller dollarwise than stock commissions, simply sell the profitable call. By doing so, you don't have to incur the additional commission expense.

profit, let alone a $9 profit. A 180 per cent gain in the value of a call during a short period of time represents the exception rather than the rule in call buying. One alternative, therefore, is to sell the call and take the 9-point profit.

But, as with virtually any investment decision, this has its drawbacks. By taking the profit, the option buyer denies himself the opportunity to participate in any future gain in the underlying stock during the life of the option. It also protects him, naturally, from any subsequent decline in the stock that might occur prior to expiration.

Another alternative is to continue to hold the call. Having earned $9 on the call, the call buyer might decide to simply hold the option and do nothing. At expiration, of course, he'll be forced to take action if he wishes to gain his profit. Obviously, this tactic is somewhat more risky, since the stock could easily fall back below the call's strike price of 45 and he could actually realize a 100 per cent loss on the initial 5-point option investment. On a more positive note, the stock could continue to rise and he could fully participate in the move. Selling the call or doing nothing are two obvious alternatives with which most option buyers are familiar. But what about the option buyer who wants to utilize a more sophisticated strategy that will enable him to perhaps earn more profit but without the risk of losing everything in the event of a market decline?

One strategy is to take profits on the 45 call and immediately buy a higher-strike call—a process known as *rolling up*. In this instance, with the stock at $57 per share and the 45-strike call selling for $14 per share, the call buyer might sell the 45 call for $14 per share and immediately buy two 55-strike calls for, let us say, 3½ points each, or a total of 7. Now, having invested $5 for the initial purchase of the single 45 call, the call buyer sells the call for $14 per share. His profit is $9, of which he pockets $2 and immediately reinvests the remaining $7 in two 55-strike calls. The advantage of this strategy is that the call buyer is using his profits to purchase two new calls. Since the calls are slightly in-the-money, they will retain some cash value even if the stock remains at $57 per share. If the stock rises, of course, the results will be even more encouraging. At 70 the two 55 calls will return $30. In addition, the call buyer will have the initial $14 he received when selling his 45 call. Once you subtract the $5 cost of the 45 call and the $7 cost of the two 55 calls, the net is $32 per share, or $3,200 before transaction costs. When you compare this to a profit of $20, or $2,000 for the single 45 call (70 − 45 = 25; 25 − 5 premium = 20), you can see how the profits can magnify. At worst, if the stock declined in price after the call buyer rolled up to the 55 options, he would still retain a profit of $2 that he pocketed before reinvesting in the higher-strike 55 calls. For this strategy to work best, you want the stock to continue to rise.

Yet another alternative is to continue to hold the long 45 call and *sell* a higher-strike, out-of-the-money call—a technique known as *spreading*. (For additional information on spreads, see Chapter 5). In this instance, having purchased the 45 call, you might *sell* an out-of-the-money 60-strike call and *receive* one point in writing income. With the stock at 60, you will receive a total of $15 a share on the 45 call ($60 − $45 = $15) and another point for writing the 60 call. The total gain on the transaction will be $16 *if* the stock is trading above 60 at maturity of the options. The short 60 call will lock out any additional profit above 60, but it will ensure you at least another point of profit regardless of where the stock ends up. By spreading, you have *lowered* your overall cost from 5 to 4, a 20 per cent reduction. When the stock is at 59, the 45 call will have only $14 of profit. But when you add the writing income from the 60 call—which will be abandoned as worthless by its buyer if the stock stays under 60—the net gain is 15 points. Thus, the writing or selling of the 60-strike call adds a degree of insurance to the trade that it otherwise would not have had. This strategy can only be used by option traders who maintain a margin account with their brokerage firm and who have been approved for spreading. The minimum required for a spreading account is generally about $2,000. This strategy works best if you anticipate that the stock will stay relatively unchanged, or move slightly lower.

Now let's compare the four strategies. The spread tactic will prove the wisest if the stock remains relatively unchanged after you write the higher-strike option and the spread is in place. If the stock makes a precipitous decline after rising sharply, the wisest decision you could have made would be to liquidate the call once you earned the profit; the worst mistake in this situation would be to do nothing and watch your profits disappear. For a moderate rise, the do-nothing strategy will result in additional profits. And for a sharp rise, the aggressive strategy of rolling up your options and buying more calls at a higher strike will result in the greatest gains.

None of these alternatives are mutually exclusive, however. You might decide to liquidate half your call position on a price rise, for example, and continue to hold the other half. You might liquidate half your position and roll up the other half. Or you might roll up half your position and spread the other half. The number of combinations are many. The important thing is that you have a plan for exiting the market and dealing with profitable situations when they develop. In buying options you can make a lot of money on a very small investment. But to do so, you must try to make the odds as favorable as possible whenever you purchase an option. The option buyer must always be aware that there is an excellent chance he will lose his entire investment. One way to cope with this possibility is to diversify your option buying. With experience and skill, you'll lose on a few but hopefully recoup your losses and profit on others.

4

Option Writing

Just as buying listed stock options is akin to betting against the house in Las Vegas, the selling, or writing, of listed stock options is akin to *being* the house in Las Vegas, booking the bets of eager gamblers all looking to make a score. And just as, occasionally, the house loses, so must the option writer on occasion. But over time, the writing side of the option equation is apt to produce the most consistent and reliable profits. Option writing, which may be viewed as either highly conservative or highly risky depending upon one's market exposure, falls under two main categories—*covered writing* and *uncovered* or *naked writing*. Because the two writing techniques are so different in terms of risk exposure, they are likely to appeal to different types of investors, and we'll treat each separately.

COVERED WRITING—A CONSERVATIVE APPROACH

Covered writing, which involves writing options on securities you own, is considered a relatively safe, conservative investment technique. You may buy stock to write options, or you may already own stock and decide to write options. In either case, you'd be considered a covered writer. What happens when you write a call option? You are paid a premium for writing a call. In return, you may be asked to give up your stock at the agreed-upon strike price. Whether your stock is called away or not, the premium you received when you write an option is yours to keep. If you write an option that is *not* exercised, you have the best of both worlds— you profit by receiving the premium income, and you get to keep the stock.

Covered writing is considered conservative because the worst that can happen is that you'll have to give up your stock—stock which you may have acquired at a much lower price and hence will have a profit in. When you write a call, you are said to be short a call. You may continue to hold the short call until expiration—in which case your obligation to deliver shares of the underlying stock at the strike will persist—or you may get out of your obligation at any time by *covering,* or buying back, the same call that you previously sold. The price difference between where you sell the call and where you cover the position will constitute your profit or loss. The fact that you sell first and buy later makes no difference in the profit calculations. The profit is calculated only on whether you sold higher than where you bought. The order in which you buy and sell in the options market is unimportant.

Once you sell a call against stock you own, your risk is that the stock declines in price. If the stock falls 3 points and you only received 2 points for writing the call, you'll have a net loss. If, however, the stock declines just 1 point and you receive 3 points for writing the call, you'll have a 2-point profit—and, of course, if the option remains out-of-the-money, you'll get to keep the stock.

Since most stocks don't soar out of sight every three months, covered writers base their strategy on the idea that occasionally they'll have to give up a good stock, but more frequently they'll retain the stock and keep the premium income. Covered-writing programs have become so much a respected and conservative means of generating income in the stock market that bank trust departments, pension funds, and the insurance industry have all received the approval of their respective governing bodies to engage in this low-risk trading strategy. Moreover, a number of brokerage firms offer covered writing programs especially designed for IRA and Keogh retirement accounts. Because covered writing is a form of hedging one's stock position, it has come to be viewed as more conservative than owning stock. This is understandable, since the covered writer has a cushion against a market decline and the stock holder does not. In addition to gaining a modest amount of protection against a decline in the market value of his portfolio, the covered writer stands to increase his yield on his investment portfolio.

How does covered call writing work in practice? Let's say you purchase 100 shares of IBM common shares at 55 and the price rises to, say, 57½. You might then write an IBM April 60 call for a premium of 1. Should IBM common stock rise above 60 by the April expiration, your shares will be "called away" and you will be paid $60 a share. In addition, you'll be able to retain the writing income of $1 a share you received for writing the call. Thus, above 60, your gain will be $5 on the stock and $1 on the option, for a total of $6 in profit. Should IBM fail to rise above 60, the call option will prove worthless to its buyer and it will be abandoned. In that instance you'll still retain the $1 per share you received as premium income. Once the April option expires, you'll be free to write another covered option and receive more income.

The covered call writer operates in a risk-free situation, because he has the shares to deliver in the event that the stock stages a rally. Obviously, if the writer knew in advance the stock would rally, he probably wouldn't write a call. But since he operates in a world of uncertainty, he writes calls, knowing that the income will be welcome during periods of stable stock prices and that he'll relinquish his shares should prices rise and the stock is called away.

The covered writer is selling time value in return for current income when he writes a call. As the option approaches maturity, the time value of the call will diminish at a more rapid rate, hopefully returning a profit to the covered writer. The covered writer's risk is a rally in the underlying stock—an event that will result in the price of the call likewise rising. Because he owns the stock, however, the covered writer's loss on the option will be offset by the gain in the stock, and no real loss will occur. Typically, if he has purchased the stock at a lower price, he will already have a profit in the stock position and an additional rise will only lock out additional profits above the strike price of the short call.

The call writer is giving up the upside potential of his stock in return for the call premium. In the illustration of the IBM April 60 call, the covered writer has agreed to let his IBM shares be called away at a price of $60 a share. This is fine if the investor is pleased with the profit he makes on the stock plus the writing income. But the covered writer always has the option of *buying in* his call if he wishes to hold on to the stock. For instance, let's say the April expiration is approaching and IBM shares are threatening to go over 60. One alternative is for the covered writer to do nothing and hope the shares stay under 60 prior to expiration. Should this happen, the call option will expire worthless and the covered writer will retain the stock. Another alternative is to take a more aggressive approach and buy in the short April 60 call. Depending upon the price of the stock and the amount of time left to expiration, the April 60 call might be selling for more than the original selling price of 1. Let's say the option is selling at 2. By buying back the IBM April 60 call in the secondary market, the covered writer is now out of the options market—albeit at a loss, since he paid $2 for an option that he previously sold for $1. But he no longer has an obligation to let his shares be called away. He is free to participate in any rise in the price of the stock. Thus, to terminate his obligation to deliver stock after writing or selling a call, a covered writer need only buy back his option for the current premium.

This notion of taking an active approach to covered writing is an important one to remember if you are not to be locked out of profitable situations. Covered writing lends itself to a passive approach to the market. You write options on stocks you already own, and you sit back and await developments in the market. If the stock rises above the strike price of the option you've written, the stock is called away. If the stock doesn't rise, you retain the stock. In either case, you still gain the premium income. The buying-in approach, however, calls for taking defensive action to prevent losing a potentially profitable move in the stock for a small option premium. It is one thing to earn consistent premium on a number of stocks by writing calls. But occasionally you'll write a call on a stock that plummets in price and you'll ride the stock down in hopes of ultimately recouping your losses. Now what have you achieved? A series of small gains resulting from writing calls and a huge, disastrous loss by holding on to a stock too long. Occasionally, of course, the stock you own will soar in price. Un-

less you quickly buy back your short calls, you are going to miss
the bull move in the stock, however.

SETTING UP A COVERED-WRITING PROGRAM

One method of setting up your covered-writing program is to
plan in advance precisely what you will do if the stock rises or
falls more than you initially anticipate when you write the call.
For instance, let's say you are bullish on the long-term prospects
of XYZ stock, but over the near term you decide to pick up some
writing income by selling calls. We'll assume XYZ is trading at
$41 per share, with a 40 call available for $3 per share. You write
the 40 call and receive the premium of 3. Your plan is to buy
back the call at some time in the future when the wasting time
value will erode the premium to, say, 1. Upon expiration, if XYZ
stays at 41, the 40 call will be valued at $1 and you will have a $2
profit on the option if you buy it back prior to it being exercised.
But instead of XYZ's price staying stable, let's assume bullish
news hits the market and the stock and option begin to gain
ground. The stock moves up to 43 and the 40 call now has a value
of 4. If you want to avoid losing the stock, you must be prepared
to buy in the call option at a loss. To avoid losses it is necessary
that you decide beforehand to take action at a specific price. Let's
say you decide that if the stock goes to $44 a share, it will go
much higher, since that price represents a breakout on the charts.
At $44 the 40 call may be selling for 5 or 6 and you will have to
buy back the option at a loss. At this point you must gather the
courage to take the loss in the option in order to hold onto the
stock. Not to do so will only mean you will be locked out of a nice
move in the stock. In the heat of battle, so to speak, taking a loss
in the option position will often prove difficult. The tendency will
be to await a decline in the market to get out of the option. But
hesitation usually proves fatal in this situation. A week later the
stock may be at $47 and the option you sold at 3 may be trading
at 8 or 9. To avoid trouble, simply tell your broker to buy back
your short 40 call if the stock reaches $44. If the timing proves
wrong, you can always write another call and recoup your writing
losses.

On the downside you likewise have to make a decision. Using

the same example, we'll assume you initially purchased your XYZ shares at 35. With the stock at 41, you are sitting on a $6 paper profit in the security and pick up another $3 in income by writing the 40 call. In this situation the stock would now have to fall all the way to 32 before you'd have a loss. But let's say you're determined not to let the profit slip away, and you decide that if the stock declines to 38, you'd rather not prefer to hold it any longer. You simply tell your broker to sell the stock at 38 and liquidate the option position at the same time. Of course, the 40 call will have minimal value when the stock is at 38, but the potential always exists for a rally. Unless you want to be a naked writer—which you'll be once you sell the stock and continue to hold the 40 call—you must exit the option position when you sell the stock.

ROLLING DOWN

If you are reluctant to sell your stock, there's an alternative you can use that will soften the decline and hopefully help you emerge a winner even if the stock decline is prolonged. This strategy involves selling more calls as stock prices decline at progressively lower strike prices. Known as *walking down* or *rolling down* the option, this strategy continues to generate income and serves to protect the value of your stock portfolio. Ideally, as you continue to sell calls, the writing income offsets the decline in value of the stock.

Again returning to our previous illustration of XYZ common shares at 41, let's assume you sold the 40 call for 3 and the market for XYZ shares falls to 38. You buy in your 40 call for, say, ½ (representing a gain of 2½) and immediately write a 35 call for, say, 4½. (If you are to remain fully covered at all times, you must liquidate one option before you write another one. We are assuming here that you own just 100 shares of XYZ and you will only hold one short option at a time.) Continuing its decline, the stock then falls to 33, and you buy in your short 35 call for ½ (a gain of 4) and write a 30 call for 4. Finally, the stock stages a rally to, say, 36 and you buy back your short 30 call for 6 (a loss of 2). You now have a total gain of 6½ for the two profitable short calls and a loss of 2 on the one unprofitable call. The net gain is 4½ on the calls, but this is offset by a loss of 5 points in the stock.

Disregarding transaction costs, the net loss is just ½ point. When you consider that the stock investor who doesn't write options would have a loss of 5 in this situation, representing more than 12 per cent of his initial investment, the rolling-down strategy makes sense. While it isn't especially profitable, rolling down your options does serve to minimize the damage of a declining market to your stock portfolio.

Since the purpose of a covered-writing program is to generate income on stock you own and perhaps will continue to own for a long time, the prospects of having to roll down options as a defensive strategy to prevent a loss are not very inviting. In a stable market the opportunity for profit as a covered writer is considerably greater, since the call writing should generate income and the stability of the underlying stock should maintain your principal in addition to throwing off dividend income. The best neutral strategy is to write options that are at or near the current market price. The reason for this should be fairly obvious. These options have the greatest time value. In addition, out-of-the-money calls will provide little income, while the in-the-money calls are almost certain to consist of a large amount of intrinsic value and relatively little time value. Most importantly, the in-the-money calls are subject to premature exercise, a situation you are trying to avoid since you are fundamentally comfortable owning the stock.

The decision to take defensive action will be one you'll have to make based on your attitude toward the stock. On the one extreme, there are covered writers whose only interest is maintaining a steady cash flow from their writing activities. They owe no allegiance to any particular stock. If a call they've written is in-the-money and in danger of premature assignment, they'll be prepared to deliver their shares without hesitation. In short, they play the averages and are quite willing to lose a few profitable stocks in pursuit of consistent profits from their writing activities. On the other hand, there are investors who are committed to a certain stock and will readily buy back an option that turns unprofitable. For this investor, continual ownership of the stock is important—not the short-term writing income. This covered writer reasons that writing income is welcome during periods of stable or declining stock prices. But his long-term outlook is one of bullishness on the stock—a viewpoint he is willing to back up with dollars by buying back unprofitable short call positions.

A CONSERVATIVE STRATEGY

Most covered writers will fall somewhere in between the two extremes—committed to writing income or long-term security ownership. That is, they'll purchase stocks solely for the writing-income potential in addition to buying stocks they genuinely like for a long-term capital gain. Since stock ownership far exceeds participation in the options markets, it shouldn't be surprising that most covered writers already owned stock when they got interested in options rather than the reverse situation of an interest in options trading generating an interest in stock ownership.

Given the overwhelming downward trend in stock option premiums since the advent of options trading, it should come as no surprise that more and more investors see the writing side of the market as the most consistently profitable. Following the introduction of listed options trading in the early seventies, premiums took a dive, since the buyers soon found themselves with continued losses. As a result of the drying up of buyers and the growth in the number of writers, the institutional investors among them (who soon caught on to the profits to be made writing calls), the premiums had nowhere to go but down. Now that so many investors feel that writing options is a profitable venture, it makes sense to begin to consider option buying purely from a contrarian standpoint. When too many investors seem to feel option writing is a good thing, it is only a matter of time before the majority will be proven wrong.

Nevertheless, covered writing enjoys widespread popularity—and deservedly so. Stocks are notoriously vulnerable to a host of economic conditions ranging from high interest rates to the fickleness of consumer demand. Covered writing enables the stock investor to hedge his bets on the market. It provides the stock investor with a measure of protection he otherwise wouldn't have. When this very conservative market technique is viewed against the traditional notion that the options market is risky, the paradoxical nature of options trading becomes quite clear. Yes, options trading can be risky. Yet the covered writer is engaging in a market strategy that is as close to a sure thing as you will ever find in any investment. The covered writer receives income for agreeing to sell stock that he already owns at a price that may very well guarantee him a profit. In return for giving up the opportunity to participate in the potentially significant profits above the strike price (which may not materialize), the covered writer settles for an immediate gain. His real risk is that the stock may decline further than he anticipated—and that the income he received for writing the call won't offset that decline. But even in this situation—as we've seen in the rolling-down example—the covered writer may recoup some of his paper loss on the stock by writing lower-strike calls.

PREMATURE ASSIGNMENT

The covered writer can count on losing his stock if prices rise above the strike price of the call. As an option writer you must be prepared for *premature assignment* at any time when you hold a short call that is in-the-money. Premature assignment simply means the stock will be called away from you. The Options Clearing Corporation makes the assignments on a random basis to the various brokerage houses. The brokerage houses, in turn, then call in the stock among their customer accounts according to whatever method they've decided to use to deal with options being exercised. Rather than thinking your short option will be overlooked when it comes to premature assignment, it is better to be prepared to deliver the shares at any time the call is in-the-money. If you are not psychologically prepared to have your stock called away, be quick to take defensive action by buying back short calls, buying more stock, or whatever method you've decided to use in such a situation. Having your stock called away is a part of option writing. Obviously, when the price is stable and you've sold an at-the-money or out-of-the-money option, the chances of having the option exercised is diminished considerably. But the risk of losing the stock, albeit at a profit, remains whenever you write options. Look upon your writing activities as a way of playing the averages and you'll find you have an attitude toward the strategy that will enable you to win consistent profits. You'll win some; you may lose on others. But over time, if your covered writing program is properly executed, you'll find the strategy profitable.

If you are inclined to hang on to your stock as a covered writer, you'll want to be aware of certain situations when the threat of a premature assignment is greater than at other times. One particular situation to be mindful of exists in a dividend-paying stock right before it goes ex-dividend. As you well know, the owner of the stock at the time it goes ex-dividend receives the dividend. Accordingly, call buyers who may be planning to exercise their calls are apt to call in stock just before the ex-dividend date. Their reasoning should be obvious. As holders of long call options, they stand to gain nothing when a stock goes ex-dividend; as owners of stock, however, they receive the dividend. As a covered writer, therefore, you had better not count on receiving that final dividend before expiration of the option you've written. If the option is in-the-money, chances are the option buyer will exercise his option and you'll be asked to deliver your shares and miss the dividend altogether. Moreover, the larger the expected dividend, the greater the chances of having the stock called away on the strength of the dividend alone.

The drawbacks aside, the covered writer enters into this strategy knowing that the risks involved are minimal. In the event of soaring stock prices, the writer's stock is simply called away at the strike price. True, there will be a certain "opportunity cost" involved. The bulk of the rise in the stock's value will then go to the option buyer. But consider the numerous times when stock prices were stable and stock owners gained nothing for their patience. Covered writers look for a steady income. On a percentage basis the income may seem small, especially when compared to what the buyers gain when a stock takes off, but the consistent nature of the premium income should prove appealing. If you can make just 7 per cent on a quarterly basis writing covered options, that translates into 28 per cent annualized. Few stocks gain 28 per cent in a year. For the covered writer the 28 per cent is available in a stable market in which the underlying stock doesn't have to gain even a single percentage point to return income from option writing.

SELECTING THE PROPER OPTION DURATION

What duration option should you write? That depends, in part, on your analysis of future stock prices. If you think your stock may soar in value at some future date, you are better off writing shorter-duration calls. This will enable you to gain income on an option that you may be able to sell again at a higher price when the stock shows signs of bullishness. For instance, with your XYZ common shares at $27, you may be able to write a call with a 25 strike for $2¼. But at $31 the same option will go for $6 or more, a considerable difference. Remember, as a covered writer, you can always buy back a short option and again write another option of a higher strike or longer duration. When you write a single long-term option, you tie up your capital for a relatively long period of time in return for a single premium. Moreover, since option premiums decrease at an increasing rate once expiration approaches, the longer-duration option—all other things being equal—will retain its value longer.

SELECTING THE PROPER STRIKE PRICE

Calls with lower strike prices will command higher premiums. But a large percentage of such in-the-money call premiums will consist of intrinsic value and relatively little time value. In deciding on the proper strike price call to write, you want to concentrate on capturing time value as compared to intrinsic value. The reason for this is that time value will surely erode, whereas intrinsic value will only decrease if the stock declines. Let's assume you own Shell Oil common stock trading at $35 a share and you are looking for a call option to write on Shell. You glance in the newspaper and find that Shell has options trading at three different strike prices (Table 8).

Table 8

CONTRACT MONTH/STRIKE	PRICE
May 30	5
May 35	2½
May 40	1

Establishing the time value in each option is very simple, since you can subtract the strike price from the market price to arrive at the intrinsic value. Thus, in the case of the May 30, the intrinsic value is 5, the full price of the option. The May 30 has no time value since it is selling at its cash value, 5. The 2½ premium of the May 35, however, represents time value alone since it has no cash value. And the May 40 has a time value of 1. Clearly, the option with the greatest time value is the May 35. If we assume that Shell remains at $35 a share at expiration of the May calls, the May 30 will be exercised and the writer will break even, having given up 5 points in the stock and having received 5 points for writing the call. The May 35s and 40s, however, will expire worthless and the writer will retain the full premium.

Had Shell risen to $40 a share by expiration, the situation would be different. In this instance, the May 40 would clearly be the ideal call to write, since the writer would still receive the premium income and retain the stock. What if Shell had declined to $30 a share at expiration of the calls? In this instance, the May 30 would have been the ideal call to write, since it would fully compensate the writer for the 5-point decline in the value of his Shell common stock. As you can see, the correct strike price to write is determined by what the underlying stock is likely to do. Unfortunately, it is not always easy to determine the future course of a stock when you write a covered call.

Some rules: *if you think the stock will rise, write the higher-strike call option; if you think the stock will decline, write the lower-strike call.* Also: *in the absence of bull or bear expectations, write the option with the greatest time value.* This will generally be the option with the strike closest to the market price.

The return in a covered writing program is usually measured in terms of return on equity. Thus, if you purchased 100 shares of a $100 stock for $10,000 and wrote calls that threw off $3,000 a year in premium income, you'd have a return of 30 per cent on your investment. One popular method of generating a greater percentage return on your money in a covered-writing program is to purchase the stock on margin and write calls against the stock. Given a 50 per cent margin requirement, you can now buy 200 shares of the $100 stock and write twice as many calls, thus doubling your writing income. In this instance, by purchasing a stock

on margin, you increase your percentage gain on the same investment. You also heighten your risk in the event of a declining
market, however. But in the options market, whether you are engaged in covered writing or some other market strategy, risk is always commensurate with reward.

ROLLING OUT THE CALL

Having written calls, whether you've purchased the underlying
stock for cash or on margin, you should be prepared to monitor
the market. The astute covered writer will look for the time value
in the calls he's written to decline and will be quick to buy back
the options at a lower price and then look for an opportunity to
write another option of a different strike or duration. For instance,
let's say you own 100 shares of Dow Chemical that you purchased
at 18 and it is now trading at 24. You might write a Dow Chemical June 25 call for a premium of $1. As the June expiration
approaches, the premium will fall should Dow remain below the
strike price of 25. The premium may fall to ¼ point or even ⅛ or
$\frac{1}{16}$ point. Rather than persist in holding on to the short call in
hopes of gaining the remaining ¼, ⅛, or $\frac{1}{16}$ point, buy back the
short June 25 call and sell a September or December 25-strike call
on Dow Chemical. This strategy, in which you buy back a previously sold option and sell another at the same strike price with a
longer duration, is known as *rolling out* the option. It has the advantage of immediately generating more income and will not keep
you tied to a position with a maximum profitability potential of an
eighth or a sixteenth.

In rolling out an option, try to think in terms of a spread order
in which you are concerned with the net credit rather than the absolute price you buy and write the options for. In the Dow Chemical example, you may be able to buy the June 25 call for an eighth
and write the December 25 for 1⅛. Rather than specifying a
price, tell your broker to buy a June 25 and sell a December 25
for a net credit of 1. Thus, you may buy June at, say, ⅞ and sell
December at 1⅞. Or buy June at ⅛ and sell December at 1⅛. In
either case the net credit to your account will remain the same.
Exactly what will constitute an acceptable profit will depend on
the initial value of the option and the stock as well as the stock's

prospects. Typically, when the price of an option falls to a fraction, it is time to start looking for new writing opportunities. Not to take profits as they are generated in a writing program just doesn't make sense. Anytime you can write an option for 3 or 4 and buy it back for ½ point or less, you should do so.

Another reason for rolling out your call is that the downside protection offered by the option will have disappeared once it falls to a fractional amount. If you buy stock at 25 and write a 25 call for 3, you have protection on your stock position down to a price of 22. But what will happen if the stock declines to, say, 22½, and the call is trading at ¼? In this situation you have lost virtually all of your downside protection—right when you need it most. Rather than continue to hold the short call, it is better to buy it back for a quarter point or whatever it will bring in the market and write a longer duration 25 or even 20 call to generate a larger premium offering more downside protection.

ROLLING UP THE CALL

When the stock turns bullish, you may not have the luxury of rolling out your call, since the option you wrote may actually increase in price. In this situation you'll want to *roll up* your call options in order to hold on to the stock. This means you'll buy back the option you previously sold and sell an option of the same duration but of a higher strike. Using the Dow Chemical example above, let's say, having written the June 25, you suddenly become bullish on Dow's prospects and you want to hold the stock for a few more points while still receiving writing income. To roll up you would buy back the June 25 call and write a June 30 call. Having rolled up your option, you would now be able to participate in an additional 5 points of Dow's rise and still receive some writing income by selling the June 30 call. The general rule is to try and capture additional time value in options you write. In this instance, with the stock trading higher, you are reinstating the same relationship between stock and strike price that you previously had—albeit at a higher level. Not to have rolled up, of course, would have meant you would have had the Dow stock called away at $25 per share in the event of a bull move.

Unfortunately, rolling up is not always a painless process. On the one hand, as long as you hold an in-the-money short call option, you are locking out profit on your stock position. On the other, it may cost you money to exit the option position and roll up to a higher strike. Whenever you roll up, you must ask yourself: how much of a debit am I giving up in return for gaining 5 points in the stock? Again using the Dow Chemical example, let's assume the June 25, for which you initially received 1 when the stock was at 23, goes for 4 when Dow trades at, say, 28. At the same time, a June 30 call might be available for 1. You could now buy back the June 25 for 4, sustaining a loss of 3 on the transaction ($1 - 4 = -3$), and sell a June 30 for a premium of 1. The net debit on the transaction would be 3, since you paid 4 for the June 25 and received 1 for writing the June 30 call. As you can see, rolling up can be painful, since you didn't initially write the June 25 in order to take a loss. On the bright side, however, you've freed yourself of the obligation of selling your Dow Chemical stock at 25 when the prevailing market price is 28. In fact, you stand to earn 2 more points should the stock rise to 30 or above. Whether this strategy of rolling up proves profitable will depend on where the shares are trading upon expiration of the option. When Dow is trading at 30, your position will have 2 points of profit that it otherwise wouldn't have had had you not rolled up—plus, you'll retain the stock. Above 30 the stock's profits will go to the call buyer.

The most disappointing situation will occur when you roll up to the higher strike and the stock declines on you. When this happens you lose in the stock and you lose on the lower-strike option you initially wrote and bought back in anticipation of higher prices. In our Dow Chemical example above, any move back to the $23 area will result in insufficient writing income to offset the loss on the stock. Having been caught in such a situation, you may want to think about rolling down or even selling the stock.

When the stock shows signs of rising, you may want to combine rolling up and rolling out. Specifically, you cover your lower-strike call at a debit—say, 1½ points. Next, you sell a *higher-strike, longer-duration call* for more than the initial debit. You may, for instance, decide to sell an October 25 for 2½ rather than selling the shorter-duration July 25 for 1½ and pick up another point in writing income. The only disadvantage to this strategy is that the

October 25 will retain its time value for a longer period of time than the July 25. And you may have to hold the position longer as a result. But when you see it in terms of the cost, the October 25 makes sense. Ask yourself: what will it cost me to capture 5 points in the underlying stock? If you must pay a debit of 1½ to exit the short 20 call and this is offset by selling a 25 call for 1½, it costs you nothing to capture the 5 points in the stock. Better yet, if you are able to sell a longer-duration 25-strike call for 2½, you have actually *gained* a point. The net result will be a 5-point gain in the stock (assuming it rises to the higher strike of 25) plus another net point for selling the longer-duration October 25 call for 2½.

BE FLEXIBLE

Finally, as a covered writer you can buy back your short calls and simply hold the stock. Even if you find covered writing a profitable strategy, there will be times when you'll want to be out of the options market altogether. Under such circumstances your stock position alone will determine the profitability of your trading account. In general, regardless of the market strategy you employ, it pays to be flexible, to change with market conditions. Being long stock is often the safest and best response to a market that shows signs of gaining strength and moving higher. In such a market, don't feel bad about abandoning covered writing temporarily. No single strategy, no matter how profitable, can be expected to work without fail consistently. Covered writing is no exception.

Unlike buying shares of stock, in which the outcome of the investment can be quite unpredictable, covered writing involves a maximum ceiling on profits no matter how high the stock rises (assuming, of course, that defensive measures are not taken). For this reason you should make it a practice to monitor your covered-writing program continually and calculate the maximum gain every time you complete a covered-writing position. For instance, let's say you purchase 100 shares of Delta Air Lines at 31 and write an October 30 with more than six months left to expiration for a premium of 5. Assuming you hold this short call for six months and it is exercised at expiration for 1 (when the stock is still at 31), you would have realized a net profit of 4. By taking the profit and dividing by the investment of 31 (the price of the stock), you arrive at the percentage gain of 12.9 per cent. Annualized, this comes to more than 25 per cent. For most covered writers this would be an acceptable return on their investment. The point is, in return for that maximum return, you are assuming the risk that the stock will not decline more than 4 points, and you are giving up the opportunity to make more than 4 points on the stock. The maximum return is fixed in advance, and no matter what happens to the underlying stock, the return will not improve beyond that maximum return. On the downside, of course, the situation could deteriorate quite severely, since covered writing only protects your long stock position to the extent of the premium you receive for writing the call.

In addition, when you factor in the expense of commissions, the profit situation may not seem to be quite as promising. On a percentage basis commissions tend to be substantially higher on one or two options than they would be in larger multiples. Since the cost of executing 100 option trades on the same stock isn't significantly higher than executing a single option trade, your brokerage house understandably provides discounts to high-volume traders. As a result, the percentage cost of covered writing for an individual trading one or two options at a time is considerably higher than the percentage cost of a large institution that routinely trades 50 or 100 options. Therefore, because of the commission cost and the tiny margins of profit that are involved in covered writing, the covered write that a large institution finds profitable may not likewise prove profitable in your own covered-writing situation. Watch commission costs. They can change an otherwise profitable writing program into a losing one.

Operating on thin margins of profitability in a handful of stocks, the covered writer must also take pains to monitor his covered writes for signs of declining profitability. Since you know at the outset of a covered write the maximum profitability, you must be quick to take losses when the stock price shows signs of declining. Using the Delta Air Lines example above, you know when you purchase 100 shares at 31 and write an October 30 call for 5 that your margin of safety extends down to a price of 26. Below that price you will incur a real loss, since the premium income of 5 won't offset a decline in the price of Delta shares below 26. The logical strategy to take, therefore, is to place a stop-loss order *for the stock* at 26. This will ensure that you don't hold on to a losing stock in pursuit of writing income which isn't sufficient to pay for the stock losses. Should this hypothetical situation occur, of course, the October 30 call would no doubt sink to just a fraction and you would gain the bulk of the original 5-point premium you received for writing the call. Since the possibility always exists that the underlying stock may stage a rally, you should tell your broker to liquidate the option position at the same time the stock stop-loss order is activated.

It is important to decide in advance of adversity what your reaction will be. Professional traders regard trading losses as part of the game. They never claim to have a flawless record, and they are quick to admit a trading mistake. Unfortunately, for less seasoned traders, taking quick, small losses is psychologically difficult to do. The discipline to take losses by setting your loss parameters in advance when writing options is an important part of an overall profit strategy. Most losing situations go from bad to worse. Never hang on in the hope that a deteriorating situation will improve. Instead, take small losses and let writing profits continue to grow.

STOCK SELECTION

An integral part of any covered-writing program will be the selection of good stocks to buy as writing candidates. It is in this area that the art of covered writing is most complicated. Deciding what stock will best serve your writing needs is often hard to judge, but let's outline a few of the characteristics of a good stock to purchase for a covered-writing program. First and foremost, of course, the stock will have to be one which has listed options trading on one of the major options exchanges. This should be obvious. Second, you'll want a stock that you feel comfortable owning —one that you may want to hold on to for long-term growth. On this score there are two approaches to stock ownership for the covered writer. One is to write calls on stock you already own, stock which, most likely, you didn't acquire for the purpose of writing covered calls. The second approach is to purchase stock for the specific purpose of writing calls. In the first instance the covered writing takes a secondary importance to the stock ownership. In the latter, chances are you only plan to hold the stock as long as it serves your covered-writing goals. Assuming the latter for the moment, a word of warning: among the most dangerous stocks to acquire for writing purposes are the high price/earnings stocks, the highfliers which are routinely touted for so-called aggressive growth. The reason? These volatile stocks, while they may have options trading for high premiums (meaning high income for the call writers), tend to rise and fall quickly. In pursuit of a high premium, therefore, you may find yourself on the losing side of a stock that falls rather precipitously just after you purchase it. This disastrous state of affairs can be avoided by avoiding high P/E stocks for your covered-writing program.

KEEP YOUR INVESTMENT CAPITAL WORKING

While the emphasis on a covered-writing program is to collect as much of the initial premium as possible, you must decide when you've received the bulk of the maximum gain in a writing situation and take your profit. For instance, if you write an out-of-the-money 25-strike call for 1 and after an appropriate amount of time the option falls to $\frac{1}{16}$, you've gotten more than 90 per cent of the maximum potential gain in the writing situation. With so little value remaining in the call, you should buy back the short option and write another one against your stock position. As long as any amount of time remains in a stock option, it will retain *some* time value no matter how far out-of-the-money the option remains. It makes sense not to tie up your invested capital in a situation that will only return an additional $6.25 when you've already received $93.75 on a potential gain of $100. You should always think in terms of the capital investment you are making in purchasing stock for covered writing. Assuming you purchased a $20 stock for cash, a $93.75 writing gain only translates into a little better than 4 per cent on your $2,000 investment. But if you can write ten options per year on the same stock and remain fully covered the whole time, the 4 per cent grows to 40 per cent—a very welcome return on an essentially riskless transaction. It is for this reason that you must be quick to take profits when they become available—and leave the additional fractional profits for someone else.

MONITOR PREMIUM LEVELS

Since you enter into a covered-writing program to generate income off your invested capital (the money you've invested in purchasing the stock), you want to make sure the return you're receiving is comparable with the risk of stock ownership. After all, if you are receiving less than you would on virtual riskless investments—government high-grade debt instruments and the like—why fool around with covered writing? Set your sights on short-term profit goals that will justify the work you have to put into covered writing on an annualized-return basis. Since premium levels change, there's a good chance a stock that might be ideal for covered writing today won't be a good covered-writing candidate six months from now. Fine. When a stock no longer serves the purpose you purchased it for—in this instance covered writing—sell it and look for another optionable stock. What should your criteria be? That depends on a number of factors. Be mindful of a need to make a certain percentage per year off your writing activities. If you need 8 per cent per quarter from your writing to make the profits meaningful, you can readily judge whether a particular situation warrants purchasing the stock and writing options against it. Moreover, you may want to pursue your writing activities in terms of what kind of downside risk a particular option offers. If you have a $65 stock and you want to hedge against a 6 per cent decline in the value of your shares over the next four months, you'll need an option with an expiration date four months distant that has a premium of at least $4. Since a 6 per cent decline in the value of a $65 stock would reduce the value to just over $61 a share, a call with a strike price of 65 and a premium of $4 would be ideal. But if the premium were only, say, $2, you wouldn't have the downside protection you seek and you might be better off selling the stock and looking for a better writing opportunity.

DISCIPLINE IS THE KEY

The most important rule for covered writers is to have a disciplined approach to their market activities. The "wait and see" attitude applied to options trading rarely makes good sense, simply because you frequently become a prisoner of your own mistakes and compound your errors by making an untenable situation intolerable. Consider the stock investor who purchases stock with an eye toward writing calls against the stock but awaits higher prices. If the stock declines before he has an opportunity to write a call, he misses out on the downside protection provided by the short call and he sustains a real loss in the stock. If, having waited and the stock declines, he then writes a lower-strike call, the stock may even be called away from him at a price at which he has a locked-in loss. The number of things that can go wrong are many. Strive to take a disciplined approach in which you purchase shares because you know you can write specific options at specific premiums that meet your investment needs. At worst in this situation, if the strategy doesn't work out, you have a disciplined and planned approach to minimizing your mistake and you are looking ahead to another writing situation that meets your criteria. To ensure that you follow your own rules, write them down on a piece of paper and don't act unless the conditions are right. Remember, discipline is what separates the winners from the losers in any investment activity.

NAKED CALL WRITING—A HIGH-RISK/HIGH-GAIN STRATEGY

Naked writing involves selling calls on stock you do not own. The naked writer is said to be an *uncovered writer;* this is in contrast to covered writing, which is a strategy used by an investor who actually owns the underlying shares of the stock he writes the options on.

In contrast to the covered writer, who undertakes a conservative strategy in writing calls on stock he owns, the naked writer engages in a highly speculative venture when he writes calls. Since he doesn't own the underlying shares, he has two choices when the underlying stock stages a rally and soars above the strike price. On the one hand, he can enter the stock market and purchase shares for delivery against his short call; or, on the other hand, he can buy back his short call in the options market. In either case he'll sustain a loss in the process. The loss may be small or large depending upon when the naked writer decides to take action or

How to Profit From SELLING Options

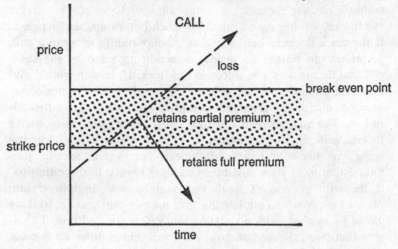

CALL

price

loss

break even point

retains partial premium

strike price

retains full premium

time

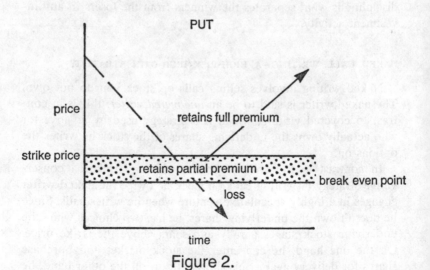

PUT

price

retains full premium

strike price

retains partial premium

break even point

loss

time

Figure 2.

when the shares are called in. The important point, however, is that in return for a fixed potential gain (the writing premium), the naked writer faces unlimited liability, since the underlying stock, at least theoretically, can rise to infinity.

Let's take a simple example. The naked writer sells an uncovered call on XYZ stock with a strike price of 35 for $1½. At the time he writes the naked option, XYZ shares are at, say, $27 per share. If XYZ is trading below $35 per share at expiration, the naked writer will be able to retain the full $1½-per-share premium, since the call will not be exercised. Assuming the naked writer maintains sufficient margin, he may write as many calls as he wishes—and he may be able to retain all the premium income he receives. But if XYZ stages a significant rally prior to expiration, the naked writer may find himself in considerable trouble. When the stock is at $36½, for example, the call will command at least its intrinsic value of $1½, the full amount of the premium the naked writer received when writing the call. Actually, the premium will be somewhat higher than that when you factor in whatever time value the option commands. With the stock at $38, the call will have a value of at least $3, and the naked writer will have sustained a 200 per cent loss on the income he received for writing the call. By the time it reaches $43, the 35 call will have a value of at least $8 per share, and the naked writer will be required to pay that amount to buy back his short call—a call that only gave him $1½ in writing income. With XYZ at $50 the naked writer is out $15 minus his $1½ writing income. And so on. As you can see, the naked writer can get in a lot of trouble fast—if he isn't careful. If he doesn't decide to buy back his call in the secondary market and the option is exercised, he will have to buy the shares in the stock market. If the stock rises to $50, therefore, he will have to pay $50 for a stock he will only receive $35 for, ensuring a loss of 15 points.

Naked writing is fraught with risk—no doubt about it. Since you are only trying to gain a relatively small premium for writing naked calls, why, you may ask, in the light of the obvious risk, should you engage in this practice? The answer has to do with percentages. If you know what you are doing, and if you are willing to cut short your losses, naked writing can be consistently profitable—a real sure-thing trade. The odds of an out-of-the-money call rising above the strike price prior to expiration will vary from option to option. On options trading near the strike price, the stock may very well go over the strike price, resulting in a loss to the naked writer. On options which are well out-of-the-money, the odds may well be astronomical that the underlying stock will rise above the strike price. Typically, the premiums will reflect the unlikelihood of out-of-the-money proving profitable. Consider a stock selling at $27 per share having a call option with a 35 strike. For the option to have value at expiration, the stock must rise 30 per cent in that limited amount of time. Since most stocks don't rise 30 per cent over a year's time, let alone two or three months, the premium of such an out-of-the-money call is apt to be small, perhaps as low as $\frac{1}{8}$ or $\frac{1}{16}$. Such low-priced options will only appeal to exchange-based market makers, who do not pay commissions. They make their money by writing these low-priced options in large quantities. An out-of-the-money call written for $\frac{1}{8}$, for instance, will only return $12.50 to a naked writer, but 100 such calls will return $1,250. If the level of commissions can be reduced to a level where this return is acceptable, even an option trading for a small fraction offers naked-writing possibilities.

MARGIN REQUIREMENTS FOR NAKED WRITERS

Because selling options without a position in the underlying stock is a risky venture, the exchanges and brokerage houses have established margin requirements for naked writers. There are minimum margin requirements set by the exchanges and suitability requirements imposed by some brokerage houses that don't want to encourage their clients to engage in naked writing. The minimum exchange requirements every naked writer must conform with; the brokerage house suitability requirements, however, vary from house to house, and you can shop around for the brokerage firm whose requirements are suitable to you. It is important to understand that the brokerage house is accountable to the clearing house for every order it transacts. If you are undermargined, or get yourself in a situation where you are unable to meet your obligations as a naked writer, your position will automatically be liquidated. But in the meantime, someone has to make good on your losses. If you can't, the brokerage house will be asked to come up with the funds. Hence the suitability rules. Although couched in terms of being in the client's interest, the suitability rules are in fact designed to protect the brokerage house *from* its clients.

Writing a naked option is a credit transaction. This means you receive money as soon as you write a naked option. Were it not for margin requirements, anyone could simply call a broker and write dozens of options—and leave town with the cash. Fortunately, safeguards have been established that prevent this from occurring. To protect the integrity of option contracts, writers are required to deposit margin equal to 30 per cent of value of the underlying stock. But this is only part of the requirements for writing options. How far an option is in- or out-of-the-money will also affect the margin requirement. For instance, let's say you write a call with a strike of 40 when the stock is at 35. The call might be trading for 1. But if you write a call with the same 40 strike when the stock is at 45, the premium is going to be much higher—perhaps 5½ or 6. As a result, for margin purposes in-the-money options are treated differently than out-of-the-moneys. The second margin requirement calls for adding a dollar requirement in margin for every dollar the stock is over the strike price in the case of a call, or in-the-money option. For out-of-the-money options, a dollar can be reduced from margin for every point the stock is out-of-the-money. For instance, let's say you write an out-of-the-money 75-strike call for a premium of $1 when the stock is at 69. What is your margin requirement? Well, 30 per cent of $69 is $20.70. And since the call is 6 points out-of-the-money, you can subtract $6 from the margin to arrive at $14.70. From this amount you can subtract the premium you received for writing the call; this lowers the requirement to $13.70 per share. If the difference between the market price of the stock and the strike price is large enough to lower the margin requirement below $2.50 per share, however, the requirements call for a minimum $250 per option margin on every naked option.

All naked options are marked to the market every trading day. This means that you may be asked to supply additional margin if the underlying stock rises and the call becomes more valuable to the buyer. Remember, you are the one who supplies the winnings to the call buyer whose judgment proves correct. Thus, even if your overall, long-term judgment ultimately prevails, your naked option position must be fully margined throughout the time you hold the short option. These interim short-term rallies in the option and stock can have an adverse effect on your margin position. The key to successful naked writing, therefore, is to have sufficient cash on hand to margin every position you write.

To see just how rapidly the margin requirements may increase, let's look at an example. Assume XYZ stock, selling for $52 a share, has a 60-strike call selling for 1. The naked writer wishes to sell an XYZ 60 call because he believes the chances of the stock rallying more than 8 points in the near future is quite unlikely. What is his initial margin?

If you take 30 per cent of $52, you get $15.60 ($52 × 30% = $15.60). Next, you subtract $8 from this amount, because the stock is 8 points out-of-the-money. This will give you a margin requirement of $7.60 per share; lastly, you subtract the premium of $1, which reduces the margin by another dollar to $6.60 per share. For the 100-share contract, this translates into a minimum margin requirement of $660 to write the XYZ 60 call. If you are trading multiples, of course, the margin would likewise increase: 10 options would require $6,600 in margin; 100 options, $66,600; and so on. But working with the $660 minimum margin required to write a single call, let's assume the underlying shares stage a rally and the stock goes to $61 after you write the option. When XYZ is at 61, the 60 call may well trade at $2, since the stock's prospects are much improved. Now the margin on the short call is calculated on a higher stock value and the call is in-the-money. Since 30 per cent of $61 is $18.30 plus an additional dollar because the call is one dollar in-the-money, the margin is $19.30. But since your initial premium was 1, the margin is reduced a dollar to $18.30 per share, or $1,830 on the short call. Percentagewise, the increased margin requirement is 177 per cent higher than the initial margin—all to capture the initial $1 premium, which has since disappeared. If the stock were to rally even higher, the margin requirement would increase at an even faster rate.

The point is, as a naked writer, you have to have an ample supply of cash to see you through those inevitable setbacks when you'll be asked for additional margin. Not to be well financed as a naked writer means you'll be prematurely forced out of a short position every time the stock rallies. This is not to suggest, however, that you'll want to continually meet margin calls when a stock rallies after you've written a naked call. On the contrary, the fact that the stock has behaved contrary to your expectation suggests your initial judgment was wrong—and that you should take appropriate action without delay. But there will be times when you'll want to stay with the short option position—and that requires additional cash.

TAKE LOSSES QUICKLY

Knowing when to take a loss quickly and without hesitation or regret is an important aspect of any naked-writing program. Losses must be kept to a minimum. To ensure the smallest possible loss, you must be rigorous with yourself and not merely sit back and watch a deteriorating position in hopes of recouping paper losses. One method is to use a mental stop-loss order when an option position goes against you. Since intraday fluctuations can be considerable, you are probably better off using close-only stops (on paper since the exchanges don't allow stop-loss orders in the options markets) that you can monitor on a daily basis. You could also ask your broker to do this for you. If you were to write a call for 3, for instance, you might then want to liquidate the position if the option closes at 4 or higher.

In using this approach you decide in advance what adversity you are willing to withstand—and then you exit the market if the mental stop is hit. Discipline is the key to using this approach. It may sound easy on paper to say you'll take a loss at a given point, but in practice this is much harder to do. Your emotions will tell you to hold on just a little longer. You may be convinced that the rally in the stock was purely technical and the option will certainly be trading at a lower price tomorrow. Your broker may even cite some news for a "temporary" rally. But don't listen to this information. Take the loss and look for another writing situation. Remember, some stocks rally and never come back. For the naked writer the refusal to take a loss in such a situation could prove disastrous.

Another strategy is to take a loss on an option based on what the stock does. Since the stock represents the key motivating force in the option's valuation, when the stock price reaches a key resistance area and penetrates the resistance, you can use this as a sign to exit your option position. Let's say the stock is trading at $40 and you write an out-of-the-money 45 call. You might decide you want to get out of your naked call when the stock rises to $46 a share since that price might represent a breakout into new high ground.

How you get out is less important than cutting losses. Just make sure you never allow a small loss to grow large by overstaying a market. All good traders know they will make mistakes; everyone does. But the seasoned trader will quickly cut his losses—and look for another profit-making opportunity. Rarely, by the way, do losing trades develop into winning trades; once you get behind in a market, the situation usually goes from bad to worse. Most winning trades, on the other hand, are winners right from the start. Learn to go with the winning ones and exit the losing ones.

Apart from the money you save by exiting a losing trade fast, there is still another reason why this advice should be heeded. Naked writing requires margin. Thus, the more margin you have available for winning trades, the more money you'll make. If you're writing naked options with, say, $7,000 in your account and $5,000 of that money is tied up in a losing option trade that has gone against you and is threatening to use up additional margin daily, the money simply isn't working for you; rather, it is tied up trying to hold on to a deteriorating market situation. By exiting the trade that is tying up your margin uselessly, you are now free to pursue a better opportunity.

Where to get out? Some traders, in using mental stop-loss guidelines, place an emphasis on a percentage of capital. Five per cent of one's working capital is often cited as a number to follow. By following this guideline a trader must make 20 consecutive losing trades before he would exhaust his funds. But let's consider the relationship between option price and stock price to see if we can pinpoint a spot where it is advisable to take losses. Below the strike price a call premium will move up only fractionally as the underlying stock moves up a point. But as the strike price is approached, the call option will rise in price at a faster rate until, once above the strike price, the option will move point for point with the stock. Since the naked writer wants the option premium to *decrease* after he writes the call, any increase in the premium comes right out of his pocket. The logical place to cut one's losses, therefore, is just below the strike price, assuming, of course, that one is writing out-of-the-money calls. Just below the strike, the call's total value is still comprised of time value. But as it rises above the strike, the call gains intrinsic value, and the naked writer soon finds himself asked to deposit additional margin funds.

Let's consider an example. When a stock is at $33, it might have a call with a 35 strike trading at $2. The $2 premium might be available to the writer for margin of $5.90 per share, or $590 to make $200. Depending on how close the option is to expiration, the rise in the stock may not cause a significant increase in the option premium as long as it remains below the strike price. A gain of 1⅞ points in the stock to 34⅞, might translate into a 2¾ premium, or a ¾-point gain in the option. Rapidly decreasing time value may even hold the option premium steady in the face of a rising stock. But above the strike, the relationship between the option and stock prices changes dramatically, since the option and stock will track point for point. With the stock at 36, the call option will have an intrinsic value of 1 plus whatever time value remains, perhaps a point or more. The 35 call will be worth at least 2 when the stock trades at 37. At that point, the profit situation has disappeared completely for the hapless writer. Rather than allow an out-of-the-money call to be an in-the-money call, the naked writer should exit the market just below the strike price, where the whole point gains in the price of the stock only translates into fractional gains in the price of the call. Not to take corrective action at that stage (when, by the way, the opportunity still exists for the stock to retreat and the option to expire worthless), only invites trouble.

If you have any doubts about the necessity for cutting losses below the strike price, consider how the margin situation deteriorates once the stock begins to rise. When the stock is at $33 and the call is trading at $2, you'll be required to post $590 in margin to capture a potential gain of $200. But as the stock rises, so does the margin requirement, and the naked writer finds himself posting additional margin to capture the same $2 maximum premium. A 2-point gain in the stock to $35 would require the naked call

writer to post $850, a 44 per cent increase. Should the stock rise
another two points to $37, the naked writer will most likely be in
a loss position, since he only received $2 for the call that now has
an intrinsic value of $2. To hold the short 35 call when the stock
is at $37 will require $1,110 in margin, an 88 per cent increase on
initial margin; and at $42, where you are a net loser of at least
$500, and perhaps more, the margin will amount to $1,760,
nearly a 200 per cent increase. If you were writing 10 calls, a
$5,900 initial margin commitment would have grown to $17,600,
including a $5,000 paper loss—all in pursuit of a $2,000 maximum gain. To avoid this kind of situation developing, cut your
losses while they are still small.

Now that we've looked at the negative things that can happen
to the naked writer, let's examine the positive side of things—the
profits to be had. Naked writing can be very profitable on a consistent basis—simply by playing the percentages in the stock market. If you make it a policy to write out-of-the-moneys, chances
are you will collect a substantial number of premiums without
having to buy back your options or otherwise sustain losses. The
reason? Very simply, on the average, stocks do not gain that much
in value over a short period of time. For the option buyer of an
out-of-the-money call to make money, the stock must rise above
the strike price within the life of the option—which could be as
short as three or four days, or as long as nine months. On the average, stocks don't climb steadily; even in bull markets they rise
and fall, and often mark time trading sideways. For the call writer,
who sells out-of-the-moneys, the chances of being exercised are
simply not that great. There will, however, be times when bull
markets make call buying profitable. But in the meantime—which
has been most of the time in recent years—stocks have not made
the sharp rallies that would enrich call buyers.

CONCENTRATE ON OUT-OF-THE-MONEYS

To capitalize on the law of probabilities, concentrate your
naked-writing activities on out-of-the-money options. Granted, in-
the-moneys will return larger premiums initially. But how much of
this money will you get to keep? When you write an in-the-money
option, most of the premium consists of intrinsic value which

you'll just have to give up when you liquidate the option or buy the shares in the event of exercise. By writing out-of-the-money calls, you'll be selling time value alone. Unless the stock can move higher, therefore, you'll win. Moreover, the in-the-money margin requirement is higher. You must put up 30 per cent of the value of the stock *plus* the difference between the strike and the market price. For the out-of-the-moneys, chances are the full premium will be yours to keep free and clear as a naked writer. Assume you sell a 20-strike call for a premium of $1 per share on a stock that is at 19 with two months to expiration. Even if the stock rose 5 per cent in a two-month interval, you would still get to keep the full premium. If this seems like a small gain, consider that a stock that gains 5 per cent in value in two months would rise 30 per cent on an annualized basis—an unlikely occurrence but not outside the realm of possibility. The point is, the naked writer has the best of the options equation, and at very low risk *if* he is careful.

Like covered writing, naked writing should be an ongoing process in which you continually take profits and look for new writing opportunities. As long as you keep your margin tied up in an unproductive writing situation, you won't be maximizing your return. Strive to continue writing new options, therefore, as you take profits in other situations, reinvesting your profits as you go along. With a stock at 49, you might write a 55-strike call for 1¼. With time and the absence of movement in the price of the stock, the time value will begin to diminish and the call may fall to a value of ½ point. Having made over 50 per cent of the available profit in the naked option, you'll then want to buy back your short call and look for another writing situation. Anytime you make over 50 per cent of the maximum profit in a naked write, you should consider looking for other options to write. The reason for this rule is that the last eighth or quarter may require a great deal of patience, since almost every option, no matter how far out-of-the-money, will retain some value. Rather than continue to hold a short option, therefore, take your profit whenever you obtain 50 per cent of the maximum gain.

Since writing naked options is such a risky undertaking, limit your exposure in any one writing situation by diversifying your writing activities. Occasionally, you'll write an option and the market will go against you immediately. Rather than risk losing a substantial amount of your writing capital in such an unfortunate way, protect yourself by writing a number of different options. Chances are, for every one option you write that results in a loss, you'll have five or six winners. The point is, if you plunge heavily on the short side of any one option and some such dramatic event as a takeover hits the market, you could be in serious trouble. Avoid even the remote chance of this happening by spreading your risk among a group of options. Unfortunately, if the market as a whole makes a broad upward move after you write a number of calls, you could lose on the whole group. To avoid this you might consider staying on the sidelines if you fear a sharp market rise, or hedge your short market commitment in the new stock market index futures, which will be discussed in a subsequent chapter.

For the naked call writer, the volatility of the underlying stock is an important factor to consider. While high-volatility stocks will tend to have larger premiums than low-volatility stocks, the likelihood of a high volatility stock making a substantial rise (resulting in a substantial loss to the naked writer) is somewhat greater. Stock traders place considerable emphasis upon such easily identifiable factors as previous highs and previous lows, interim support and resistance levels, cyclical price movements, and a number of other technical indicators that are readily known. By acquainting yourself with the stock's past history, you'll be in a better position to spot situations that may prove troublesome to the naked writer. Avoid the stocks that have a history of sudden, rapid price rises—unless, of course, you have reason to believe such a stock is way overbought and likely to decline during the time you'll be short the call.

As a naked writer you must remember that your exposure is virtually unlimited. You can lose many, many times your initial margin if the stock stages a rally and the call begins to move against you. To minimize your exposure, concentrate on selling calls with limited time left to expiration. The less time remaining in a call, the less opportunity for things to go wrong. There is also another reason for this rule: options tend to hold their time value pretty well during the early life of a call, but time value deteriorates at an accelerated rate once maturity approaches. Thus, the shorter-term options will offer the best writing opportunities with the least risk.

In naked writing good timing is essential. This is in contrast to purchasing stock, where there are no limitations on how long you can hold a position. In naked writing, however, you have little room for timing errors. The stock must stabilize or move lower once you write a call; if it does not, you are going to find yourself in a losing position almost immediately and you'll be asked for additional margin. Thus, if you fail to take appropriate defensive action, you may find yourself losing $10 in pursuit of a $1 premium —an unattractive, not to mention potentially disastrous, situation.

WRITING PUTS—BETTING AGAINST THE BEARS

Puts, being the mirror image of calls, share many of the same characteristics. While a call gives the holder the right to *buy* 100 shares of a given stock within a given amount of time at the strike price, the put provides the holder the right to *sell* shares of stock at the strike price. Hence, the put buyer pays a premium to sell shares at a given price. In purchasing a put, he anticipates lower prices and hopes to profit by selling high (at the exercise price) and buying lower. The put *writer,* therefore, agrees to purchase shares at the strike price in return for a premium. Typically, he writes the put because he anticipates the stock will stay at its current level or trade higher. As a seller of puts, he hopes to gain premium income in the same fashion the call writer does by writing options which are abandoned by their buyers.

Like the call writer, the put writer stands to earn a fixed rate of return from his writing activities—namely, the premium income he receives for writing the put. But he, too, faces virtually unlimited risk (though his exposure is not quite as unlimited as the call writer's, since a stock may only fall to zero) when he writes a put. If he writes, for example, a put with an 80-strike price and the price of the underlying stock falls to 60, he'll be asked to pay $80 a share for a stock that he can sell for only $60 a share. But if he writes the same 80-strike put and the stock moves *above* the strike, the put will be abandoned by its buyer and the premium will be the writer's to keep.

Put options were only introduced on the listed options exchanges after call options proved themselves as viable speculative and hedging investment vehicles. Puts have never been as popular as call options—perhaps because buyers, in general, prefer being optimistic about equity prices and hence share a bullish bias. As a result, the premium level of puts has never been comparable with that of calls. And this presents a problem for put writers, who will tend to earn smaller premiums. Another reason for the popularity of calls versus puts is that whereas a stock can only fall to zero, it can rise to infinity. Thus, the call presents an opportunity for almost unlimited gain to the buyer, whereas a put only presents an opportunity to profit from the difference between the strike price and zero. For the seller, of course, whether you engage in writing puts or calls, the maximum gain is always limited to the size of the premium.

When you sell puts, you must remember that any offsetting transaction you take to liquidate your position must be in another put with an identical strike and expiration. If you write a July 30 put, and you wish to buy back your option, you must buy another July 30 put on the same stock. You cannot, for instance, sell a July 30 put and buy back a July 30 call and expect to be out of the market. Puts are not offset by calls. All offsetting transactions, whether in puts or calls, must be in identical options with identical strike prices and expiration dates.

PUT WRITING MIRRORS CALL WRITING

Put writing mirrors call writing in that the maximum amount of income the put seller can derive by writing a put is the premium he receives in initiating the trade. Thus, if you write an out-of-the-money 20 put for a premium of ½ point when the stock is at $23, the most you can make on the transaction is that ½ point. The 20-strike put would require that the stock trade *below* that price at expiration for the option to have intrinsic value. In the above situation you are betting that the stock will remain above the price of $20 a share when you write the put.

As with naked call writing, naked put writing is best accomplished by writing out-of-the-moneys. These puts have only time value and won't be exercised unless the stock declines below the strike prior to expiration. The put writer looks for high premium coupled with bullish stocks or market conditions which are stabilized to bullish. Since put premiums tend to increase on falling stocks and decrease on rising stocks, good writing opportunities exist on stocks that have recently had a decline but show signs of bottoming. Such stocks will have overpriced put premiums (the high premiums reflecting continued bearishness), and the out-of-the-moneys should be particularly attractive, since you'll be receiving time value alone—the total amount which must disappear by expiration. In a put the premium level reflects how bearish investors are on the continual prospects of a stock. Since no stock ever rises or declines without hesitation, it stands to reason that there will always be opportunities to write puts at relatively high premiums purely on the notion that the market has become oversold and the degree of bearishness has carried too far. The put writer, in a sense, bets that the bearishness of a stock will not continue. Like the call writer, the put writer doesn't need news or any fundamental factors to influence the stock. On the contrary, the put writer—especially when he's writing out-of-the-moneys—only needs conditions to stay as they are (the stock unchanged) and he will profit.

The put writer must meet the same margin requirements as the naked call writer. That is, he must deposit 30 per cent of the value of the underlying stock and add point for point the amount the option is in-the-money or deduct point for point the amount the option is out-of-the-money. Lastly, he can deduct the amount of money he received for initially writing the option.

Let's say you write a Mattel 15 put for 1¼ when Mattel shares are trading at 16. Thirty per cent of the value of the underlying shares would amount to $4.80 ($16 × 30% = $4.80). Since the stock is one dollar out-of-the-money, you subtract one dollar to arrive at $3.80. Lastly, you subtract another $1.25 per share, the amount you received for writing the put. The net amount, therefore, is $2.55 per share or $255 in required margin to generate $125 in income. Transaction costs aside, this comes to a healthy 49 per cent in income generated on invested capital. Should Mattel shares decline after you write the put, it will become more valuable and you will be required to deposit additional margin.

While much emphasis has been placed on the conservative nature of *covered* call writing and the relative risky nature of *naked* call writing, when it comes to put writing, you have to think in terms of naked call writing to find a comparable strategy. The reason is, you really can't write a covered put. You might say a short put against a short sale in the common stock would be a covered put. But while this minimizes the downside risk, the short sale in the stock creates additional risk on the upside if the stock rallies. For instance, let's say you sell stock short at 44 and write a 45 put for a premium of 2. If the stock declines to 40, the put will have a value of at least 5 (a 5-point loss for your short put). Thus, having gained 4 points in your short stock position, you will have sustained at least a 3-point loss in your short 45 put. When you subtract the 2-point gain in writing income from the 5-point loss in the short 45 put, you get a net loss of 3. In the event of a rally to 50, the short stock position will have lost 6 points and the short put will have profited the full premium, 2. After you write a put, you can never receive more than your initial premium. At 50 the 45 put will expire worthless. But selling stock short against a short put is not a good way to be covered when you write puts.

The only true way to be covered or hedged when you write a put is to be long a comparable put on the same stock with a longer or similar expiration period and at the same or lower strike. The only problem with this kind of protection is that it defeats the reason for writing puts in the first place—namely, income.

The put writer, therefore, should think in terms of the strategies of the naked call writer. He'll want to write short-term, out-of-the-money puts in hopes of capitalizing on rapidly declining time value and roll over into other writing situations as his writing activities yield income.

The put writer, like the naked call writer, has virtually unlimited risk, although his exposure stops when the stock hits zero. Granted, this is small consolation if you write a 70-strike put for a premium of 3. But chances are, if the market crashed after you wrote a put, your broker would exercise his right to close out your position the first time you showed any hesitancy to replenish your dwindling margin. Better yet, it behooves you to exercise all the caution exercised by naked call writers once they write a position —namely, cut your losses quickly and look for other, more profitable writing opportunities.

The same problem of having your option exercised against you applies to put writers as it does to call writers. Anytime the stock is below the strike price, a put is in-the-money and may be exercised. To prevent an unwanted exercise in which the shares are *put* to you at the strike price, you can use some of the same defensive strategies discussed in the section on naked and covered call writing. For instance, with stock at $25½, let's say you write an XYZ 25 put for a premium of $1 per share. As the shares fail to hold ground and begin to decline, the put will become more costly and you may want to buy it back before the damage becomes too severe. You may then want to roll down to the 20-strike puts as the stock declines further. Since you don't have a stock position, the fact that the stock is declining will only affect your short put options. If you still feel that the stock is ready to stabilize, you may write puts at a lower strike.

As we've already mentioned, some option traders write puts to secure stock at an advantageous price. Let's say you want to pick up a certain stock currently trading at $34 for $32 or less. If you can write a 35-strike put option for a premium of 3 or more, there's a good chance you'll get your price. If the stock is put to you at 35—and it probably will be if it remains below the strike price—your net cost is only $32 a share, since you received a premium of $3 for writing the put. There's no guarantee the stock will rally from whatever level it has fallen to when you have the shares put to you. But at least you will have received your intended purchase price of $32.

The objective of put or call writing is to generate income on a fairly consistent basis. Since stocks are more apt to stay precisely where they are rather than make sharp rises or declines, the option writer, as opposed to the option buyer, tends to find himself in the winner's column more frequently. Whereas the option writer selects a fixed and relatively small reward for his market activities, the option buyer is much more apt to seek substantial—and sometimes unrealistic—gains. The writer, in a sense, is betting that things will stay pretty much the same; the buyer expects action. The buyer pays for his anticipated reward in the form of premium payments to the writer, who, being of a more conservative bent, is often content to make money a bit slower yet on a more consistent basis.

5

The Option Spread

Option spreads are among the most popular trading strategies used by investors in the options market. Their popularity stems from two characteristics: they are normally lower in risk than outright buying or selling trading strategies, and they are highly adaptable to specific market conditions. Since there are many types of spreads, you'll probably find one that suits your trading needs. Don't shy away from spreads for fear they are too complicated. Once you fully understand the advantages and disadvantages of spread trading and compare the risks with the respective rewards, you'll be glad you have this technique at your disposal. Spreads are designed to limit risk, and in most cases they do this quite effectively—again, if you the investor know what you are doing.

WHAT IS A SPREAD?

All spreads have certain common characteristics. All spreads consist of long, or purchased, options and short, or written, options on the same stock. The options thus bought and sold will have different strike prices or different expiration months, or they may have both different strike prices and different expiration months. Generally, when you *put on,* or *place,* a spread, you simultaneously buy and sell options. In taking off a spread, also known as "lifting" the spread, you also do the buying and selling—albeit in reverse order—simultaneously. An option trader who bought an Exxon January 25 call and sold an Exxon January 30 call would be spread. So would the trader who bought Exxon January 25 calls and sold Exxon April 25 calls. The trader who simply bought an Exxon January 25 call, however, and then proceeded to sell an Exxon January 25 call would not be spread, since he only offset his initial position. He would be out of the market with no position at all. Thus, the long and short positions must be in *different* options, according to striking price, expiration month, or both.

Since the only determining factor in whether you make a profit or sustain a loss in the market is the difference between where you buy and sell, the option investor who spreads is primarily concerned not with the profit or loss on any one leg of the spread but the net difference between the final results of the two individual legs. Most of the time, with a few possible exceptions, one leg of a spread will prove profitable and another will sustain a loss. The spreader merely wants the profitable side of the spread to generate greater profits than the losing side sustains losses. Thus, if you put on a spread and one side earns $300 while the losing side loses $100, the net profit on the spread, disregarding commissions, is $200.

Let's say you can buy a call option on XYZ common shares with a striking price of 90 for a premium of 8. At the same time, a call with a strike of 100 on XYZ shares is available for a premium of 3. You might take the spread by instructing your broker to buy one XYZ 90 call and sell one XYZ 100 call with a limit of 5, the difference between the two options. We'll assume you are able to put on the spread for a debit of 5. Now you've paid $800 for the 90 call and received $300 for writing the 100 call. Let's assume the market moves up and both calls increase in price. In addition, we'll assume the 90 long call moves up faster than the 100 short call. What has been the result on the spread? If the XYZ 90 call moves to 15 and the XYZ 100 call only moves to 5, you'll have a profit of $500 on the spread. Having purchased the 90 call at 8, you will have a profit of 7 when it trades at 15; having sold the

100 call at 3, you will have a loss of 2 when it trades at 5. Table 9
lists the transactions in this spread.

Table 9

OPENING		DEBIT/CREDIT
TRANSACTION: Buy one XYZ 90 call.	Sell one XYZ 100 call.	
Pay: $800	Collect: $300	−$500
CLOSING		
TRANSACTION: Sell one XYZ 90 call.	Buy one XYZ 100 call.	
Collect: $1,500	Pay: $500	+$1,000
		Net: +$500

$700 profit on XYZ 90 call
−$200 loss on XYZ 100 call
$500 profit on spread, exclusive of commissions

Whether the option you purchase or the option you write in a
spread transaction proves profitable is unimportant as long as the
winning leg outpaces the losing leg. When you place a spread, you
are betting on the price differential working in your favor. The
overall profitability of the spread will be determined by how skillful you are in selecting the different months and strikes to spread.

MANY TYPES OF SPREADS

Spreads fall into two basic groups depending upon their key
characteristics. These are the *vertical* and *horizontal spreads.*
There are subcategories of spreads which share characteristics of
these two major groups. The most popular spreads will generally
be one of the types listed below.

1. The Time Spread. Also known as the *horizontal* or *calendar
spread,* the time spread is the purchase of a listed call or put option and the sale of a listed call or put option having the *same exercise price but different expiration months.* Using calls, this
spread is known as a *call time spread;* using puts, this spread is
known as a *put time spread.* An example of a call time spread
would be a long XYZ June 15 call and a short XYZ December 15
call. The longer-duration option is generally purchased using this
spread strategy and the shorter-duration option is generally written. The spreader seeks to profit by having the shorter-term option
lose time value faster than the longer-duration option. The term

"horizontal spread" refers to reading across the columns of numbers on the listed options quotations pages in the financial press.

2. The Vertical Spread. This spread, which is also called a *money* or *price spread,* consists of a long and short position in listed options having the same expiration month but different strike prices. The term "vertical spread" refers to reading up and down when reading options quotations. A spread consisting of a long XYZ February 70 call and a short XYZ February 80 call would be an example of a vertical spread. Vertical spreads can be designated as either *bull* or *bear spreads* depending upon whether the higher or lower strike price option is purchased or sold.

3. The Diagonal Spread. This spread consists of the purchase of a longer-duration option and the sale of a shorter-duration option at different strikes. A popular variation of the bull spread, the diagonal seeks to capitalize on decreasing time value in the shorter-term option that you write. Assume you put on a diagonal spread on January 1 by purchasing an XYZ August 50 call and simultaneously writing an XYZ February 60 call. With the February option rapidly approaching expiration, the rate at which it loses its time value will increase in terms of the longer-term August call option. Assuming the higher-strike February 60 expires worthless (and you get to keep the premium you received as a writer), you would then have the opportunity to write a May 60. This is known as *rolling over* when you replace one month with another of the same strike. After the May option expires, assuming the stock is in the right place, you may want to write an August 60 against your August 50 call and convert the diagonal spread into a simple vertical spread.

4. The Butterfly Spread. The butterfly spread is simply a combination of *two* vertical spreads. One half of the butterfly spread consists of a *bull vertical spread,* in which the lower-strike option is purchased and the higher-strike option is sold, and the second half consists of a *bear vertical spread,* in which the higher-strike option is purchased and the lower-strike option is sold. As the respective names suggest, the bull vertical spread is designed to take advantage of an upward move in prices and the bear vertical spread is designed to take advantage of a downward move in prices. Also known as a *sandwich spread,* the butterfly involves

four options and three different strike prices. When properly executed, the spread offers a good return on a relatively broad range
of prices. An example of a butterfly spread would be one long 15
call, two short 20 calls, and one long 25 call. The bull spread
would be one long 15 call and one short 20 call; the bear spread
would be one short 20 call and one long 25 call; together they
make a butterfly spread with the two short 25 calls sandwiched in
between the two long calls.

THE ADVANTAGES OF SPREAD TRADING

The key advantage of option spreading is that of limited—and
predetermined—risk. To understand how important managing risk
in options trading can be, you have to remember that both option
buyer and seller can lose considerable portions of their investment: the naked option writer faces unlimited risk, whereas the
option buyer stands to lose 100 per cent of his premium money.
Since neither alternative is encouraging, option spreading, in
which you are both long and short option contracts, provides a
less risky, but by no means risk-free, alternative.

Let's examine a spread in terms of its two components, a long
option and a short option. You might buy an August 30 call and
simultaneously write an August 35 call. You are now spread.
What you paid for the August 30 will be offset in part by the premium you received for writing the August 35. By placing the
spread you limit the profit zone but you also limit your risk.

For the August 30 call to prove profitable at expiration, the underlying stock must rise above the striking price of 30. If the underlying stock fails to rise, the August 30 call may be sold prior to
expiration at a loss, in which case you'll recoup at least a portion
of your premium cost; if held to expiration, however, and the underlying stock remains below 30, the call will expire worthless,
resulting in a 100 per cent loss. A more promising alternative, of
course, is that the stock stages a rally and the August 30 call
proves profitable to the buyer.

The other side of the spread is represented by the short August
35 call. In return for writing the naked August 35 option, you'll
receive the premium paid by the option buyer. This premium is
yours to keep regardless of what the stock subsequently does. In

the event of a rally in the stock, the 35 call will almost certainly be exercised and you'll be required to deliver 100 shares of the stock at a price of $35. Your only alternative to having the stock (which you do not own) called away is to enter the options market and buy back your 35 call—at a loss. Above the strike of 35, the option will gain point for point with the stock. So the potential loss is considerable. But unlike the naked writer, who is in serious trouble if the stock rises, the spreader simply misses out on an otherwise profitable move. The reason? He is long stock at 30 by virtue of having purchased the August 30 call. He has the stock to deliver at 35 should the higher-strike short call be exercised.

The spreader has neither the risk of the call buyer or of the seller. The long 30 call provides him with the opportunity to purchase shares of the underlying stock at 30 no matter how high the stock rises. Since he can purchase stock at 30 and sell it at 35, he has a potential built-in profit of the difference between 30 and 35 should the shares be called away. The potential profits above the higher strike of 35 will be lost to him, of course, since he sold a 35-strike call. Should the stock rise above 35, all the profit from 35 upward will go to the *buyer* of the 35 call. On the downside, the premium received for writing the 25 call will, in part, offset the loss of the premium paid to purchase the long 30 call. As a result of putting on the spread, the option trader finds himself with a lot less risk than a naked writer and the owner of a call with a 5-point potential. Moreover, the price he'll pay for that call will be less than the outright call buyer will pay, since the premium is offset in part by income generated by writing the 35 call. It is true that you can make a lot more money by simply buying calls on a stock in a runaway bull market, or, for that matter, writing calls in a declining or sideways market. But who's to say precisely what a stock will do next? Spreads offer a convenient, and safe, alternative to simply buying or selling calls. They are especially useful when the prospects for the stock seem limited and the future uncertain.

THE BULL SPREAD

Let's assume, in the example cited above, the lower-strike 30 call is available for 2½ and the higher-strike 35 call is available for

1. By buying the August 30 for 2½ and writing the August 35 for 1, you put on the spread for a debit of 1½ (2½ − 1 = 1½). This type of spread, in which you purchase the more expensive lower-strike call and write the less expensive higher-strike call, is known as a *bull spread*. It is always done at a debit, and as a result, no margin is required as long as you hold the long lower-strike call. This lowers the cost of being potentially long the stock and changes the break-even point. Here again, spreads have an advantage over outright short or long positions. To simply buy the 30 call would mean the option would not be profitable on expiration unless the stock were at $32½ or higher. After all, the first 2½ points over the strike of 30 would only compensate the call buyer for his premium cost. But by writing the higher-strike 35 at the same time you purchase the 30 call, you *lower your overall cost* to $1½, resulting in a significantly lower break-even point. Since your cost in putting on the spread is 1½, you'll now have a break-even point of $31½ and a profit above that level. Contrast that with the single 30 call buyer, who will still require the stock to rise to $32½ to reach break-even.

Now, what about profitability? The maximum profit in using this spread would exist at the higher strike of 35. At that point the 30 call would have a value of 5 and the 35 would expire worthless. Since you put on the spread for a debit of 1½ and could receive a total of 5 for the 30 call, your maximum profit would be the difference, or 3½. Above a stock price of 35, the gain on the long 30 call is exactly offset by the loss on the short 35 call, so you won't be able to improve profitability as long as you remain spread. And on the downside you stand to lose a total of $1½ a share if the stock remains below the lower strike of 30. The $1½ represents the total amount you paid to put on the spread. With the stock trading below $30 a share, both the 30 and 35 calls will expire worthless. At that price or lower, you'll sustain your maximum loss in the spread, 1½ points.

As you can see, the bull spread, which consists of buying the lower-strike option and selling the higher-strike option, serves to enhance your profit opportunities over a very narrow range—at and just above the lower strike to the upper strike. Above the upper strike, the bull spread is no help at all, since it locks out profit, and its value is only minimal on the downside. Because it enables you to receive income, the bull spread lowers your over-all cost of what amounts to a proxy for a long option position.

THE BEAR SPREAD

If you are bearish on a particular stock, and if you wish to avoid the risks of naked call option writing, it usually pays to use a *bear spread,* in which you purchase the higher-strike call and write the lower-strike call. You will make a little more by simply writing a naked call on a declining stock. But you'll achieve a certain peace of mind by using bear spreads. When you write a naked call and the market price of the underlying stock rises, you are responsible for either delivering the stock when it is called away from you, as it most certainly will be, or you must exit the market by purchasing the short option at a higher price. The bear spread relieves you of this responsibility. With a bear spread you are potentially long at the higher strike.

As the name suggests, a bear spread will make money when the market declines. On one side of the spread, you'll sell a call that will result in a credit. On the other side, you'll purchase a higher-strike but less expensive call. Since you will receive more than you will spend in putting on this spread, you'll have a net credit.

Let's assume XYZ stock is selling at $80, with six months to run in the July calls. The July 70 might be available for a premium of $12 per share, and the July 80 might be available for $5. If you are bearish on the XYZ stock, you might sell the higher-priced, in-the-money July 70 for $12 and simultaneously buy the lower-priced, but higher-strike, July 80 for $5. The result is an immediate credit of $7 ($12 − $5 = $7) for putting on the spread. Even though you receive a credit, you'll still have to post margin. In this instance the margin requirement will be the difference between the credit you received and the distance between the respective strike prices. Since you spread a July 70 against a July 80, the difference in the strikes is 10 points. The credit for doing the spread was 7. Thus, the difference of 3 will constitute the margin required. In addition, you'll have to wait until you close out the spread position before withdrawing your credit from your trading account.

The maximum profit potential will exist in this spread at or below the lower strike, the point at which both options will expire worthless. Thus, at 70 or lower neither option will have any value and you'll be able to retain the full credit of 7 points on the spread. Given a margin requirement of $3, this translates into a maximum profit potential of 233 per cent. This percentage is calculated by dividing the maximum profit by the margin requirement.

As the stock rises above 70, the profit situation in the spread will lessen somewhat and range from good to bad as the stock moves higher. With the stock at 72, for example, the option you received 12 for will still be worth 10, and your net profit will have dropped from $700 to $500 before commissions. With the stock at 78, the 80 call will still be worthless, resulting in a total loss of the $500 premium. The short 70 call will still retain a value of at least 8, however, and perhaps a point or two more. Since you received 12 for writing the short 70-strike call, you will now have a $400 profit if the 70 call falls to 8. But this profit will be offset by a $500 loss sustained in the long 80 call. The result: a loss of $100 plus commissions. Fortunately, the situation stabilizes around $80, because you gain on one leg what you lose on the other above that price. But the fact is, you'll still have a loss, although it will be relatively small compared to what a naked option writer can lose.

THE BUTTERFLY SPREAD—
A BULL SPREAD AND A BEAR SPREAD TOGETHER

The risk-limiting feature of spreads is perhaps best illustrated by the butterfly spread, which, as we've mentioned, combines a vertical bull spread with a vertical bear spread. The advantage of the butterfly spread is that it offers profitability over a broad range of prices.

The butterfly consists of four options on the same stock with identical expiration dates and three different strike prices. For instance, you might set up a butterfly spread by buying a July 25 and July 35 and writing two July 30s in the middle. Or you could set up the spread with the two long positions in the middle—short a July 25 and 35 and buy two July 30s. In either instance the butterfly consists of a vertical bull spread and a vertical bear spread combined. The rule is that for quiet markets, the two short legs of the butterfly are placed in the middle; for volatile markets, you do the reverse with the two long legs in the middle.

Let's consider an example in which you anticipate a stable market and place the two short positions in the middle with the long positions at a higher and lower strike. We'll assume the underlying stock is at 33 with the October 25 call available for 9, the October 30 call at 5, and the out-of-the-money October 35 call at 2. Table 10 shows the butterfly spread.

Table 10

Buy 1 XYZ October 25
Sell 2 XYZ October 30
Buy 1 XYZ October 35

Since the investor received $10 for writing the two October 30s ($5 × 2 = $10) and paid $11 for the long October 25 and 35 ($9 + $2 = $11), his debit on the spread is $1. Ideally, in using the butterfly you want a debit equal to zero, or less than $2 per share. As long as the stock doesn't move above the higher strike of 35 or below the lower strike of 25, the spread will prove profitable.

When the stock is at 30, the two October 30s will expire worthless along with the October 35, and the spreader will get to keep the full 10 points he received for writing the two October 30s. He'll sustain a loss of 2 on the October 35, but this will be more than offset by the 5-point gain he'll make on the long October 25. The net gain will be $4 per share before commissions. The calculations are in Table 11.

Table 11

STOCK AT 33

Sold 2 XYZ Oct 30	@ 5 =	10
Bought 1 XYZ Oct 25	@ 9 =	(9)
Bought 1 XYZ Oct 35	@ 2 =	(2)
		(1)

STOCK AT 30

Bought 2 XYZ Oct 30	@ 0 =	0
Sold 1 XYZ Oct 25	@ 5 =	5
Sold 1 XYZ Oct 35	@ 0 =	0
		5

5 − 1 = 4 net income

As you move the price of the stock higher or lower, the gains will diminish. But the profit range is sufficiently large. Above the price of 30, the profits on the two short October 30s will decline as the spreader must give up some of his writing income. Below 30 the October 35 remains worthless and the value of the long 25-strike call will decrease, until, at 25, it also becomes worthless.

In using a butterfly spread with the two short positions in the middle, you want the stock to be stable and you want the stock to be trading near the middle strike at expiration. In addition, you want to be able to place the spread at a zero or small debit. The best candidates for this spread are those expensive stocks where the legs can be placed 20 points apart. Teledyne, with strikes placed at 10-point intervals from 120 to 170 readily comes to mind. Marathon Oil and Digital Equipment are two other stocks with strike prices sufficiently far apart, although these have not exactly been stable stocks in recent years.

As with any spread, in a butterfly you are on both sides of the market at the same time. Typically, what you lose on one leg (in this case, on the bull or bear vertical spread), you gain on the other, and vice versa. Yet with a butterfly, unlike the bull or bear spread, which are its components, you are indifferent to the direction of the underlying shares within certain limits. The stock may move up a little or it may move down a little and the results to your account will be the same. The important point is that the stock not move too much lest you sustain a loss, albeit a small one, on the spread.

BULL MARKET SPREAD STRATEGIES

The bull vertical spread is used to capitalize on rising markets. Often used as a proxy for an outright call purchase, the bull spread has the advantage of being less expensive than a simple call purchase and thus has less risk attached to it. Moreover, within a narrow price range, the bull spread offers a better return on invested capital than does the outright call purchase.

The most widely used bull spread consists of a long in-the-money call and a short out-of-the-money call. Ideally, you want at least two to three months left prior to expiration when you initiate the spread. And you place the spread with the intention of generally holding it to expiration, since you want the higher-strike short call to lose all of its premium value.

A bull spread will always be a debit spread, since lower-strike calls are always more expensive than higher-strike calls. Because you'll be buying the lower-strike call, you'll be paying more than you'll receive for writing the higher-strike call. As with any spread, you want one leg to gain more in value than the other leg loses. In this instance, the lower-strike long call is expected to gain more than the higher-strike short call, resulting in a net profit.

The difference between what you pay for the long call and what you receive for writing the short call is known as the *basis*. You want the basis—which in this case is a debit—to be as small as possible, since this amount constitutes your cost. As with purchasing an outright call, the cost of the bull spread is the maximum amount you stand to lose regardless of the subsequent movement of the underlying stock. Nevertheless, if the market price of the underlying stock goes down after you put on the spread, you'll lose the full debit you paid, or 100 per cent of your invested capital in the position.

On the other hand, if the underlying stock moves upward in price as you anticipate, the maximum amount you can gain is also known. The maximum profit of any bull spread is the difference between the initial debit and the difference between the two strike prices. Thus, if the difference in the two strikes is 10, and the cost of the spread is 6, your maximum potential profit is $4. As a general rule, if the stock moves 10 per cent in four weeks, the profit before commissions should be greater than 50 per cent of the basis. Thus, if you paid 6 for a bull spread and you had a 3-point profit in four weeks, you'd be wise to take the profit. After all, if the maximum profit was only 4, you'll only be giving up an additional point by closing out the spread prior to expiration.

In a bull spread, which is put on at a debit, you are said to *buy the spread,* since a cash payment is involved. This is in contrast to a bear spread, in which you receive a credit—a technique known as *selling the spread.* Regardless of whether you buy or sell a spread, the profit will come from the changing relationship between the two option prices.

Let's assume you look in the financial pages and find the options on a stock you are bullish on trading at the following prices (Table 12) in relation to the stock.

Table 12

OPTION SERIES	PRICE	STOCK PRICE
XYZ May 25	3½	26
XYZ May 35	½	26

Since you are bullish on the stock, you'll buy the May 25 for 3½ and sell the May 35 at ½. Your basis, or debit, on the spread is 3 (3½ − ½ = 3). This constitutes your entire cost, the most you can lose if the spread doesn't work. If you are bullish on the stock, of course, you have the alternative of simply buying the May 25 for 3½. But this would cost you another ½ point.

Unlike the naked option writer, you are fully covered against loss on your short May 35. You are considered fully margined if you have purchased an option with a lower strike than the call you have written. The long call serves as your margin on the short call in a bull spread. By writing the short call, you not only lower your cost from 3½ to 3, but you also lower your break-even price from 28½ to 28. This may not seem a significant advantage, but when you consider the percentage gain, the advantage becomes easier to see. You have a 16 per cent gain in the spread when the stock trades at 28½. With the stock at 28½, the comparable outright call position would have a zero percentage gain.

Now let's consider the price of the respective options if the underlying stock moves to 31 by expiration. Look at Table 13.

Table 13

OPTION SERIES	PRICE	STOCK PRICE
XYZ May 25	6	31
XYZ May 35	0	31

At this point the bull spread is worth 6. Since the cost of the spread was 3 points, the net profit is the difference, or 3. Had you not been spread, and simply purchased the outright long May 25 for 3½, your cost would have been 3½ and the net profit (before commissions) would be 2½ (6 − 3½ = 2½). Again, the ½-point difference may not seem significant, but on a percentage basis the difference is 83 per cent versus 100 per cent.

Since you paid 3 for the spread and the difference in the two strike prices is 10, the maximum potential profit on the spread is the difference, or 7. This maximum profit will exist at the upper strike at expiration when the May 35 will have no value, permitting you to retain the ½ point you received for writing it, and the May 25 will be worth a value of 10, or the difference between 25 and 35. Above 35 the bull spread ceases to gain in value, since the May 35 position loses value point for point above that price. The long May 25 will gain in value point for point with the stock above the strike of 25, but once 35 is reached the gain is offset by a corresponding loss on the short May 35 call. With XYZ common shares trading at 35, the point of maximum profitability for the spread, Table 14 shows how the prices would appear at expiration.

Table 14

OPTION SERIES	PRICE	STOCK PRICE
XYZ May 25	10	35
XYZ May 35	0	35

You should note that prior to expiration the May 35 will have some time value left. To earn the full 7 points in maximum profit, therefore, you have to wait until expiration for the May 35 to lose all its value.

Since the cost of the bull spread was less than the cost of simply buying the outright position, you should remember that even at the upper strike, the bull spread will give you a better return on your money. Above the upper strike, of course, the single long May 25 call will continue to gain in value, whereas the bull spread will not.

One situation we haven't dealt with here is that of a bull spread in a declining market. On the one hand, the short option will provide a small protection against loss by lowering your overall cost. On the other, however, you still stand to lose your entire investment if the stock declines below the lower strike. The bull spread doesn't offer you a great deal of protection against falling prices. But once you take the spread, you must decide either to hold it until expiration in hopes of the stock rallying or cut your losses by taking whatever you can get. As long as the stock remains above the lower strike, the long option will retain both intrinsic and time value. Once the stock falls below the lower strike, however, the time value alone will account for the premium, which is apt to be quite low.

We've defined the bull spread as a long in-the-money call and a short out-of-the-money call. But in fact, this is just the most popular type of bull spread, known as an *at-the-money spread*. The price of the underlying stock may be below the lower strike of a bull spread. Or the price of the underlying stock may be above the higher strike of the bull spread. The former is known as an *out-of-the-money spread* and the latter as an *in-the-money spread*. Both are worth considering for their respective advantages and disadvantages. The out-of-the-money spread, in which the price of the stock is slightly below the option you buy, is highly speculative, because unless the stock stages a rally prior to expiration, both options are going to expire worthless. In fact, even a small drop in the price of the stock will make them virtually worthless, since the long option will be even further out-of-the-money with time value eroding daily. On the plus side, an out-of-the-money bull spread can be taken at relatively low cost. For example, with XYZ common shares trading at a price of 84, you could probably buy the 90 call for 1 and sell the 100 call for ¼, or perhaps even less. Your cost only amounts to $75 for the spread. But the chances of the stock rallying more than $6 a share in three months may make you reluctant to risk even this small amount. On the positive side a genuine rally above 90 could result in a huge percentage gain. When the stock trades at 94, the 100-strike call would be worthless and the long 90-strike call would have a value of $4 per share. Considering that you paid just $75 for a spread that is now worth $400, your percentage gain is 433 per cent. The maximum gain would occur at the upper strike of 100. At that price you would have a gain of $9¼, or $925 on your $75 investment. You may ask, if you're going to trade low-priced options, why spread at all? Does the $25 in writing income on this spread warrant locking out all that profit above $100 per share? It may seem like a small amount of money, but in terms of investment it lowers your cost by 25 per cent, from $1 to $.75. Moreover, with the stock at 84, chances are that you won't see the rally to 90—at least during the next three months—let alone a rally to 100.

When you put on an in-the-money bull spread with the stock

trading above the higher strike, you're dealing with a completely different situation altogether. In the previous example, the opportunity, no matter how remote, existed to make a large potential gain. In the case of the in-the-money bull spread, however, you are counting on time value decreasing to provide your profit—not the price of the long call increasing. And the gain that you are likely to get is limited. In this spread you are selling the higher strike in hopes that its future time value exceeds that of the lower-strike option you buy. With eroding time value the higher-priced option should decline in value faster than the lower-priced option. If you are not to sustain a loss on this spread, the price of the stock must stay above the higher-strike option. A decline in prices would mean the long call would lose value and you could lose your entire investment.

Let's consider an example in which a stock is trading at 44 and the 35 call is at $11, with the 40 call trading at $7½. You buy the 35 call for $11 and sell the 40 call for $7½, for a debit of $3½. Since the strikes are only 5 points apart, the maximum amount you can make on this spread is 5, or a net profit of 1½. If we further assume that at expiration the stock is still at $44 a share, the two options will be worth their intrinsic value alone. In the case of the 35-strike call, the value will be $9 ($44 − $35 = $9). And in the case of the 40 call, the value will be $4 ($44 − $40 = $4). Since you paid $11 for the long 35-strike call which is now worth $9, you have a $2-per-share loss on the long call. Since you received $7½ for the short 40 call which is now worth $4, your profit is $3½. Your net profit is the difference between the two options, or 1½ points. On a percentage basis this spread makes sense. But it is not without risk. In pursuit of that 1½-point profit, you might have lost the entire investment of $4 had the underlying stock declined in price. It is a simple task to calculate remaining time value in any in-the-money option simply by subtracting the price of the underlying security from the strike price. This will give you the intrinsic value. Whatever premium the option commands over this value is time value, which can be expected to erode to zero by expiration. In this instance the 35-strike call trading at $11 had a time value of 2 and the 40-strike call trading at $7½ had a time value of 3½. Since the higher-strike 40 call had more time value to lose, the spread made sense—assuming, of course, the underlying stock stayed above the higher strike price.

Given the highly speculative nature of the out-of-the-money spread and the small profits of the in-the-money spread, your best bet is probably to concentrate on at-the-money spreads with the stock trading somewhere between the two strikes. You'll pay more for this spread than you would for an out-of-the-money, and your percentage return won't be as large if you exercise it at a profit. But you probably won't have to sustain a 100 per cent loss as frequently as you would in the more speculative out-of-the-money spread.

Ideally, you would like to take an on-the-money bull spread for the cash value of the lower-strike option or less. For instance, if the stock is at $33 a share, you may be able to buy the 30 call for 6 and write the 35 call for 3. Your cost is 3, the intrinsic value of the 30 call. Now, if the stock goes to 35 or higher, you'll make the maximum profit on the spread, 2. Contrast this situation with that of the option buyer who pays 6 for the 30 call. He has a loss at 35, having paid 6 for the option.

Bull vertical spreads are a relatively conservative strategy for the option investor when he has good reason to anticipate a rise in the underlying stock. The rise he'll need to profit is modest—but rise it must if the bull spread is going to work. Every bull spread you put on will cost you money. And you stand to lose every penny you invest if your market judgment is wrong. Going into the spread, therefore, you know your ultimate risk—the cost of the basis. On the profit side, moreover, you also know what you can expect—a profit no larger than the difference between the initial debit and the distance between the strikes. Knowing the most you can gain should keep your expectations modest. It may also tell you when to exit the trade once you've gained the lion's share of the maximum profit.

TIME SPREADS

You can also employ bull market strategies using *time* or *calendar spreads*. These are spreads between options on the same stock and striking prices but different expiration dates. The bull market strategist attempts to profit by buying a longer-duration call and simultaneously selling a shorter-duration call. Typically, you'll spread call options that are out-of-the-money with the stock below the lowest strike. Should prices rally prior to expiration of the near-term option, it will lose its time value faster and hence produce a declining value in the short option, while the long option will retain its value and perhaps even advance in price.

Since out-of-the-money options are priced according to their time value alone, and since options tend to lose their time premiums at a faster rate as expiration approaches, it is only reasonable to assume the calendar spread will make money as the maturity date approaches.

For example, let's say XYZ common shares are trading at $29 per share during the first week of January, while the May 30 call is trading at 1 and the August 30 call is trading at 2. The calendar spread trader would buy the longer-term August 30 for 2 and sell the shorter-term May 30 for 1. The result would be a debit of 1. If XYZ is trading at 30 at expiration, the May 30 call will expire worthless while the August 30 call will still retain some of its time value. The degree of profitability will depend on precisely how much time value the August 30 retains, but it is likely, with three months left to expiration, the option will be worth at least 1½, resulting in a ½-point profit on the spread.

As with a bull vertical spread, in which you buy the lower-strike option and sell the higher-strike option, the calendar spread limits your risk to the initial debit you pay. But the chances of recouping at least a portion of this cost is somewhat greater with the calendar spread, since no matter how far out-of-the-money the long call stays, it will still retain some of its time value when the shorter-term option expires.

One of the advantages of the calendar spread is that it gives you a second chance. If you are trading options with a January, April, July cycle, you can start off buying July and selling January. When January expires you can then write an April call to replace it while retaining the long July call. This procedure will enable you to continue spreading—and generating income—year round.

Another advantage of the calendar spread is that you do not have to wait until expiration to take your profit. As the maturity date approaches, the time value of the near-term option will begin to decline at an accelerated rate no matter what the underlying stock is doing. This will give you an opportunity to buy back the short position and sell the long-term option to close out the spread or again write another option to generate more income against the long call.

Since the price of the longer-duration call at the time the shorter-duration call expires is the key to profitability, you'll want to have some way of judging what this value will be. We know that calls do not lose their time value at the same rate. Rather, as the maturity date approaches, the decline accelerates. Nevertheless, we would like to have an idea as to the valuation of a three-month option when the security is at the strike price. The easiest and most obvious method of making this judgment is to look at the premiums of at-the-money calls with three months left to expiration. If calls with three months left to expiration tend to trade for 2 points, there is a good chance, barring a number of unforeseen circumstances, that the at-the-money call will have a value of $2. Now, having bought a spread for a debit of 1, we can see a value of 2 in the long call at the expiration of the shorter-term option. This will result in a 100 per cent profit on the calendar spread investment. Again, transaction costs have to be subtracted from this profit. Although this estimate is not guaranteed by any means, it is a rough guideline of what to expect if the stock trades at the strike upon expiration of the shorter-term option. Put another way, you are betting on a 100 per cent decline in the value of the option you've sold versus a much less precipitous decline in the value of the option you've purchased. The reason: the slow erosion of time value for longer-term options versus the rapid erosion of time value for options about to expire.

As you can see, there is no definitive way to determine what the value of the calendar spread will be in advance. It is unlike the vertical spread in this respect. But several observations can be made. The value of the calendar spread will be greatest when the underlying security is at the strike price. Above the strike price the shorter-term call will begin to gain intrinsic value and *gain* value on the longer-term call. This is precisely the situation you want to avoid. In the above example, if XYZ had risen to, say, 35, the May 30 call would have a value of at least 5 plus whatever time value it had remaining. The August 30 would also be at 5 plus whatever time value it retained. But chances are, the longer-duration August call wouldn't command more than a dollar premium.

If this were indeed the case, having bought the spread for $1, there would be no profit left. Given still higher prices, the August call's time premium would no doubt erode even further, resulting in a loss on the spread.

In a down market the profit situation is likewise dismal. Just because the shorter-duration option expires worthless doesn't mean the longer-duration option will retain a great deal of value, especially if it is far out-of-the-money. With a need to capture at least a point in profit to reach break-even, the calendar spreader will have a hard time of it if the price of the underlying stock declines.

If it is beginning to sound like you can't win with a calendar spread, rest assured that you can. In fact, compared to the bull vertical spread, in which you stand to lose your entire investment if the stock doesn't stage a rally, the calendar spread is quite attractive. The reason? No matter how far the underlying security rises or falls, the spread will still be worth something. At worst, you'll lose a portion of your investment. In the event of a decline in stock prices, both options will lose value and the nearer option will no doubt expire worthless. But the longer-duration option will still have value. Conversely, no matter how high the underlying security rises, the two premiums for options that are at least three months apart will never be the same—the longer-duration option will *always* be worth more than the shorter-duration option. The bottom line is that you'll get something back on a calendar spread, and you may very well make a nice profit.

DIAGONAL SPREADS

Another type of spread that works quite effectively when the underlying stock is rising in price is known as the *diagonal spread*. The diagonal spread is a sort of calendar spread with different strike prices. It combines a long and short position in different contract months *and* different strike prices. When XYZ common stock is at $27 per share, you might be able to buy the lower-strike, in-the-money August 25 for $3½ and simultaneously write the out-of-the-money, shorter-duration May 30 for $.75. The result would be a diagonal spread.

We'll assume it is mid-February, with a little over three months left to run in the May contract and over six months left to expiration in the August contract. The option series, option premiums, and stock prices are in Table 15.

Table 15

OPTION SERIES	PRICE	STOCK PRICE
XYZ Aug 25	3½	27
XYZ May 30	¾	27

This is a debit spread, since you'll be paying 3½ for the August 25 and receiving only ¾ for the short May 30 call. As long as the stock stays near 27 or higher at the expiration of the May 30 call, the spread will make money. With XYZ trading at 27 upon expiration of the May 30 call, the August 25 call will still have at least a value of $2 per share (its intrinsic value) plus whatever time premium it can command. With XYZ at 27 the May 30 call will expire worthless, resulting in a break-even situation or better on the diagonal spread. Should the underlying stock rise to 30 upon expiration of the May 30, the profit situation will improve considerably, however. The spread will earn ¾ from the expiration of the worthless May 30 call option. In addition, the in-the-money August 25 will now be worth at least 5 plus its time value. Thus, a spread that cost just 2¾ (3½ − ¾ = 2¾) will have a value of at least 5 points, and perhaps ½ to 1 point more.

With the stock at $30 upon expiration, the option series, option premiums, and stock prices would appear as in Table 16.

Table 16

OPTION SERIES	PRICE	STOCK PRICE
XYZ Aug 25	5+	30
XYZ May 30	0	30

The diagonal spread works so well in rising markets because you are selling rapidly declining time value and buying slowly declining time value. Time value does not erode at the same rate throughout the life of the option; on the contrary, it erodes slowly at first and then much, much faster as the option approaches expiration. As a result, the premium income you'll derive by writing the nearer-term option will be greatest on a per-week basis in the shorter-term option. The shorter-term option *must* lose all its time value by expiration; the longer-term option, on the other hand, may lose only a tiny fraction of its time value during the same period of time. In the illustration above, two adjacent months were spread. Had the spread been put on earlier, however, you might have sold February and purchased the more distant August. Then as the February contract matured, you might have rolled over into May while staying long the August contract.

The nearer-term contract will always have the highest future time value on a percentage basis. This spread strategy capitalizes on the rate at which time value declines by writing the shorter-duration option and buying the longer-duration option. When the long option is in-the-money, as it was in this example, and the short option is out-of-the-money, you are writing pure time value —which, in the illustration above, constitutes 100 per cent of the May 30 call premium. This is not the case with the August 25 call, however. Less than 50 per cent of the $3½ premium of the August 25 is time value. On a cash basis alone, the August 25 was worth at least $2 when the stock was trading at $27. Given a market that doesn't collapse, there is room for profit in this spread, with a fixed level of risk limited to the cost of the initial debit.

Another way to look at a diagonal spread is as a cheap form of covered writing, since the long call serves as a potential long stock position. The advantage over covered writing is that you don't have to come up with the cash for the stock. With a diagonal, therefore, your leverage is enhanced and you can continue to write higher strike calls against the position as a means of generating income.

BEAR MARKET SPREAD STRATEGIES

The bear spreads, which are designed to make money on declining stock prices, are vertical spreads in which you buy the less expensive, higher-strike call option and sell the more expensive, lower-strike call option. Since the option you buy is worth less than the option you sell, this spread will always be done at a credit to your account. You will, however, be asked to deposit money with your broker to put on the spread. The margin required will be the difference between the initial credit you receive and the difference between the two strike prices. A spread which is done for a credit of $6 per share when the two strikes are 10 points apart will require a margin of $4 per share.

Just as the bull spread could be considered a proxy for a long call, the bear spread can be viewed as a proxy for a short call, or naked writing. By virtue of being spread, however, the option investor doesn't expose himself to the risk of the naked writer when he uses a bear spread. The long call, which is purchased at the upper strike, ensures the spreader of a long position at that upper strike should the underlying shares rally. The long call, in this instance, should be seen primarily as a cheap form of insurance—a policy he'd rather not collect on, since he anticipates lower prices.

The strategy with a bear spread is to have the underlying security decline, enabling the spreader to keep the credit he initially received in putting on the spread as the lower-strike, short option expires worthless—or, at the very least, cheaper than it was when the spread was first put on. For example, let's consider a bear spread (Table 17) with the options shown.

Table 17

OPTION SERIES	PRICE	STOCK PRICE
XYZ June 60	4½	61
XYZ June 65	1½	61

The bear spread can be put on for a credit of 3 (4½ − 1½ = 3). You buy the higher-strike June 65 for a debit of 1½ and simultaneously write the lower-strike June 60 call for a credit of 4½. The difference represents a credit of 3, which will immediately be applied to your account. The margin requirement for the spread will be 2, since the strikes are 5 points apart and your account has already been credited for 3 when you put on the spread. To collect the full credit of 3, the stock need only close at 60 or less on expiration. When the stock is at 60, both options will expire worthless and the net credit of 3 will be yours to keep. With the stock trading around 60, however, the June 60 will have cash value. Above 65 the June 65 will have cash value as well. Since you received a credit of 3 for selling the spread, your break-even point will be $63 per share in the underlying stock (transaction costs aside). At any price above 63, the spread will have a loss, with the maximum loss occurring at the price of 65. At 65 the short 60 call will have a loss of 5 and the long 65 call will be worthless. Thus, when the underlying stock trades at 65 at expiration, you will have a loss of 2 on the spread, since the June 60 call will be worth 5 points and you received a net credit of 3 points when you initiated the position.

Returning to the ideal situation, in which the price of XYZ is 60 or lower upon expiration, both the calls would have zero cash values (Table 18).

Table 18

OPTION SERIES	PRICE	STOCK PRICE
XYZ June 60	0	60
XYZ June 65	0	60

Accordingly, a declining stock price would result in the bear spreader being able to retain the full credit of $3 per share that he received for selling the spread. This favorable result would only occur upon expiration, however, since the two call options would continue to retain time value until the maturity date.

IN-, OUT-OF-, AND ON-THE-MONEY BEAR SPREADS

Just as bull spreads can be categorized according to whether they are in-, out-of-, or on-the-money, the same subheadings can identify bear spreads with one very important qualification. Whereas the bull spreads were considered *in-the-money* when the stock price was *above* the higher strike, the bear spread is considered *out-of-the-money* when the stock price is *above* the higher strike. The bear spread is *in-the-money* when the stock is *below* the lower strike. And the *on-the-money* bear spreads have the stock price *between* the two strikes. Assume the stock is at 21 and you want to put on a bear spread by writing the 20 call and buying the 25 call. This would be an on-the-money spread, since the stock price falls *between* the two strikes. In the same example, however, if you used a 25 and 30 strike for the bear spread, it would be in-the-money; a 15- and 20-strike bear spread in the same stock would be out-of-the-money.

The in-the-money bear spread is perhaps the least popular, because it requires the most capital and can result in sizable losses should your judgment prove incorrect. In this spread the underlying security is already trading at or below the lower strike. For example, let's say the stock is at $68 per share and the July 70 call is available for $4½ and the July 80 call for $1. You sell the lower-strike July 70 for $4½ and buy the higher-strike July 80 for $1, resulting in a net credit of $3½. Since the strikes are 10 points apart, however, and you've only received a credit of $3½, you have to post a margin of the difference, or $6½. If you are correct on the downward direction of prices, of course, you'll earn the full credit of $3½ if the stock fails to rise above $70 by expiration. But in the event of a rally in the stock, you'll be unprotected above 73½, the break-even point. On a risk-reward basis, you stand to gain only about half of what you put up. Moreover, you could lose the full 6½ if the stock rallies to 80. On the positive side, the stock need only stand still at 68 and the spread will prove profitable at expiration. To prevent a spread like this one from sustaining losses, you should make it a policy to close it out even if the profitability is threatened. Let's say the stock rallies to 72 after you put on the spread, and, given the time value that the calls will retain, the spread may be worth less than a point. In this instance, close it out before the profitability disappears and look for a more inviting bear spreading opportunity. It doesn't make sense to stay with any position in hopes of a favorable move. If the spread doesn't work initially, you are better off getting out.

With the on-the-money bear spread, the stock price is somewhere in between the two strikes, meaning the income you derive from writing the lower-strike call will have a cash value that will decline only if the stock declines. In the absence of that decline, however, you'll have to give back all or part of the income you derived for writing the call. Assume a stock is trading at 22 with an April 20-strike call available for 4 and an April 25-strike call available for 1. The bear spread can be done for a credit of 3 and a margin of 2. As you can see, the maximum loss is somewhat less with this on-the-money bear spread than it was in the previous example. At a price of $22, the stock must decline below 20 if the bear spreader is to derive the maximum benefit of the spread. Moreover, his upside break-even is only a single point higher. The maximum possible percentage gain here is considerably greater with this spread than it was in the previous example. Should the stock decline to 20 by expiration, both options will expire worthless and the bear spreader will make a profit of 3 on a margin of 2, or 150 per cent on his funds at risk.

The most popular type of bear spread, the out-of-the-money, has the dual attractive features of being relatively inexpensive to accomplish and promising significant percentage gains in the event it proves successful. In the out-of-the-money bear spread, the market price of the stock is *above* the higher strike. As a result, the calls are deep in-the-money and the income derived from shorting the lower-strike call will be significant. With two months prior to the expiration of the April calls, a stock trading for 35 might have an April 25 available for $10\frac{1}{2}$ and an April 30 available for $6\frac{1}{2}$. The bear spread, therefore, might be accomplished at a credit of 4 points ($10\frac{1}{2} - 6\frac{1}{2} = 4$) with a margin requirement of one point. (Note: the strikes are just 5 points apart.) The cost is low. Unfortunately, however, the situation is not quite so promising if the stock remains at 35. At that price the April 25 will still command a premium of 10 (almost the entire income taken in by writing the April 25) and the April 30 will be worth only 5 ($1\frac{1}{2}$ less than you paid for it). The net result would be a loss of 1, or $100 plus commissions per spread. The point is, the stock *must* decline if you are going to make money on this spread. Break-even (excluding commissions) will occur at $29 per share in the underlying stock when the loss on the short April 25 will be equal to the initial net credit. At any price above 29, you'll have a loss of $1, the initial margin you posted. On the plus side, as the stock declines below 29, you're making rapid percentage gains, since your only investment was the $1 per share initial margin.

One drawback of this bear spread strategy is that you may be letting yourself in for premature exercise by holding a deep-in-the-money short call. At any price above 25, the April 25 will retain cash value and you may be asked to deliver 100 shares of stock against your short position. From your point of view, this amounts to shorting stock, since you must go into the market and borrow stock to deliver against the call. You must pay commissions to do this. Moreover, you must ultimately cover your short by buying back the stock. Once you cover your short stock, you are relieved of any additional obligation. But you are no longer spread. You could reinstate your short option position. But this has the drawback of inviting another premature exercise, in which case the process will have to be repeated all over again as you borrow stock and cover the short position, all the while paying commissions and providing cash margin for the short stock position.

If all this sounds a bit confusing, there's yet another market condition you have to be on guard against that will almost certainly result in a premature exercise against your stock option position. And that is if the option is on a dividend-paying stock that is about to go ex-dividend. The option will almost certainly decline the day the stock goes ex-dividend. Oftentimes, if there is not a great deal of time value left in the option, this decline in the option will result in a situation where the option is trading at a discount to its actual cash intrinsic value. Although the discount will be small, probably only ¼ or ½ point, the discount will encourage professional arbitrageurs, who track these things with computers, to buy up the options and exercise them. They will then simultaneously take delivery of the stock they call away from you and other in-the-money writers and sell the stock in the market at a fractionally higher price. The result is a profit for the arbitrageurs but a premature exercise against your short in-the-money call. How to prevent this type of unwelcome premature exercise? Simply check to see that the lower-strike call you write when you do a bear spread retains a fair portion of time value. If the time value is sufficient, and the stock goes ex-dividend, the decline will not be large enough to encourage premature exercise, since the option will not be at a discount to the stock.

The closest thing to a sure-thing trade exists in the options market when you have an opportunity to put on an out-of-the-money bear spread with the difference in the prices of the calls equal to the difference in the exercise prices. For this ideal trade to exist, however, you'll want to be bearish on the stock. Typically, you'll only find the calls trading at a difference equal to the difference in exercise prices just prior to expiration. So the time element will be working against you, since you must have the stock decline prior to expiration. At worst, however, you'll only lose commissions, which isn't so bad considering the low cost of putting on the spread and the profit opportunity.

Such an opportunity existed recently when Disney shares were trading at 52 with the soon-to-expire January 50 call at 2¼ and the lower-strike January 40 call at 12¼. Since the difference in the price of the calls was $10 ($12¼ − $2¼ = $10) and the difference in the strike prices was also 10 (50 − 40 = 10), the bear spread could have been put on for a credit of 10 points by buying the higher-strike January 50 call for $2¼ a share and simultaneously writing the lower-strike January 40 call for $12¼ a share. The margin requirement on this spread, incidentally, would be the minimum set by your brokerage firm, perhaps as low as $250.

With only a couple of weeks of time left in the options prior to expiration, the bear spreader was counting on a decline in Disney share prices. As anticipated, the decline occurred and Disney fell to $49, below the higher strike of 50. When the stock is at $49, the initial credit of 10 on the spread is reduced to a credit of 1. The short 40 call, which initially was sold for a credit of 12¼, is worth 9 upon expiration, with the stock trading at 49. With the stock trading at 49, therefore, the spread will have a net credit of 3¼ points on the January 40 call (12¼ − 9 = 3¼). From this credit, however, must be subtracted the cost of purchasing the January 50 call, which, at expiration, is without value. The net result, therefore, is a credit of one point (3¼ − 2¼ = 1)–a healthy percentage gain on margin as low as $250 within two weeks' time. Annualized, such a gain would be truly considerable. But such opportunities do not come along every week.

When the conditions are met, this out-of-the-money bear spread offers low risk coupled with possible huge percentage gains. In the illustration above, had Disney shares plummeted 15 per cent in value to, let us say, $44, the profit would have been $600 on a $250 investment. Below 40 the spread would have realized the full 10-point gain. Since many option traders put on 10 or 20 or more spreads at a time, you can see how the profits could be considerable. Unfortunately, this spread opportunity will only be found close to expiration, when the downward potential of the stock is limited by time.

Ideally, you want to buy the strike just below the market price of the stock and write the lower strike with considerable cash and time value. Moreover, you want to look for a sharp rally in the stock to proceed putting on the spread. At that point the stock may be overbought and due for a price correction. Understandably, volatile stocks with high Betas work better in this type of spread than low-volatility stocks, because the price swings, both up and down, are apt to be more substantial. Since you need a downward movement in the stock price for the difference in the price of the calls to narrow, the high-volatility stock is a better candidate. Remember, the key to success is receiving an initial credit equal to the difference in the strike prices. If the strikes are 10 points apart, you want a credit of $10; if the strikes are 5 points apart, you want a credit of $5; and so on. In placing the order, if you specify a limit of a credit of 5 points or whatever distance separates the strikes, you'll make sure you obtain the spread at a favorable differential—one which will work in your favor if prices decline and will minimize the losses to the cost of commissions if you are wrong and prices stabilize or rally.

Since the calls you'll be spreading are deep-in-the-money, your short call could very well be exercised and you'll be asked for delivery. If the stock is above the higher strike when you have the lower-strike call exercised and the shares called away, simply exercise your long call and deliver against the short call. The net result of this transaction will be that you will pay out what you received and you'll have no profit on the spread—only a small loss due to commissions. If the lower-strike short call is exercised when the shares are below the higher-strike long call, however, your higher-strike long call will have no cash value, since it is out-of-the-money. You may then want to use the funds you received for delivering the stock as collateral against a loan from your broker for the short sale. If the shares move higher, your long call will prevent additional loss. But if the shares move lower, you'll profit point for point on the short position in the stock while sustaining only the cost of the higher-strike long call as a loss.

VARIABLE SPREAD STRATEGIES

So far, we've discussed spreads in terms of one-to-one ratios in which there is a long option for every short option. Another spread technique, however, varies the ratio of short to long options to capitalize on specific market conditions. It is this type of market flexibility that makes listed options trading so interesting and, very often, so profitable.

Take a simple bull vertical spread in which you've purchased the lower-strike call and written the higher-strike call. By changing what is known as the *mix* between long and short positions—that is, varying the numbers of longs against shorts—the profit situation will change depending upon market conditions. Let's say you decide to write twice as many options as you buy. You will have an immediate lower overall cost in the spread. After all, the short options generate income immediately, income which is used to offset the funds paid to purchase the long call at the lower strike. We'll assume there's a July 20 call available for $2¼ and a July 25 call available for $.25. On a normal bull spread, you'd have a debit of $2. But if you write twice as many calls as you buy, the writing income would now amount to $.50 and the net debit on the spread would be $1¾ ($2¼ − $½ = $1¾).

With lower costs you now have a lower break-even point, and the stock doesn't have to travel as far to generate a profit. Above the higher strike of 25, however, you'd have a bit of a problem, since only one short July 25 is covered by the single long July 20 call. Above the price of 25, therefore, you'd have to buy back one naked short July 25 *or* deliver shares, which you may or may not own, against the short July 25 should the stock remain above the strike. The point is, a variable spread strategy that involves writing more calls than you buy can be profitable within a rather broad range. The maximum profit in this spread, of course, will occur at the higher strike. At that price both short July 25s will expire worthless, allowing you to keep the full ½-point income, and the long July 20 will be worth $5. With stock at 25 you'll derive the maximum profit available in the spread, $3¼ a share. That maximum profit is derived by taking the initial debit of $1¾ and subtracting it from the value of $5 that the July 20 will have if the option expires when the stock is at $25.

Looking at the same spread another way, you can also buy twice as many options as you write. In this case let's say we buy two July 20s for $2¼ each for every July 25 we write for $.25. Our cost now has risen dramatically to $4½ for the long side of the spread versus just $.25 in income from the short side. The spread, therefore, will be put on for a debit of $4¼. The break-even point in the spread has now risen. In order to generate a profit in the spread, the stock must be trading at 22⅛ or higher at expiration.

As the stock moves higher and higher above the strike at 25, the spread improves in profitability, since the second long July 20 option will gain point for point with the stock. Above the price of 25, the first long option's gains will be offset by comparable losses on the short option.

Margin considerations aside, there are no rules concerning how many long and short positions you may have on either leg of a spread. You can buy 15 options on one leg, for instance, and sell 20 on another—or buy 20 options and write 15. For margin purposes you'll be asked to deposit funds for any options you remain naked, just as if you were a naked writer. But on a one-to-one basis, your brokerage house should give you the spread margins. Since long calls are purchased for cash, there are no margin requirements involved if the number of longs exceeds the number of shorts. If the number of short positions, however, exceeds the number of long positions, you'll be treated as a naked writer—and be expected to post margin—on those short calls that aren't offset by long calls at a lower strike.

TWO-TO-ONE RATIO WRITES

A popular variable bull spread strategy is known as the *two-to-one ratio write*—a spread transaction between options of the same stock and expiration month but at different strike prices. To set up this trade, you should buy at least two options of the lower strike and write four options of the higher strike.[1] This strategy is particularly attractive when you can accomplish it at a zero debit, because it means you can walk away from the trade should the stock price decline without a loss. Better yet, try to get a net credit when you initiate the spread, and it will protect you, in the event of a rally, to one strike above your highest strike price.

[1] As a general rule in trading two-to-one ratio writes, you should always buy at least two lower-strike options and sell twice as many higher-strike options. By trading multiple contracts in this fashion, you'll minimize commission costs which can cut into profitability. Thus, a two-to-one ratio write may consist of two long calls against four short calls or four long calls against eight short calls. The ratio—not the absolute numbers—is important. For purposes of illustration, however, we'll discuss the strategy in terms of one long call and two short calls.

A recent example is provided by the Fluor call options. With Fluor stock trading at 23, the October 20-strike call was available for a premium of $6 per share and the October 25-strike call for a premium of $3 per share. By buying one October 20 and simultaneously writing two October 25s, you could have put on a two-to-one ratio write that would return a profit all the way up to a price of $30 in the stock—or one strike above the higher strike in the spread. This protection, therefore, extends to 30 per cent above the price where Fluor shares are trading. On the downside, you would have broken even at any price below $20 in the stock. With the stock at 20, neither call option will have value and the spread will be a wash—what you made on the two short October 25s will be exactly offset by the cost of the October 20. But in the rather broad range between $20 and $30, you make something on the spread.

The two-to-one ratio write affords the option trader *total downside protection* when the spread is placed at *zero debit or better*. It also affords reasonably good upside protection. For example, if Fluor is trading at $24 at the October expiration, the October 20 call will have a value of $4. The two short October 25s will expire worthless, allowing you to keep the total $6 premium you received. This $6 premium, in turn, was used to purchase the October 20 call option. After subtracting the debit from the credit, the net profit is $4 per share. When Fluor is at $25 per share, the two October 25s will expire worthless and the October 20 will have a value of 5 points. As you move higher, however, the spread remains profitable but only for another five points. When Fluor common trades at $29, for instance, the long October 20 will have a value of $9. This is offset, however, by a loss of $8 on the two October 25s. Each short October 25 will have a loss of $4 when Fluor trades at $29 a share ($25 − $29 = −$4). Since you have two of them, your total loss is $8. The profit on the long side, therefore—a total of $9 on the October 20—is offset by a loss of $8 on the short side, resulting in a net profit (transaction costs aside) of one point. Above $30 per share you find yourself in trouble, because the two short options are losing money faster than the single long option can make it. But isn't it reasonable to assume that a stock selling for $23 per share today won't be selling for more than $30 nine months from now? That's a difficult

question to answer. Yet the odds probably favor a profitable outcome on the spread.

In a two-to-one ratio write, you always write the higher-strike
option and buy the lower-strike option. Ideally, an attractive two-
to-one ratio write will have the stock trading just at, or slightly
below, the lower strike price. This will ensure that the spread will
be available at a zero debit or better. In addition, you'll want a
relatively high writing premium and a fairly stable stock that will
move up to the point of maximum profitability, the higher strike,
by expiration. The reason the higher strike represents the point of
maximum profitability is that at that price you earn both the full
premium of the options you have written *plus* the return from
selling the options you have purchased at a lower price. One word
of warning about two-to-one ratio writes: while this spread offers
excellent profit opportunities, you must be willing to take defensive action if the underlying stock begins to rise much above *one*
strike over the higher strike. In the Fluor example you broke even
below 20, made money between 20 and 30, and sustained losses
above 30. But whereas the profit was limited to a maximum of 5
at the higher strike of 25, at 40 the spread would have a loss of
10; at 50 the loss would be 20—four times the maximum profit.
One appropriate defensive strategy is known as *leveling* the trade,
in which you change the mix by buying back the shorts or purchasing long option positions.

USING VARIABLE SPREADS IN BEAR MARKETS

Two-against-one spreads can also be used to capitalize on bear
markets. Using the same example as in the Fluor calls above,
when the stock is trading at $23 and the October 20 call is avail-
able for 6 and the October 25 call for 3, you could accomplish a
variable bear spread by selling two October 20 calls for a credit of
12 and simultaneously buying one October 25 call for a debit of
3. The net credit would be 9 points (12 − 3 = 9). The drawback
with this spread is that it offers very little upside protection. At
25, for instance, the two short October 20s have a combined loss
of 10, resulting in a net loss of one point, since you received a
credit of only 9 for putting on the spread. When the stock trades
at $27, the spread is in considerable trouble, since you'll now have

a loss of $14 on the short options and a gain of only $2 on the single October 25 call. On a more positive note, however, the full credit of 9 is yours to keep if the stock is at 20 or lower on expiration. So you can see that having a notion of where the stock is going is quite important if you are planning to use variable spreads.

In looking for a variable bear spread, don't make the mistake of buying twice as many higher-strike options as you sell. This type of spread is known as a *volatility spread,* in which you'll only make money if the stock proves volatile and moves well away from the strikes. Should the stock stabilize, you'll find you have a loss. Again using the Fluor example above, if you buy two October 25s for a total of 6 points and write an October 20 for 6 points, you'll be able to put on the spread for a zero debit. We're assuming the stock is at 23, however, which means unless the stock makes a substantial move upward you won't be able to get out with a profit. Suppose the stock is at 28 at expiration. The short October 20 will have a loss of $8 at that price, and this will only be offset by a gain of $6 on the two long calls. Only at 30, a 7-point gain in the stock, will the spread be at break-even. And above that price you'll have profitability. When the stock is trading at $32, for instance, the loss of 12 on the short October 20 will be offset by a gain of 14 on the two long October 25s. Naturally, as the stock moves steadily upward from 30, the spread will improve. But the 7-point gain required in the movement of the underlying stock makes this far from a bear spread—in fact, the very opposite!

The calendar spread also lends itself to the variable spread strategy if you buy more of the longer-term options than you sell of the shorter-term options. Remember, the calendar spread consists of long and short positions of the same strike and same security but of different expiration months. The calendar spreader is anticipating declining time value to make the short position decline in price faster than the long position. In the bull calendar spread, which is really a substitute for a bull vertical spread, you simply buy more longs than shorts. Rising prices will result in more rapid gains on the long leg than you'll have losses on the short leg. For instance, let's say you have a stock trading at $19, with the nearer-term May 20 call trading at $1½ per share and the longer-duration August 20 trading at $2¼. You can put on the spread by purchasing two August 20s at 2¼ for a total of 4½ and simultaneously selling a single May 20 for 1½. Your net debit is 3 (4½ − 1½ = 3). Of course, this debit will be larger than would be the debit if you simply purchased one August 20 and sold one May 20. But since risk is always commensurate with reward, the return will likewise be much improved if the stock rises. If the stock stays at 19 or moves lower, you'll stand to lose the entire debit of 3. But you might recoup a portion of the debit by liquidating the spread prior to the May expiration if the stock doesn't show signs of rallying. The August 20, with several months to run, is bound to have some value even if the stock remains below $20. Thus, you might recoup a point or more of the debit of 3 even if stock prices don't rally. With the stock trading above $20, you'll be in good shape as the two long positions rapidly gain in value. For instance, with the stock trading at $27, you'll have a gain of 14 on the two longs versus a loss of only 7 on the short position. As with any calendar spread, your total risk is known at the outset, and even that amount is not likely to be lost due to the August call's remaining time value no matter how far prices decline. As for switching strategies and writing more calls than buying longs with a calendar, you're again involved in naked writing, and the risk is quite high should the stock rally.

The spread offers flexibility combined with known potential and limited risk. When you consider your exposure with most outright positions—either buying options or writing naked positions—spreads are a welcome addition to your list of strategies.

6

Straddles and Combinations

The option straddle and combination can be used to capitalize on a variety of market conditions. Until now we've discussed the use of puts *or* calls under specific and general market conditions. The option straddle and combination involve the use of puts *and* calls together. Just as buying and writing a put or call lend themselves to varying market strategies, buying and writing puts and calls together will likewise meet numerous investment needs.

THE OPTION STRADDLE

The *straddle* is the purchase or sale of both a put and call at the *same* strike price and *same* expiration on the *same* underlying stock. You may either *buy* a straddle by purchasing a put and call; or you may *sell* a straddle by writing a put and call. In its simplest form, the straddle consists of a single put and call. But some option traders use this strategy to capitalize on anticipated higher or lower prices by varying the number of puts and calls on each leg of the straddle.

Since there are two sides to every option transaction—represented by a buyer and seller (writer)—both buyer and seller stand to profit or lose by entering into a straddle. The *straddle buyer* stands to benefit if the price of the underlying stock moves sufficiently *away* from the strike price to overcome the cost of the straddle in *either* direction. The *straddle seller* stands to make the greatest gain if the shares are trading *exactly at the strike price upon expiration.* Just as a put or call buyer stands to lose no more than the cost of his premium, the straddle buyer is also limited to the initial cost of putting on the straddle. The straddle writer or seller likewise stands to earn a fixed amount from his writing activities in similar fashion to the lone put or call writer. The straddle writer will likewise face an *unlimited* risk if underlying shares move significantly away from the strike price in *either* direction. Thus, straddle buying is very much like option buying, with this exception: the straddle buyer will profit if the stock moves away from the strike price in *either* direction; this is in contrast to the position of the call buyer who must have the shares move upward or the put buyer who must have the shares move downward in order to profit.

THE STRADDLE BUYER

To see how a straddle might work in practice, let's take an example of a straddle buyer who simultaneously purchases an at-the-money call and an at-the-money put when the underlying stock is at 35. We'll assume the straddle buyer purchases a June 35 call with two months left to expiration for 1⅝ and a June 35 put for 2. His total cost amounts to 3⅝ points plus transaction fees. Being long both a put and a call, the straddle buyer can purchase 100 shares at the 35 strike at any time prior to expiration and he can sell shares at the 35 strike at any time prior to expiration. Theoretically, at least, he can make money on both legs of his straddle if prices fluctuate sufficiently above *and* below the strike; but the chances of exercising both options are slim. In order to profit, of course, the return on one or both options must exceed the initial cost of 3⅝. The only way he will suffer a total loss on the straddle is if he waits until expiration to offset or exercise his options and the stock is trading exactly at $35. At any price above or below 35, the call or put will retain *some* value at expiration—although to offset his premium costs, the straddle buyer will need a stock price at least 3⅝ points away from the strike.

BUYER'S RISK LIMITED TO COST OF STRADDLE

Having bought the straddle for 3⅝ points, the straddle buyer knows his maximum cost will be the amount he paid to purchase the straddle. In addition, he knows that he will suffer a 100 per cent loss on his investment only if the stock is trading exactly at 35 upon expiration—an unlikely event. Assuming he has an opportunity to exercise only one side of his straddle—either the put or the call—he also knows the parameters of his profit and loss zone, either 3⅝ points above or below the strike. Accordingly, if the stock is at, say, $38⅝ at expiration, the straddle buyer will exercise his profitable 35-strike call for 3⅝ point and abandon his worthless 35-strike put. He will therefore have a net loss of $3 on the straddle. Assuming the stock rises to $45⅝, however, the straddle buyer will have a $10⅝ profit on the 35-strike call and a net profit on the straddle of $7 ($10⅝ − $3⅝ = $7). Likewise, a move to the downside will prove profitable if the stock moves far enough away from the strike price. At $34⅜ the 35-strike put will have a value of ⅝ point, resulting in a net loss on the spread (transaction fees aside) of 3 points. At $24⅜ the put will be worth $10⅝ and the straddle profit will amount to $7 ($10⅝ − $3⅝ = $7).

The key point is, the stock must move sufficiently away from the strike price to overcome the cost of the straddle if this strategy is to prove profitable for the buyer. But the underlying stock does not have to move the full 3⅝-point premium cost away from the strike for the straddle to be profitable. If the straddle buyer takes a profit on both legs of the straddle, the combined profits may exceed the 3⅝-point premium cost. For example, let's say the stock moves to $33 and the put is sold for a price of $3 ($2 cash value plus $1 time value), and then the stock stages a rally to $36 and the call is sold for $2 ($1 cash value plus $1 time value). The straddle buyer will have a net profit of 1⅜ points, or the difference between his cost of $3⅝ and his return of $5 ($5 − $3⅝ = $1⅜). For the buyer, the disadvantage of a straddle is that he must pay for two premiums. The stock must travel far enough away from the strike price to overcome this initial disadvantage.

THE STRADDLE WRITER

If straddle buying has such drawbacks, one could conclude that straddle writing must have excellent profit probabilities. Straddle writing, being the *opposite* of straddle buying, involves the sale of both a put and a call at an identical strike. For the straddle writer, who is said to have a *short straddle,* the ideal situation is to have the underlying stock stay exactly at the strike price; there, neither option will prove profitable and he'll get to keep the premium income. Assuming he took the other side of the straddle in the illustration above, his maximum profit will consist of the income he received for writing the 35-strike call for 1⅝ and the 35-strike put for 2. His gain, or writing income, therefore, is 3⅝ points, or $362.50 for the two options. Like the naked call writer, he assumes a considerable amount of risk in writing a straddle, however. As a writer his exposure is unlimited on the call (since it can rise to infinity) and extends down to zero on the put, or 35 points. Like the naked call writer, the straddle writer sells time in hopes of generating income. The seller of a straddle wants the underlying stock to stay pretty much where it was when he wrote the options. In our illustration (Table 19), as long as the stock stays at or near 35, the writer stands to profit. Chances are, his net profit will be somewhat less than 3⅝, since this maximum profit will only exist if the stock is at $35 at expiration. The straddle writer, like the naked option writer, must take all the precautions associated with naked writing. He must be willing to take small losses if they occur, roll down his options if necessary, and otherwise undertake a defensive posture.

If we assume that only one of the two options the seller writes will be exercised, it becomes relatively easy to calculate the profitability zone in writing the straddle. With the 35 call selling for 1⅝ and the 35 put selling for 2, the total proceeds of the straddle would amount to 3⅝ points as indicated in Table 19.

Table 19

STRADDLE WRITING INCOME

June 35 call premium	$1⅝
June 35 put premium	$2
Total Proceeds	$3⅝

With the strike at 35, it then becomes an easy task to calculate the upside and downside profit parameters as well as the profitability zone—the area within which the straddle writer will emerge a winner. The calculations are in Table 20.

Table 20

UPSIDE PROFIT PARAMETER		DOWNSIDE PROFIT PARAMETER	
Strike price	35	Strike price	35
Straddle proceeds	+3⅝	Straddle proceeds	−3⅝
	38⅝		31⅜

Profitability Zone: 31⅜ to 38⅝

For the straddle buyer, of course, the profitability zone above will constitute the area where the straddle is *unprofitable*. Thus, the straddle writer profits in the narrow area around the strike price, and the straddle buyer profits in all the area above or below the writer's profitability zone. In the illustration above, the straddle buyer will have profits *above* 38⅝ and *below* 31⅜. This is assuming that only one option proves profitable and the other option is simply abandoned. As you can see, you can easily calculate the profitability zone of any straddle you are planning to write by adding the total premiums to the strike price and subtracting the total premiums from the strike price. By the same token, the straddle buyer knows that the stock must move out of the writer's profitability zone for his position to prove profitable.

THE COVERED STRADDLE BUYER

The covered straddle buyer deals with a three-part investment, which is also known as a *conversion*. In addition to buying a put and a call, the covered straddle buyer purchases the underlying stock. He has a definite bullish bias on the stock, since he is potentially long 100 shares by exercising his call and actually long another 100 shares in stock ownership. His long put serves as a sort of insurance policy if the market price of the stock declines. On the upside, the covered straddle buyer will profit twice as fast as the uncovered straddle buyer. A decline in the price of the shares below the strike price, however, will only result in a loss in the stock being offset by a comparable gain on the put option.

For instance, if you bought an on-the-money straddle when the

stock is at 40, paying a total of 6 in premiums, the uncovered
straddle would not be profitable until the price of the stock rose to
46 or fell to 34. But if you bought a covered straddle, having
purchased stock at 40, the cost of the straddle would be paid for
in full when the stock traded at 43—the price at which you would
have a 3-point profit on the stock and a 3-point profit on the long
call. If the price of the stock fell below 40, however, you would
not gain more on the put than you would lose on the stock. The
put's gain below the strike would cancel out any loss on the stock.
But in the meantime, you would have an overall net loss, since
you paid a premium for both the put and the call, which would
not be offset.

THE COVERED STRADDLE WRITER

The straddle may be written with or without an accompanying
stock position, either long or short. When you write a straddle and
are long the underlying security, you have a definite viewpoint on
the future direction of prices. The covered straddle writer who is
long the underlying stock has a bullish posture on the market
prospects for the stock. He is willing to sell his shares at the strike
price if the call is exercised, and he is willing to purchase more
shares at the strike price if the market price declines and the
shares are put to him.

You must understand this bullish bias of the covered straddle
writer if you are going to succeed at this strategy. By virtue of
being long the stock, you would realize the maximum profit at any
price above the strike price. But on the downside your profit situation changes dramatically from that of the uncovered straddle
writer, because you stand to lose *twice as much* in the event of a
market decline. If the stock declines in price, you'll be out a dollar
for every point the stock falls. In addition, should the stock decline, you'll be out a dollar on your short put for every point the
stock falls below the strike price.

Let's look at an example in which you write a straddle on a
stock trading at 30 for 6. You write one October 30-strike call for
3½ points and one October 30-strike put for 2½ points. Thus, you
receive a total of 6 for writing the straddle. Assuming you do not
own the underlying stock, you immediately know that you have a

profit zone of $6 on either side of the strike price—from $24 to $36 per share. Now let's say you pick up 100 shares of stock at the strike price of 30. You are now short a straddle and long 100 shares of the underlying stock. At any price above 30, the stock will be called away, since the 30-strike call will be profitable to exercise. You will lose the stock, but you will retain the premium income. But when the market declines, the straddle writer who owns the stock finds himself in a less fortunate situation. The short 30-strike put will be profitable, for example, at any price below $30 a share. Therefore, you will give up a portion of your straddle writing income every time the stock falls below or rises above 30. But when the stock falls below 30, you lose twice as much, since you are losing on both the short 30-strike put *and* the stock. With the stock at 24, for instance, the straddle writer who received a 6-point premium breaks even. But the straddle writer who owns stock loses $2 for every point decline below 30. When the stock trades at 23, the straddle writer with long stock will have lost a total of 14 points—7 points on the short put and 7 points on the stock. With the stock at 20, a 10-point decline from the strike price, the straddle writer with stock is out a total of 20 points, for a net loss of 14 points, since he was credited with 6 points for writing the straddle. By virtue of owning the stock, the straddle writer must be prepared to take defensive action sooner than the uncovered straddle writer when the stock declines. With the stock at 30, as in the example above, the straddle writer will have a break-even at 27, just 3 points below the strike. At that price he will have lost the entire 6-point writing income he received. Below that price he'll fall into a losing position.

THE COMBINATION

One method of coping with the additional risk of writing straddles against long stock in down markets is to write a put and a call which have lower and higher respective strike prices, a strategy known as a *combination*. For the writer the combination lowers the risk of short options proving profitable to the buyer, but it also lessens the writing income, since the short options are apt to be out-of-the-money. With stock trading at 30, let's say you write an out-of-the-money 25-strike put for 1 and an out-of-the-money 35-

strike call for 1½. Your writing income will amount to just 2½ as compared to an income of 6 that could be derived by writing an at-the-money straddle. But while the income is less, the risk exposure is also less. For example, you won't have a loss on the put unless the stock falls below the 25 strike, and you won't have a loss on the short call unless the stock rises above the 35 strike. Should the stock settle between those two prices at expiration, the writing income will be yours to keep. Since we are assuming that you purchased stock at 30, naturally, you'd like to see prices rise— at least as far as the upper strike of 35, the point of maximum gain on the combination with stock.

The writing income on the combination will serve to lessen any slight decline in the stock. For instance, if the stock declines to, say, 27, you'll have a 3-point loss in the stock. But this will be offset, in part, by the 2½-point writing income you derived from selling the combination. If the stock falls precipitously, of course, you'll still be in trouble using this strategy. If, for example, the stock falls to 20, you'll be out 10 points in the stock and 5 points in the 25 put. This 15-point loss will be offset only by the 2½-point writing income, for a net loss of 12½ points. Lastly, on a more positive note, a rise in the stock will enable you to keep your premium income and the stock as well—as long as it doesn't rise above the 35 strike of the call. At a price of 32 in the stock, you will have picked up 2 points in the stock and 2½ points in writing income on the combination, for a 4½-point gain on a 2-point rise in the stock. Maximum profitability will exist at the higher strike of 35, where you'll retain the full writing income plus gain 5 points in the stock. As you can see, writing a straddle or combination when you own the underlying stock makes sense when you have reason to believe the stock will rise. If you misjudge the market, however, you may regret using this strategy, since the long stock will make you twice as vulnerable on any real market decline.

The most common type of option combination involves the purchase or sale of a put and a call on the same underlying stock with different strike prices and the same expiration dates. The most popular type of combination involves out-of-the-money options. With stock at 20, for instance, you might buy or sell a 25-strike call for ¼ point and buy or sell a 15-strike put for ¼ point.

If you are a combination buyer, your cost is just ½ point, or $50 for the combination; for the writer, this amount would constitute his income on the combination.

Just as volatility is the key to success for the combination buyer, the combination seller or writer wants the market to stay stable, enabling him to capture the full premium income he takes in when writing the combination. Thus, the combination buyer seeks volatility; the combination seller, on the other hand, seeks stability. By purchasing out-of-the-money options, the buyer stands to benefit from enhanced leverage. And the writer received income which he wouldn't ordinarily have earned had he not sold options.

As you might suspect, the odds favor the combination seller. Since both sides of a combination are usually out-of-the-money when they are written, the stock must make a move up or down in order for the combination to prove profitable to its buyer. But the premiums on out-of-the-money options are apt to be small.

THE COMBINATION BUYER PROFITS FROM VOLATILITY

The combination buyer who does not hold a position in the underlying stock is neither bullish nor bearish—but he does anticipate market volatility. He believes the stock is likely to make a move in *either* direction, and he isn't particularly concerned about which direction it will take. To profit, the combination buyer wants the stock to rise above the call strike price or fall below the put strike price. Combination buyers will concentrate on high Beta stocks whose past history tend to show them outperforming the averages. Numerous highflier stocks and stock groups have come and gone in recent years that have been good combination buying candidates.

THE COVERED COMBINATION BUYER

The combination buyer may very well be long or short stock. If he is long stock, he is fundamentally bullish and views the put option as insurance against a decline in the stock. The call serves as added leverage on the upside, doubling the profits should the stock rise above the strike price of the call.

Just to compare the two situations in which you are a combination buyer and thinking about acquiring the stock, let's assume with the stock at $23 you purchase a 20-strike put for ¼ and a 25-strike call for ¼. Both the put and call are out-of-the-money. If you do *not* acquire stock, and the underlying security stays between $20 and $25, you'll lose the cost of the two premiums, or ½ point. Above $25 or below $20, you'll have a profit on either the call or the put. At $28, for instance, the 25-strike call will have a cash value of $3. Deducting your cost of ½ point, this will translate into a 2½-point gain. Conversely, at $17 you'll have at least a 3-point gain on the 20-strike put, since the put will be 3 points in the money.

But if you acquire stock at $23 and then purchase the two options, you immediately have a bullish bias. You stand to make more on the upside and lose more if the stock declines. If the stock goes to $28, therefore, you'll have a $3 profit on the 25 call plus a $5 profit on the stock ($28 − $23 = $5). This 8-point gain will be offset by the cost of the two options, for a 7½-point gain before transaction costs. Compare this 7½-point gain when you own the stock at $23 with the 2½-point gain for the combination buyer without stock, and you can see the advantages of being long stock *and* calls in a bull market. But consider the situation if the price of the security falls to $17. Now, instead of a net 2½-point gain, you have a 6-point loss on the stock which is only offset by a 3-point gain on the 20-strike put. This is a 3-point loss plus the cost of the two option premiums, resulting in a loss of 3½ points before transaction costs.

Since combinations are flexible, you can turn this situation around so that your position has a bearish bias if you wish. Simply buy a combination and sell the stock short. Now the call becomes the insurance against the short position. If the stock declines, you'll make money twice as fast, since you will profit from your short sale as well as the put. In the event of a rally, however, the short stock will prove a handicap. Using the above example, let's assume you shorted the stock at $23 and purchased the combination for ½ point. If the market stays at $23, neither option will prove profitable and you will be out the cost of the combination. The short stock, we'll assume, proves a wash, meaning you were able to cover at the same price you sold the stock for. As the stock declines, however, the profit picture brightens. At $20 the 20 put will have no intrinsic value. However, the short sale of stock at $23 will provide you with a profit of 3 points. Once you subtract the ½-point premium cost of the combination, you have a profit of 2½. Below $20, of course, things begin to look even more promising. At $17 the 20 put has a profit of $3 and the short stock has a profit of $6 ($23 − $17 = $6). Together, this results in a profit of $9, which is offset by the ½-point cost of the combination, resulting in a net profit of 8½ points. Should the stock fall to $10 per share, the stock would have a profit of $13 and the 20-strike put a profit of $10. As you can see, shorting stock along with buying a combination can be profitable in a bear market. Should the stock rally, however, the results of this strategy would be discouraging. At a price of $24, the 25-strike call and 20-strike put would both expire worthless. The short stock at $23 would have a loss of 1. The net result would be a 1½-point loss. At $30 the stock sale would have a 7-point loss ($23 − $30 = −$7). And the 25 call would have a 5-point profit. The result: a 2-point loss plus transaction costs.

VARIABLE RATIO COMBINATION BUYING

While the combination buyer might purchase or sell shares in order to enhance his profits and provide an inherent bullish or bearish bias to his trading activities, he need not use the stock market at all to accomplish his goals. Rather, he might opt to buy more calls than puts as a bullishly inclined combination buyer or buy more puts than calls as a bearishly inclined combination buyer. This strategy is known as *variable ratio combination buying*. Using this strategy, twice as many puts or calls are purchased depending upon one's bias on the market. The bull variable ratio combination buyer, therefore, will buy twice as many calls as puts and the bear variable ratio combination buyer will buy twice as many puts. The purchase of more long options will increase the combination buyer's cost. But it will also magnify his profits should his market judgment prove correct.

Assume a stock is at $25 and you buy a combination by purchasing a single 20 put for $1 a share and *two* 30 calls for $2 a share, a cost of $4. Your total cost on the variable ratio combination amounts to $5. Since you don't own the stock, the movement in the market must be sufficient to overcome the premium costs of the three options. Since this particular combination has a bullish bias, you will make more money faster if the market rises. If the market declines you can still make money with this combination— but you must have a significant decline. How significant? Well, with a 5-point premium cost to overcome and a long 20-strike put, the stock must decline to $15, or 40 per cent in value, before you will break even on the combination. Remember, your premium cost is $5. Therefore, to recoup this cost you must gain at least 5 points in one or more of the options. With just a single 20 put, the price of the underlying shares must fall to $15 a share to regain your cost. Below the price of $15, the combination will prove profitable. Looking at the upside, the profit picture is somewhat more encouraging—but only if prices rise above $30. Between the price of 30 and 20—a rather wide unprofitable zone—the three options will expire worthless. Above $30, however, you will be making two points for every 1-point move in the stock. The reason? You own two 30 calls. The break-even point on the upside, therefore, is $32½. At that price you will have a 2½-point profit on the two calls. This 5-point profit will offset your initial cost of $5 for the combination. Moving higher, the combination will generate steady profits. At $33 per share in the stock, for example, you'll have a profit of $6 on the two calls. Once you deduct the cost of $5, your profit will be $1 less transaction costs. When the stock is at $40, you will have 20 points in the two calls —or a 15-point net profit. With stock at $45 the two 30 calls will be worth 30 points—and so on. Before you go and purchase a variable ratio combination, however, take note of the significant price move you need to reach break-even.

In the above example a fall to $15 per share in the underlying security would have been required to reach break-even, or a 40 per cent decline; on the upside a rise in the security to $32½ per share would have required a 30 per cent gain. In this instance you must ask yourself, does the stock have a good chance of rising 30 per cent or declining 40 per cent prior to expiration? If it doesn't, you may want to try another strategy.

CHANGING RATIOS

To enhance your upside leverage and lower your break-even point slightly, you could simply change the ratio of calls to puts. You might want to buy three 30 calls and just one 20 put. Using the same prices, this would increase your cost to $7, since you acquired another $2 call. The impact of this decision would be to magnify your profitability *if* the shares rose above the new break-even point of about 32⅜. But on the downside the stock would have to fall to $13 per share ($20 − $7 = $13) before the single 20 put could recoup your investment. Should your market judgment prove correct, however, the three long 30 calls would significantly increase your leverage. With stock at $40 the 3 calls would be worth a total of 30 points as compared with just 20 points for the 2 calls. Even with the slightly higher cost of $7, the 3 calls would return $23 ($30 − $7 = $23) as compared with a profit of $15 ($20 − $5 = $15) on the two call position. That's an improvement of more than 50 per cent.

VARIABLE RATIO COMBINATION IN A DECLINING MARKET

No doubt, you can see how a variable ratio combination using more puts than calls can likewise work in your favor in the event you buy a combination in a declining market. In the particular illustration we've been using, this strategy has an added advantage, because the 20 put is available at a significantly reduced cost to the call. With the stock 5 points out-of-the-money on either option, the 20 put is available for $1, whereas the 30 call is available for $2. Now, if you buy twice as many puts as calls, your cost is only $4 as compared to $5 when you purchase two calls for every put—a savings of 20 per cent. Let's assume you invest a total of $4 in this combination by purchasing two 20 puts and one 30 call when the stock is at $25. We'll also assume you are neither long nor short the stock. The combination has an inherently bearish bias. The upside break-even is at 34—the price at which the single 30 call will be worth 4. The downside break-even is at 18—or two points below the strike of the put. This bearishly biased combination will now be profitable at any price below 18. Yet this decline still represents a loss in value of 28 per cent on the stock. Moreover, the upside break-even of 34 represents a 36 per cent rise in the value of the underlying shares.

In this illustration the farther and faster the stock declines, the more money you'll make. When the stock declines to $12½, a 50 per cent decline in the value of the stock, the combination will be worth 15, or 7½ points on two options (20 − 12½ = 7½). Once you deduct your premium cost of 4, this translates into an 11-point profit before commissions. Here again, you could magnify your profit picture still further by adopting a three-to-one ratio between puts and calls. Such a combination would require an initial cost of $5. It would raise the price at which the combination would turn profitable on the downside to just a little above $18¼ while raising the break-even on the upside to $35 per share. Due to the unbalanced nature of the combination, of course, the profits would multiply much faster on the downside when the price went under the strike of the put at 20. With stock at $18 it would already have 6 points of profit on the three puts, resulting in a net gain of one point on the $5 combination. This compares with the two-to-one ratio combination that would still be unprofitable at a price of $18. (The two puts would be $4 in-the-money when the stock trades at 18; unfortunately, the entire cost of the two-to-one combination is $4. When you factor in transaction costs, this one proves a loser.)

With stock at $10, of course, the three-to-one combination would be worth 30 points, since you have 10 points on three puts. Deducting the $5 cost of the combination, this leaves you with a 25-point gain on the combination. Unfortunately, we are talking about huge percentage declines in the value of the stock. For a $25 stock to fall to $10, it would have to lose 60 per cent of its value. Granted, such moves do occur. But when you use a combination, the decline must take place within the limited three-, six-, or nine-month life of the options. The combination buyer, whether he purchases his combinations in a strict one-to-one ratio or variable two-to-one or three-to-one fashion, must overcome the cost of the premiums. The odds of a stock moving significantly higher or lower in the near future is decidedly hard to predict. And you must remember, the more limited the life of the options you buy, the more limited your opportunity to close out the positions profitably. Combination buying, like outright put or call buying, is a highly speculative undertaking—one best undertaken by sophisticated option traders.

THE COMBINATION WRITER

One other side of the combination buyer's trade is the combination seller, or writer. Like the naked writer, the combination writer settles for a fixed, predetermined maximum profit coupled with unlimited liability. Like the naked writer, the combination writer knows the parameters within which his writing activities will be profitable, and he takes rigorous steps to ensure that he exits his short positions should they turn unprofitable. Not to take this defensive posture, whether you are writing naked puts *or* calls, or naked puts *and* calls, as is the case in a combination, will only result in financial disaster. Remember, the combination *buyer* is committed at the outset of the trade. His maximum potential loss is known. The combination writer, however, is facing unlimited liability. He *must* take defensive action. Having said that, which strategist faces the longest odds? Obviously, the buyer. The combination buyer needs a significant move away from the strike price to reach profitability. The combination seller only needs the short options to expire worthless—for the price to remain stable—in order to profit. Here, again, combination buying versus combination selling parallels outright option buying versus option selling. The buyer risks a relatively small amount of money in pursuit of a potentially large gain; the seller deposits margin in hopes of earning a fixed, predetermined, and often small maximum profit. Thus, the seller is looking for income, the buyer for a sudden spectacular capital gain.

SELLER SEEKS LOW-BETA STOCKS

The seller looks for stable, low-Beta stocks to write combinations on. If the buyers want to purchase the volatile, high-Beta stocks and the sellers want to write the low-Beta stocks, what brings them together? The answer is the cost of the premium. Options serve the function of price discovery. Sellers will be tempted to write the high-Beta stocks if the premium levels are high enough. Conversely, given rock-bottom premium prices on the low-Beta stocks, the buyers may feel that even if the odds don't favor the stable stocks, the risks are so low they will take a chance and buy a combination using options on stable stocks. Thus, the price of the respective puts and calls will bring buyer and seller together.

SELLING COVERED COMBINATIONS

Just as there are two ways to write straddles—either covered or uncovered—the combination writer may or may not have a related stock position. A combination seller *without* a related stock position is said to be an *uncovered combination seller;* a combination seller *with* a related stock position is said to be a *covered combination seller.* The uncovered combination writer or seller is neutral on the prospects for the stock. He expects both options to expire worthless and for the stock to remain pretty much where it traded when the combination was written. The covered combination writer or seller, who has a related stock position, is willing to sell his long position at the strike price of the call or to add to his stock position should the shares be put to him at the strike price of the put. The two premiums he receives for writing the combination serve to lower his effective cost in the case of acquiring shares or raise his selling cost in the case of selling of shares.

While most covered combination writers are long the underlying stock (own the stock), some writers are short the stock (have sold the stock short). The seller who is short stock is willing to cover his short positions (buy back the shares) at the strike price of the put—the price at which, should the put be exercised, the shares will be put to him. Since this is a somewhat more complex strategy, let's look at an illustration in which a combination writer is short shares of the underlying stock.

Let's assume the stock is at $28 a share and the writer sells short 100 shares at that price. At the same time, he writes a combination by selling a July 25 put for ½ point and a July 30 call for 1 point. His income from his writing activities is now 1½, and he is obligated to buy back the 100 shares of the stock he sold short. Since the seller of the out-of-the-money options in a combination wants both options to expire worthless, the profit zone in which the writer will capture the entire 1½ premium will be between $25 on the downside and $30 on the upside. Moreover, since this seller is short stock at $28 a share, he wants the market to decline so that he may buy back his shares lower. The point of maximum profit to the combination writer, therefore, will be 25 or lower. When the stock trades at 25, both the put and the call will expire worthless. Moreover, at 25, the short stock position will have a 3-point profit. Thus, when the stock trades at 25 at expiration, the combination writer will pick up $1½ off his writing activities and $3 on his short stock position ($28 − $25 = $3), for a net gain of $4½. Should the price of the shares fall below $25, the writer will lose money on his short put. This loss, however, will be exactly offset by a comparable gain on his short shares.

Should the option expire below the strike price of the put, the shares will be put to the writer at a price of $25—thus locking in the difference between $28 and $25, a net gain of $3 on the short stock position. On the upside, the call becomes unprofitable to the writer once it rises above $30 and gains intrinsic value. When the stock is trading above $30, the shares will be called away. Since the writer doesn't own shares (indeed, he is already short 100 shares and is obligated to buy them back at the market price at the time he decides to cover), he will sustain a loss not only on the call but also on the shares he sold at $28 and may have to cover at a higher price. When the stock trades at $28 per share, the short seller will neither lose nor gain on the short sale, with the exception of commission costs. In fact, should the two options expire when the stock is at $28, neither will have value and the writer will receive the full 1½-point premium. As the stock rises, however, the writer must realize that he has a limited amount of protection on the upside. In fact, he has precisely 1½ points of protection. Because he sold shares at $28, therefore, his break-even point will be at $29½ per share. At that price the short sale in the stock will have a loss comparable to the premiums he received for writing the put and the call. When the stock rises above $29½ per share, a loss on the short shares will result comparable to the income derived from writing the options.

At the same time, the short 30-strike call is about to become unprofitable. Thus, above the price of 30, the combination writer who is short shares at 28 loses two points for every 1-point gain in the stock. He loses a point on the short stock and he loses a point on the short call. To see how a potentially rewarding position, whose maximum potential profit was just $4½, can deteriorate in a hurry, you have to appreciate the magnifying affect of leveraged options trading. Remember, the short call and short put only generated 1½ in income. When the stock is at $34, the call is 4 points in-the-money and the writer of the combination has a 2½-point loss (1½ − 4 = −2½). But when you factor in the loss resulting from the short sale of stock at 28—a 6-point loss—the loss increases to 8½ points. Considering the maximum gain on the combination and short sale was only $4½, this is truly an unwelcome situation. How best to avoid this happening? Take defensive action long before the situation is allowed to deteriorate to this level. You should set limits on where you will buy back your stock *and* your short call. In pursuit of the maximum 4½-point potential gain in this illustration, you may be willing to lose, say, 3 points in the stock. This would require you to repurchase shares at $31 ($28 − $31 = −$3). When the stock is trading at $31 per share, the 30-strike call might be available for $2. This would result in a 1-point loss on the call, or a ½-point loss on the combination, since you initially received 1½ points. Taken together, a $3 loss in the stock and a ½-point net loss on the put and call would constitute the most you would want to lose on this position. Not to take defensive action at this stage in the rally would probably only invite additional losses—a situation you want to avoid at all costs, since the combination and short stock sale were limited in their profit potential at the outset.

VARIABLE RATIO COMBINATION WRITING

The combination writer may decide to write an unequal number of puts and calls, depending on whether he has a bullish or bearish outlook on the market. The combination writer who is bearish on the particular stock he writes options on will write a greater number of calls than puts. Conversely, the combination writer who is bullish on the stock will write a greater number of puts than calls. Just as the combination buyer can use additional options as a proxy for being long or short stock, the writer can use the same strategy and sell more of one option than of the other. By doing so he will increase his income if his market judgment is correct. At the same time, he will increase his risk exposure if his judgment proves faulty.

SELL TWO PUTS AND ONE CALL

Let's examine a hypothetical variable ratio combination from the seller's point of view. With stock at 56 and an August 50 put with more than three months of life remaining available for 1 and an August 60 call available for 2½, let's say the combination writer sells two 50 puts and one 60 call. By selling twice as many puts as calls, the writer, on the one hand, increases his writing income from 3½ to 4½, a 28 per cent gain. He does so because he expects the stock to stay stationary, or move up to the higher strike of 60 at best. At any price between 50 and 60, he'll be able to retain the full 4½-point writing income. Remember, he receives two points for writing two August 50 puts and 2½ points for writing one August 60 call. At the outset, therefore, he knows his maximum profit zone exists between 50 and 60. He also knows that below the lower strike of 50, he'll lose two points for every one point decline in the stock. With stock trading at 48, therefore, the two short puts will have losses equal to 4 points, and at 47¾, the combination writer will just break even. At that price the combination writer will have a loss of 4½ points on the two short puts, just equal to his writing income. Below 47¾ the combination writer will experience a loss. When you write twice as many puts as calls, the losses on the downside mount quickly. With three puts for every call, you are losing 3 points for every point decline in the stock below the lower strike. At the same time, the additional short put only adds one point in writing income. Had you written a three-to-one ratio of puts to calls, you would have 3 points of income from the puts and 2½ points of income from the single call. This 5½-point income would be offset by less than a 2-point move below the strike price of the put.

With just a single short call with a strike of 60, you will lose just 1 point for every 1-point rise in the stock above the higher strike of 60. Thus, the break-even point for the two-to-one ratio combination will be 64½. For the three-to-one ratio combination, you'll have another point's worth of protection before reaching break-even, or 65½. Thus, even if the stock rises to, say, 64, a 14 per cent gain in value, the variable combination will return a profit to its writer. Since the total income derived from writing two puts and one call was almost the same on each leg—2 for the puts versus 2½ for the call—the profit zone, both above and below the strike price, would be somewhat comparable.

SELL TWO CALLS AND ONE PUT

Had you written twice as many of the more costly calls, however, the protection to the downside would be substantially increased along with the writing income. The bearishly inclined combination writer who writes two 60-strike calls at 2½ each, for example, generates 5 points in income. By writing a 50-strike put, he also picks up another point, a total of 6 points on the combination. Having received 6 points for writing the combination, he can lose 6 points before going into a loss position. With a single 50-strike put, the writer won't experience a loss unless the stock falls below 44. This represents a 21 per cent decline in the stock's value. Thus, by writing more of the more costly calls, the combination writer can extend his profit zone from 44 on the downside to 63 on the upside. The upper-level break-even of 63 was derived by taking the 3 points the options would be in-the-money at 63 and multiplying by two. This loss of 6 would exactly offset the gain the writer received for selling the combination. An important point to remember is that these prices represent the price of the stock *at expiration*. Prior to expiration the options would retain some time value, and the combination writer would find himself with losses at 63 and 44. At 63, depending upon the amount of time left to expiration, the 60 call might be trading at, say, 4. This would represent an 8-point loss on the combinations which only generated an initial 6-point gain. At expiration, however, if the stock is at 63, the 60 call will have a value of 3, the two calls a value of 6. The same, of course, is true if the stock fell below the strike price of the 50 put, or, for that matter, even threatened to go under 50 with sufficient time left in the option. With stock at 50 upon expiration, the 50-strike put would have no value; but at 50, with two months left to expiration, the premium might be as high as 2 or even 3, depending on investor attitudes toward the option and the stock.

In the example above, the variable combination writer could sell his combination either covered or uncovered. The uncovered writer, of course, owns no stock. The covered writer, who sells two out-of-the-money August 60 calls, might also own 200 shares of the underlying stock. Being covered in this manner lowers the risk, but increases the net investment, since the combination writer will probably have more than $10,000 invested in purchasing the stock.

STRADDLE AND COMBINATION MARGINS

As a writer of a straddle or a combination, you'll want to acquaint yourself with the margin requirements. Knowing the margin, you can easily calculate the maximum percentage return to expect on any given straddle or combination. To calculate the margin on a straddle or a combination, you simply take the margin on the naked call and the margin on the naked put (naked put margins are calculated in the same manner as naked calls), and then you take the larger of the two. By allowing you to collect almost twice as much income on the same margin, the exchanges make straddle and combination writing very attractive. In addition, when you write a straddle or combination, you deduct *both* the put and call premiums that you received for writing the option straddle or combination.

ONE HUNDRED PER CENT PROFIT POTENTIAL

To take an example, when U.S. Steel recently traded at 24⅝, you could have written the nine-month 25 call for 2 and written the nine-month 25 put for 1⅞. Together, the two options offered a maximum profit of 3⅞ on the straddle. What was the margin requirement? Well, taking first the call, which was ⅜ out-of-the-money, the margin amounted to about $7. The put will have the larger margin requirement, however, because it is slightly in-the-money, and will require a bit more margin—about $7.75 per share. Subtracting the premium from both put and call, however, lowers this cash-up-front margin to just $3.87 per share, or $387 for the

entire straddle. Since the maximum possible return on the straddle
was the same amount, the maximum possible percentage return
amounts to 100 per cent. As you can see, a $387 return on $387
in margin is considerably better than the mere $187 return prom-
ised to the put writer alone.

As a rule, straddle and combination writing offer better rewards
per dollar invested in the form of margin than does simple naked
writing. The drawback with a straddle, however, is that it is almost certain that you'll have to give back at least a small portion
of your writing income. Why? Well, unless the stock trades exactly
at the strike price at the close of trading on the day of expiration,
your put or call will expire with *some* value, no matter how small.
Straddle writers, therefore, must be willing to deduct a certain
portion of their writing income in order to cope with this problem.
Combination writers, however, have it somewhat better; a combination can easily have the stock close between the strikes of the
put and the call, resulting in the writer keeping the entire com-
bination-writing income.

STRADDLE AND COMBINATION WRITERS MUST LIMIT LOSSES

The straddle or combination writer must take efforts to calculate precisely where he will exit the market if losses develop. All
the rules that we suggested for the naked writer apply to the straddle or combination writer. The market exposure is similar, and the
writer is threatened with intolerable losses if he doesn't take defensive action when losses occur. As a rule, calculate your maximum potential gain, your target level of profits (which should be
somewhat less than the maximum potential gain), and then set up
a contingency plan for exiting the trade if the stock hits a predetermined stop-loss level or if one of the options reaches a point at
which you wish to take losses. Not every straddle or combination
will prove profitable to its writer. Nor does every straddle or combination have to be profitable for you to win on a fairly consistent
basis. But you must learn to keep the losses small when they
occur. By doing so you'll be playing the options market like a professional, and you'll have the long-term profits to show for your
efforts.

USING CONTRACT MONTHS OF DIFFERENT DURATION

Straddles and combinations, as we've seen, can be tailor-made to fit special situations in which the buyer and seller is biased toward the long or short side of the market. So far, we've discussed straddles and combinations in terms of using the *same* contract month for both the put and the call. But what about using *different* contract months? If, for instance, you are a long-term bull on a particular stock, but you anticipate temporary reactions in the stock price, you can buy a short-term, three-month put and a long-term, nine-month call. Any temporary adversity in the price of the stock would serve to make the put profitable; you can then hold the longer-term call for the full duration of the option and end up exercising both sides of a straddle or combination. Conversely, if you anticipate short-term strength and long-term weakness in a stock, you can buy a three-month call and a six-month put.

Straddles and combinations offer a variety of profit-making strategies for buyers and sellers. The successful listed option trader has only to select the correct method to capitalize on existing conditions.

PART THREE

Understanding the Basics of Listed Commodity Options Trading

7

Options on Futures Contracts

Commodity options, which were first known as *privileges,* began trading on the Chicago Board of Trade in 1865. Declared illegal 20 years later by the Illinois Supreme Court, options appeared again in the nineteen thirties, but abuses in their marketing led to a ban on all so-called domestic commodities that were once regulated by the Commodity Exchange Authority. In the early seventies, the commodity option surfaced again—this time on what was known as the unregulated "world" commodities, such as sugar, coffee, cocoa, silver, and copper. But these off-exchange options, despite catching the attention of an eager investment community, proved fraudulent as well. Unsavory promoters soon created a Ponzi-type scheme in which winning option buyers were paid off with the new premium money coming through the doors. When the word got out that huge profits could be made at very little risk by purchasing the new commodity options, investor enthusiasm grew and grew. Soon option promoters were sponsoring seminars at which hundreds of eager new investors were shown how they, too, could get rich in the booming commodity options market. Within months the business mushroomed as millions of dollars were invested in the high-flying options game. But the bonanza proved short-lived. When the leading options marketing firm— Goldstein, Samuelson—was placed in involuntary bankruptcy in

1973, the commodity options business collapsed with it, along with the hopes of thousands of unwary investors. By the time the authorities closed down the naked[1] options game, the public had lost millions of dollars—and the idea of the commodity option as a legitimate trading vehicle was doomed for several years to come.

NAKED OPTIONS

In the aftermath of the naked options scandal, a few firms turned toward the legitimate London options which are still traded today. But even London options, which had been traded success-fully for more than a hundred years, achieved some notoriety as their stateside marketing firms were less than honest about their dealings in London. Indeed, in a repeat performance of the naked options scandal, a number of firms purporting to sell London op-tions simply pocketed the premiums and closed their doors—or had their doors closed for them by regulatory authorities. By the mid-seventies the Commodity Futures Trading Commission had come into existence, and it promptly brought *all* commodities traded in the U.S. under its regulatory umbrella. After much re-search and study, the CFTC permitted a number of firms to offer unlisted options on commodities to their customers. Unlisted op-tions never achieved the success of their naked counterparts—per-haps for good reason, since their premiums were prohibitively expensive.

In September 1981 the Commodity Futures Trading Commis-sion approved a pilot program for exchange-traded options on the nation's leading futures exchanges. Each commodity exchange was invited to submit a proposal for trading options on one of its fu-tures contracts. Although final approval for the exchange-traded options has been agonizingly slow, the first options began trading in October 1982. Given the success of listed stock options in the seventies, the new commodity options are likely to become the booming success story of the eighties.

[1] So-called naked *unlisted* options which were sold by a number of West Coast-based firms in the early seventies are not to be confused with writing naked *listed* options on the nation's regulated commodity exchanges. The safeguards and margin requirements on listed options are such that the in-tegrity of every option bought and sold on a regulated exchange is entirely protected.

HOW THE NEW PUT AND CALL MARKET WORKS

Just as listed put and call options on securities enable you to sell or buy a specified amount of stock at a given price within a given time frame, puts and calls on futures enable you to sell or buy a given *commodity futures contract* at a given price during a specified time frame. Instead of taking possession of 100 shares of a common stock, however, the commodity option enables you to take possession of a *long* futures contract, in the case of a call, or a *short* futures contract, in the case of a put. To be long futures means to be a buyer of the underlying commodity; to be short means to be a short seller of the underlying commodity. Most futures contracts are not held to maturity. Thus, buyers rarely take delivery as they are obligated to under the terms of the contract; and, conversely, short sellers are rarely obligated to give delivery of the commodity. Rather, contract positions are offset prior to maturity, and the buyer or seller profits or loses according to whether he buys and sells at favorable prices. The prices at which the buyer agrees to buy and the seller agrees to sell are established on the floor of the exchange at the time they enter into the contract.

A futures contract is not the actual underlying commodity or financial instrument but rather a legally binding agreement enabling you to either buy or sell a specified amount of the underlying commodity or financial instrument at a specified price. Any given commodity will be quoted in terms of a given trading month. Thus, there will be a June Treasury bond contract, a September Treasury bond contract, and a December Treasury bond contract all trading at different prices. The prices reflect traders' estimates of precisely what those financial instruments are worth with the different maturities. As the contracts mature, buyers, who have purchased the futures by posting only a good-faith margin deposit, post the full contract value of the commodity and *take* delivery. Conversely, sellers, who have likewise posted a good-faith margin to make good their losses in the case of price adversity, must *give* delivery of the specified underlying commodity or financial instrument.

The major drawback of futures trading is that of *unlimited risk* for both buyer and seller. Whether you purchase or sell a futures contract short, you are liable for any and all adversity in the price movement of the full value of the underlying commodity. For example, if you sell short one futures contract of gold for $300 an ounce and the price of gold *rises,* you are liable for the entire price rise. Since a standard gold contract contains 100 ounces of gold,[2] a $10 rise would constitute a $1,000-per-contract loss. A $100-an-ounce rise, therefore, would constitute a $10,000 loss. Since the initial margin on a contract of gold might be $2,500, you can see how you can lose many, many times the cost of your initial investment. For the buyer of a gold futures contract, the liability exists if the market *falls* after purchasing the contract. A $100-an-ounce decline in the price of gold following the purchase of a contract would constitute a $10,000 loss, again even if initial margin were only $2,500. The point is, when you purchase or sell a futures contract, you have *unlimited liability.*[3] When you purchase a *put* or *call option* on a futures contract, however, your risk is *strictly limited to the premium cost* of the option.

Why options on futures contracts? Why not options on the cash commodity? For one thing, the futures markets provide the price discovery function that is often not available in the cash markets. Futures prices are arrived at in a competitive marketplace with continuous price dissemination. The abundance of buyers and sellers meeting in a single, centralized location ensures that you will receive the most competitive price available at that moment in time. This works in the interest of both buyer and seller. In contrast, a public market doesn't exist for the underlying cash commodity or financial instrument in many cases. For another, futures markets are liquid. With an option on a futures contract, you can do one of two things: you can exercise the contract and take delivery of a *long* or *short* futures contract, depending upon whether you have a call or a put; or you can simply sell the option in the liquid secondary market for options and receive a competi-

[2] The MidAmerica Commodity Exchange trades futures on "mini-size" contracts which are one third the size of the Comex gold futures contract. It is expected to have an option on its gold contract as well.

[3] For additional information on the commodity futures market, I suggest you read my prior book *Winning in the Commodities Market,* Doubleday & Co., 1979.

tive price. Of course, if after purchasing an option you find it unprofitable to exercise, you can simply abandon the option altogether. But chances are, an option with remaining time value will command some value in the secondary market, no matter how small. A major attraction of futures trading is leverage—which will carry over to an option holder of a futures contract. Since a futures contract doesn't require full advance payment (only a margin payment which serves as a good-faith deposit), the buyer of a futures contract which increases in value, or a seller of a futures contract which decreases in value, can realize a profit which is substantial in value relative to the small commitment in margin funds.

OFF-EXCHANGE OPTIONS VERSUS LISTED EXCHANGE OPTIONS

When you compare a listed exchange-traded option with an off-exchange option, for which no secondary market exists, you can plainly see the difference. For one thing, the premium of an option that is not traded on a regulated exchange is determined by what the traffic will bear. That is, the seller sets the price. For this reason, any option you buy off the floor of a commodity exchange is apt to be overpriced.[4] Secondly, once you buy an unlisted option, you must either exercise it or abandon it; most firms selling unlisted options will not buy them back prior to expiration. As a result, the buyer is locked in his option position once he decides to purchase an unlisted option.

OPTIONS ON FINANCIAL INSTRUMENT FUTURES

Since the most popular options on a futures contract promise to be those on the enormously successful U.S. Treasury bond contract traded at the Chicago Board of Trade, the most widely traded futures contract in the 135-year history of the exchange, we'll look at an example using bond options. First and foremost, you must understand that bond prices move *inversely* to interest rates. That is, as interest rates *decrease,* the price of a fixed-interest bond will

---

[4] This was clearly the case on the over-the-counter puts and calls market for securities that thrived for many years prior to the opening of the Chicago Board Options Exchange.

rise—and vice versa. Let's say, therefore, that in anticipation of
falling interest rates, you purchase a call option on U.S. Treasury
bonds, because you anticipate that bond prices will rise. Just as
with a listed stock option, you are asked to pay a *premium* to
purchase a call with a fixed *striking price*.[5] Let's say you pay a
premium of $1,500 to purchase a call option on a U.S. Treasury
bond future with a striking price of 60-00. (Treasury bonds are
quoted in points equal to $1,000 and in 32nds of a point, or
$31.25 per 32nd. For instance, 60-00 means 60 points and no
32nds; 60-24 means 60 points and $24/_{32}$; 61-12 means 61 points
and $12/_{32}$, and so on. A move from, say, 60-00 to 63-00, therefore, would be worth 3 points, or $3,000. Every quoted price of a
U.S. Treasury bond or U.S. Treasury bond futures contract corre-
sponds to a specific interest rate yield on the 20-year 8%
$100,000 Treasury bond. For instance, when the price of the
bond is 76-00, or $76,000, the yield equivalent on the 8% bond is
10.989 per cent; when the bond is quoted at 60-00, the yield is
14.001 per cent.) Returning to our example, let's say the purchaser of the call option anticipates lower interest rates to result in
an increase in the value of the underlying U.S. Treasury bond contract. In paying $1,500 for the call, the buyer knows he needs at
least a 1½-point upward move in the price of the bonds to reach
break-even, since each point move equals $1,000. Assume that in-
terest rates drop ½ point to about 13½ per cent and the price of the
bond rises two points to 62-00. Now, the call can be exercised
(or, more likely, the call sold in the secondary market) and the
underlying bond position subsequently sold for $62,000. The re-
sult would be a profit on the option of 2 points or $2,000
($62,000 − $60,000 = $2,000). The buyer of the call earns a
$500 profit on the call, since he initially paid a premium of
$1,500.

Had the underlying bond contract *not* risen by 2 points but
rather declined by 4 points to 56-00, the call would become
worthless upon expiration. To the call buyer, however, the rise in
interest rates and the corresponding decline in bond prices would

---

[5] The writer of the option, who *receives* the premium, must post margin
that is marked to the market daily. If the option moves against the writer,
he could lose a substantial amount of money *unless* he takes defensive action to cut his losses.

have only resulted in the loss of the premium paid. As a result, the call or put buyer always has a *limited amount of investment risk*. This is a major advantage, since the buyer of a bond futures contract at a price of 60-00 would have a loss of 4 points, or $4,000 on the decline to 56-00. Thus, the limited risk aspect of options on futures contracts becomes a key advantage for any investor looking at the financial instruments market.

Since financial futures have been notoriously volatile in recent years, the limited-risk aspect of options on U.S. Treasury bonds becomes doubly important when you consider that the new options offer the investor *staying power*—the ability to maintain a position despite the vagaries of the market. When you first take a position in the futures market, you are asked by your broker to deposit what is called *initial margin,* a good-faith deposit to ensure you'll pay any losses that result in the position. The exchanges require that any futures position meet the slightly lower *maintenance margin* requirements as well. When the amount of money you have on deposit with the broker falls below the minimum maintenance margin, you receive what is known as a *margin call,* and you are asked to deposit additional funds immediately. If you don't meet this margin call, your position is automatically liquidated.

For the holder of an outright futures position, the margin calls can mount steadily if you are on the wrong side of the market. As a result, you can lose an unlimited amount of money in a futures position if the market goes against you. In fact, you can lose all your investment or speculative funds protecting a single futures position. But with an option on a futures contract, the entire risk is limited to the initial premium paid when you purchase the option. No matter how far the market goes against your position when you purchase an option, your risk is known. As a result of the staying power that the option provides, you can await a favorable trend in the market to get yourself back in a profitable position. By virtue of owning an option, therefore, you have less concern with *timing*. Again, the only cost is the initial premium payment.

To summarize: options on futures contracts work in the same manner as options on stocks. The difference rests with the underlying security. In the case of a stock option, the underlying security is 100 shares of whatever stock the option covers; in the case of an option on a futures contract, the underlying security is the futures contract on which the option is written. The futures contract becomes the cash commodity at the *maturity date of the futures contract*. The maturity date of the option on the futures contract will tend to fall about one month *preceding* the maturity date of the contract itself.[6]

Options on futures have terms similar to options on stocks. The buyer of the contract pays a *premium* to the seller or writer of the option contract. Both puts and calls have *striking prices* and *exercise* or *maturity dates* just like stock options. A *call option* gives the holder the right to *purchase* the underlying futures contract at the striking price prior to expiration; and a *put option* gives the holder of the contract the right to *sell* the underlying futures contract at the striking price prior to expiration. From the buyer's point of view, the *simplest strategy is to purchase a call in anticipation of higher prices in the underlying futures contract and to purchase a put in anticipation of lower prices in the underlying futures contract*. There are, of course, many more sophisticated strategies that can be used to capitalize on these new and versatile investment vehicles. As with stock options a liquid secondary market will exist for the options on futures contracts; as a result, a holder of an option on a futures contract can easily take profits or losses on his option by simply liquidating the option in the secondary market. One area where the options on futures will differ from stock options is in how they are quoted. Options on futures will be quoted in terms of the point values of the underlying futures contract—not the point values of the stock market. In the case of U.S. Treasury bonds, for instance, the options will be quoted in 64ths; at first, this may seem confusing, since the bond contract itself is quoted in 32nds of a point. But a 64th of a point is simply one half of a 32nd of a point. Since a point in the bond market is valued at $1,000, the value of a 32nd is $31.25 and the value of a 64th is one half as much, or $15.62½. For example, a June 60 call might have a premium of 3-00, or $3,000. This

---

[6] The exception exists in the new option on S&P index futures and Kansas City index futures which expire on the same day as the underlying futures contract. The reason that index options expire on the last day of trading is due to the cash settlement provisions of index futures.

means 3 points and no 64ths. At the same time, the underlying June U.S. Treasury bond futures contract might be trading at 60-24. This means the value of the contract is 60 points and $2\frac{4}{32}$, or $60,750 ($60,000 + [24 × $31.25] or $750). The reason the options are quoted in 64ths as opposed to 32nds is to ensure greater liquidity. Unlike stocks, where every point is equal to one dollar, the value of a point in the commodities market varies according to the size of the underlying contract and how the futures are quoted. Gold options, for instance, will be quoted as so many dollars per ounce; the per-ounce price, therefore, will be multiplied by the standard 100-ounce contract. Thus, if your broker tells you that an option on a June 300 call is $16.20, you'll know that the premium will be 100 times as much, or $1,620. In the sugar market, where the standardized contract consists of 112,000 pounds of raw sugar, the value of a 1-cent move is $1,120. Since sugar is quoted in 100ths of a cent—or one point—the minimum move is equal to $11.20. One hundred points in sugar equals 1 cent. Thus, a premium of, say, 280 for a sugar call will amount to $3,136 (280 × $11.20 = $3,136). Options on Standard & Poor's 500 stock index futures are quoted in terms of dollars which are $\frac{1}{500}$ the value of the underlying contract. Thus, a quote of 7.00 for a June 125 S&P call would cost $3,500 (7.00 × $500 = $3,500). Your broker can fill you in on the point value of any futures contract on which you intend to purchase an option.

BUYING OPTIONS IN COMBINATION WITH FUTURES

The introduction of options on futures literally opens the door for a host of new trading strategies that were not available prior to the introduction of the new options trading vehicles. Now, for the first time, futures traders can manage their risks in the futures markets without having to resort to stop-loss orders. One of the most popular new strategies should prove to be the *"trading against"* concept, which enables short sellers in the futures market to purchase calls and thereby limit upside risk, while long futures traders can purchase puts to limit their downside risk. Because this concept is undoubtedly new to most, we'll consider the pros and cons of each position.

Clearly, the risk of a futures trader who goes long a futures contract is that the price of the underlying futures will decline; conversely, the risk of a futures trader who goes short a futures contract is that the price of the underlying futures will rise. In the case of an outright futures position, moreover, the risk is unlimited, since the futures trader must make good the entire difference between the price at which he buys and that at which he sells a futures contract when his market judgment is wrong.

When you purchase an option in conjunction with trading a futures contract, however, your risk situation changes. The trader who is long a futures contract, for example, might purchase a put option to hedge his downside risk. Buying a put to limit losses in a long futures position is a strategy that can be tailored to suit your risk management requirements. Think of the put premium as the cost of the "insurance" to limit risk.[7] You can think of the put premium as the "deductible" cost in a typical insurance policy. Thus, if you pay a $500 premium for the put, you're willing to pay for the first $500 in losses on the long futures position. Beyond that cost, you want the put option to "insure" you against additional loss.

There is no one-to-one requirement when purchasing puts for insurance when you hold a long futures position. You can "fine-tune" your risk-management strategy to fit your particular needs by purchasing two puts for every long position or by purchasing in- or out-of-the-money puts as you desire. A key consideration will be what amount of risk you wish to hedge. This will determine which put you select. While out-of-the-money puts are less expensive, their protection is somewhat less—hence the "deductible" is higher.

To illustrate how you might implement this strategy in practice, let's say you are bearish on interest rates and bullish on U.S. Treasury bond futures (remember, they move *inversely*). Assume it is

---

[7] The notion of an insurance policy is a good analogy in two other respects as well. First, the policy stays in effect until it expires. Because the protection is continuous, you can trade against the option as often as you like prior to expiration. Second, you can "cancel" your option insurance at any time by simply selling the option and receiving a "partial refund" on your insurance investment.

January 2nd and the price of the nearby March bond futures contract is 59-00. Since you anticipate a rise in bond prices (reflecting a decline in interest rates), you purchase one March U.S. Treasury bond futures contract for a price of 59-00. At the same time, because you fear that bond prices might decline during the time you hold the long bond futures position, you purchase one March 59 U.S. Treasury bond put option for a premium of $3\frac{2}{64}$, or $500. The put option provides you with the right to *sell* one bond futures contract at the price of 59-00 prior to maturity. Assuming your long position proved a loser and bond prices declined to 58-00 by February 15, your insurance will pay off by *limiting* your downside risk. The two transactions are shown in Table 21.

Table 21

BUY PUT—LONG FUTURES

January 2

FUTURES	OPTIONS
Buys 1 March U.S. Treasury bond futures contract at 59-00. (Value: $59,000)	Buys 1 March 59 U.S. Treasury bond futures put for $3\frac{2}{64}$, or $500.

February 15

FUTURES	OPTIONS
Sells 1 March U.S. Treasury bond futures contract at 58-00. (Value: $58,000)	Sells 1 March 59 U.S. Treasury bond futures put for 1-00, or $1,000.
Loss: $1,000	Gain: $500

Net Gain/Loss: −$500

Although the trade resulted in a loss, the amount lost was lessened by the ownership of the put option. An unhedged long futures position in the March U.S. Treasury bond futures would have resulted in a loss of $1,000. By purchasing a put option on the March U.S. Treasury bond contract for $500, the maximum downside risk was limited to the premium cost, or just $500. Had bond prices fallen to, say, 54-00, the wisdom of the hedged position would have become more apparent, because the outright futures trader would be looking at a $5,000 loss on the long futures position. By purchasing a put, however, no matter how far the market declined, the entire loss would be strictly limited. Conversely, had the market risen as anticipated, the ownership of the put would have only offset the profits by $500.

SHOULD YOU PURCHASE IN-THE-MONEY OR OUT-OF-THE-MONEY OPTIONS?

The degree of "deductibility" can be altered when using this trading strategy by purchasing options which are in- or out-of-the-money. In Table 21 the put option was at-the-money when the long futures position was taken. What would be the impact of purchasing a put with a strike of 60-00 or 61-00? Because the put is in-the-money (remember, put options *increase* in value as prices for the underlying security fall *below* the strike price), the premium cost will be higher. This higher premium cost will affect the overall profitability of the long-futures/long-put strategy. Should prices rise in this case, the greater cost of the put will offset a greater amount of profit. Thus, the break-even cost to the upside will be higher. Conversely, if you purchase an out-of-the-money put—one with a strike at, say, 58-00—the downside protection won't begin until prices trade below that lower strike. So, in Table 21 the trader would have lost the entire 1-point adverse move in the prices of the bonds on the long futures position had prices declined from 59-00 to 58-00 *plus* the cost of the 58-strike put premium. With March bond prices at 58-00, the put would have expired worthless. As you can see, there is a trade-off involved. Out-of-the-money put options will have lower premiums, but they offer less protection. The key is to find a balance between put prices and protection in using this strategy.

SHORT SELLERS SHOULD PURCHASE CALLS FOR PROTECTION

Just as a long put option will protect a long futures position, the purchase of a *call option* will provide protection to the *short seller* of futures contracts who anticipates lower prices. Assuming you are bearish on the stock market, you might *sell* Standard & Poor's index futures in anticipation of being able to "cover" and buy them back at a lower price. We'll assume it is June 1 and you are looking to profit from a decline in September S&P 500 stock index futures. At the same time, you decide to purchase a call on the S&P stock index futures to protect yourself from a *rise* in the S&P index. You have now sold short one September S&P stock index futures contract and purchased one September call on S&P stock index futures. We'll assume the September S&P stock index is trading at 150.00 and the premium for an at-the-money September S&P 150 call is 2.85, or $1,425. Assuming your initial judgment proves correct and September S&P 500 stock index futures fall to 110.00 by August 15, your profit and loss on the hedged transaction will appear as shown in Table 22.

Table 22

BUY CALL–SHORT FUTURES

June 1

FUTURES	OPTIONS
Sells 1 September Standard & Poor's 500 stock index futures contract at 150.00.	Buys 1 September Standard & Poor's 500 stock index futures call with a strike price of 150.00 for 2.85, or $1,425.

August 15

FUTURES	OPTIONS
Buys 1 September Standard & Poor's 500 stock index futures contract at 110.00.	September Standard & Poor's 150 call expires worthless.
Gain: $20,000	Loss: $1,425

Net Gain/Loss: +$18,575

Here again, the option provides insurance in case the trader's initial market judgment proved incorrect. Had S&P prices *risen* forty points, the loss would have been limited to the $1,425 cost of the call premium. The reason? Above a price of 150.00, the call option would have gained point for point with the loss in the short futures position. We are assuming that the option expires on August 15. In reality, it may expire as much as a week later. Even if the option still retained some value, the hedge would still work, although the profitability would be slightly less.

Assume, on the other hand, that your market judgment proved incorrect and September S&P futures *rose* forty points to 190.00. Without the protection provided by the call, the loss on the short futures position would be $20,000. By having the call option, the maximum loss is limited to the cost of the premium, or $1,425.

Just as options can be used as a hedge when purchased in conjunction with futures trading, they can also be used to *enhance leverage* when the underlying futures position and the options position are oriented toward one side of the market. For instance, you might be bearish on a commodity or financial instrument and sell short the futures. For additional leverage you might then purchase a put option which will enable you to sell additional positions at the strike price if prices decline. Why not double up and sell more futures? The reason is risk. The futures trader is liable for the entire movement of his underlying position. The difference is vitally important to understand if you are going to use options in conjunction with futures. The bullish speculator, of course, will buy futures in conjunction with calls. When you buy futures and options in this manner, you must be correct about market direction. If you are not, you will end up losing on both the futures and options. Now let's look at an example of this trading strategy.

It is June 1, and you anticipate a substantial *decline* in interest rates and a corresponding *rise* in bond prices. September U.S. Treasury bond futures on the Chicago Board of Trade are quoted at 59-00, reflecting a yield of 14.235 per cent. Your best estimates are that bond prices will rise to 67-00 by mid-August, reflecting a yield of 12.535 per cent on the 20-year 8% $100,000 standard bond contract. You decide to purchase a September futures contract at 59-00. In addition, you wish to enhance your leverage by purchasing a call option on a September bond futures contract. Your broker informs you that a September 59 call is available for 1-14, or 1-14/64. This translates into a price of $1,218 for the call option. In return for that premium, you gain the right to buy a September futures contract at 59-00 at any time prior to expiration of the call option, which will occur toward the end of August. Now, you are long 1 September futures contract and 1 September 59 call on the same futures contract. Your only cost is that of commissions plus the premium on the call of

$1,218.[8] We'll assume your market judgment proves correct and you are able to close out your bond position at a price of 67-00 on August 15. Assuming the call option is trading at its intrinsic value on that date, the transactions on the trade will appear as shown in Table 23.

Table 23

BUY CALL–LONG FUTURES

June 1

FUTURES	OPTIONS
Buys 1 September U.S. Treasury bond futures contract at 59-00. (Value: $59,000)	Buys 1 September 59 U.S. Treasury bond call option for 1-14, or $1,218.

August 15

FUTURES	OPTIONS
Sells 1 September U.S. Treasury bond futures contract at 67-00. (Value: $67,000)	Sells 1 September 59 U.S. Treasury bond call option for 8-00, or $8,000.[9]
Gain: $8,000	Gain: $6,782

Net Gain/Loss: +$14,782

While the gain on the call option was not as great as the gain on the futures position, neither were the risks comparable. The futures trader who is long bonds has an unlimited liability, whereas the holder of a call option on a bond futures contract is only risking his premium cost. In the example above the strategy worked out well, but had prices declined, the results would have been disappointing. To see how the high leverage associated with futures trading is a double-edged sword, let's consider the results if bond prices had declined to 56-00 on a modest rise in interest rates. The transactions are shown in Table 24.

[8] While futures trading requires the deposit of a good-faith margin deposit, there is no cost, aside from commissions, if you close out the trade with a profit.

[9] In this example we are assuming the speculator simply sells the call option. He could, of course, exercise the option and take delivery of a long futures contract and be credited with the difference between the strike at 59-00 and the market price.

Table 24

BUY CALL—LONG FUTURES

June 1

FUTURES	OPTIONS
Buys 1 September U.S. Treasury bond futures contract at 59-00. (Value: $59,000)	Buys 1 September 59 U.S. Treasury bond call option for 1-14, or $1,218.

August 15

FUTURES	OPTIONS
Sells 1 September U.S. Treasury bond futures contract at 56-00. (Value: $56,000)	September 59 U.S. Treasury bond call expires worthless.
Loss: $3,000	Loss: $1,218

Net Gain/Loss: −$4,218

A three-point decline in the bond market is quite modest during these interest-sensitive times. Over the past year the price of a September bond contract has moved over 27 points, or $27,000 per contract. The potential gain or loss in a bond trade is considerable.

VERY BEARISH? SELL FUTURES AND BUY PUTS

Turning Table 24 upside down, we can also see why a short sale in the futures market can be accompanied by the purchase of a put option to enhance leverage. Let's take a hypothetical example in the sugar market when October sugar futures are trading at 7 cents per pound and an October 7 put is available for a premium of 1 cent per pound, or $1,120.[10] Anticipating lower sugar prices, the futures speculator both sells an October sugar futures short *and* purchases an October 7 sugar put option for a 1-cent premium, or $1,120. Assuming the trade is initiated at 7.00 cents

10 Since a standard sugar contract consists of 112,000 pounds (50 tons), a 1-cent-per-pound move translates into $1,120. Sugar is quoted in 100ths of a cent; thus the minimum tick is valued at $11.20. A quote of .80 cents would translate into $896 (80 × $11.20 = $896). A quote of 2.30 would be valued at $2,576 (230 × $11.20 = $2,576), and so on.

per pound on July 1 and prices decline to 5 cents per pound by
September 15, the transactions would be as shown in Table 25.

Table 25

BUY PUT—SHORT FUTURES

July 1

FUTURES	OPTIONS
Sells 1 October sugar futures contract at 7.00 cents per pound.	Buys 1 October 7 sugar put option for 1.00 cent per pound, or $1,120.

September 15

FUTURES	OPTIONS
Buys 1 October sugar futures contract at 5.00 cents per pound.	Sells 1 October 7 sugar put option for 2.00 cents per pound, or $2,240.
Gain: $2,240	Gain: $1,120

Net Gain/Loss: +$3,360

Here again, the option helped magnify the profit on the futures
position. But only because the speculator's market judgment was
correct. Had sugar prices *risen* instead, the results would be far
different. Assuming a price rise to 10 cents per pound, Table 26
shows how the transactions would appear.

Table 26

BUY PUT—SHORT FUTURES

July 1

FUTURES	OPTIONS
Sells 1 October sugar futures contract at 7.00 cents per pound.	Buys 1 October 7 sugar put option for 1.00 cent per pound, or $1,120.

September 15

FUTURES	OPTIONS
Buys 1 October sugar futures contract at 10.00 cents per pound.	October 7 sugar put option expires worthless.
Loss: $3,360	Loss: $1,120

Net Gain/Loss: −$4,480

As the example shows, a put option is *not* a viable hedge for a short position in the futures market.

The two examples above illustrate how high leverage can cause both profits *and* losses to mount rapidly. Assuming that the good-faith margin required to sell short one futures contract of October sugar amounted to $1,500, the leverage in the example above would result in a 43 per cent *rise* in the price of sugar, translating into a 224 per cent *decline* in the trader's equity; that is, he would have lost more than twice as much as he originally put up in margin! But leverage works both ways. In the example in Table 25, a 28½ per cent *decline* in the price of sugar resulted in a 149 per cent *gain* on margin on the short futures contract. Added to this, of course, would be the profits on the put option. So whether or not leverage is a good thing depends on what side of the market you're trading. To win big profits you are going to have to sustain high risks. The options market, being versatile, enables you to moderate or enhance those somewhat, depending on what strategy you select.

SELLING OPTIONS IN COMBINATION WITH FUTURES

Writers of options on futures sell them for the same reason that participants in the equity markets do—namely, income. Options on futures can be written with or without a related position in the underlying futures. Since options on futures contracts are comparable to options on securities, the same drawbacks apply: as a writer of an option on a futures contract, you can lose a great deal of money, since you are responsible for the full movement of the underlying futures contract. And since futures contracts are highly leveraged, the liability can increase with great speed. On the other hand, the maximum potential to the option writer is limited to the premium he takes in when writing the option. Thus, while his potential gain is limited, his potential liability is not. The option writer, however, often feels that the premium he receives for writing the option is worth the potential risk involved.

The option writer reasons that the premium he receives will offset any loss on the position if prices move against him—at least initially. He is prepared to buy back his short option if it appears that an option is about to go into the money. In general, the option writer does not anticipate any substantial move in the underlying futures contract. He is a percentage player in the sense that he is betting that prices will stay pretty much the same.

We'll assume that it is September 15 and a prospective writer of a bond option is mildly bearish on interest rates and hence bullish on bond prices. He purchases a December bond futures contract at 57-00, reflecting a yield of 14.7 per cent, and simultaneously writes a December 57-strike call option. The premium for the at-the-money call is 1-00, or $1,000. Since the margin deposit for the futures position is, let us say, $2,000 and the call writer receives $1,000 premium income, the covered writer has taken in 50 per cent of his initial margin deposit right at the outset.[11] The writer knows that unless bond prices drop considerably, he'll emerge a winner on the trade, although his profits above the price of 58-00 will go to the buyer of the call. We'll assume that prices neither rally nor decline much between September and November 15 and that December bonds are trading exactly at 57-00 on the day the December bond call expires. The transactions are shown in Table 27.

Table 27

WRITES CALL—BUYS FUTURES

September 15

FUTURES	OPTIONS
Buys 1 December U.S. Treasury bond futures contract at 57-00. (Value: $57,000)	Sells 1 December 57 U.S. Treasury bond call option for 1-00, or $1,000.

November 15

FUTURES	OPTIONS
Sells 1 December U.S. Treasury bond futures contract at 57-00.[12] (Value: $57,000)	Allows call option to expire worthless.
Gain/Loss: None (except commissions)	Gain: $1,000

Net Gain/Loss: +$1,000

[11] In the futures market, margin requirements vary from brokerage firm to brokerage firm. Each futures exchange sets minimum requirements which all firms must honor, however, to ensure the financial integrity of every contract that changes hands. Margins will vary in accordance with volatility and price levels of the underlying futures contracts.

[12] Since no loss resulted from the trade, the initial margin is returned.

Please note that the December 57 call would probably not expire precisely on November 15 but perhaps within several market days of that date. Prior to expiration the call writer could buy back the call option for whatever remaining time value it could command in the market. This would lessen his profit somewhat. In addition, the transaction costs would have to be included in the calculations. Nevertheless, at a time when the market was *not* moving, the call writer was able to pick up $1,000 in writing income at relatively low risk.

In the example above, if you were somewhat more bullish on bond prices, you would want to write an out-of-the-money call. The out-of-the-money call would generate less premium income, but it would enable you to earn additional income on your long futures position as it rose toward the strike price of the out-of-the-money call. In the example above, the December 59 call might have been available for, say, $1\frac{7}{64}$, or about $266. While this is only about one quarter as much as the at-the-money December 57 call, the two points between 57-00 and 59-00 could generate another $2,000 in profits on the long December futures contract. The point of maximum profit, therefore, would be at 59-00 upon expiration of the call. At that price the long December futures position would have a $2,000 profit and the December 59 call option would expire worthless, resulting in an additional $266 in profit. With an out-of-the-money call, however, the long futures position has less protection in the event of a decline in prices. When you take in only $266 for writing a bond call, you only have about eight ticks of protection to the downside.[13] Hence, a decline of nine ticks or more below 57-00 to 56-23 or lower would result in an overall loss using this strategy.[14]

Another strategy using calls and futures is to write a call to protect profits on the futures position. Let's say you had the good fortune to purchase a December futures contract on gold at $300 an ounce and the price of the precious metal rises to $380 an ounce. One alternative, of course, is to simply sell the futures contract and take your $8,000 profit. Another is to write a call option.

---

[13] The value of one tick in a bond futures contract is $31.25. Eight ticks, therefore, would be valued at $250.

[14] Bond futures are traded in 32nds. The tick below 57-00 is 56-31. Nine ticks down from 57-00, therefore, would be 56-23.

Let's say a December 380 call on gold futures is available for $10 an ounce, or $1,000 on the 100-ounce contract. You can write the December 380 call and receive the $1,000 in writing income. This will guarantee that you receive the $1,000 in addition to whatever your futures contract will bring *below* the price of $380. Above the strike of $380, of course, the profits will go to the buyer of the call. But by virtue of having written the call, you'll be protected down to $370 an ounce. Should prices sell off to that level, you can sell your December futures contract for a $7,000 profit ($370 − $300 = $70; 70 × 100 = $7,000), *plus* you will have received $1,000 for writing the December 380 call option which, at $370 an ounce, will no doubt expire worthless. Below the price of $370, you'll begin to wish you had merely sold your futures contract at $380. But this insight will be quite academic at this point. Assuming the above scenario takes place on three key dates —June 15, when you take the initial futures position; October 15,

Table 28

BUYS FUTURES—WRITES CALL

June 15

FUTURES	OPTIONS
Buys 1 December gold futures contract at $300 an ounce.	No action.

October 15

FUTURES	OPTIONS
December gold futures trade at $380 an ounce, representing an $80-an-ounce paper profit on the long futures contract.	Writes 1 December 380 gold futures call for a premium of $10 an ounce, or $1,000.

November 15

FUTURES	OPTIONS
December gold futures trade at $370 an ounce, down $10 from October 15 high. Sells 1 gold futures contract at $370 an ounce.	December 380 gold futures call option expires worthless.

Gain: $7,000	Gain: $1,000

Net Gain/Loss: +$8,000

when you write the December 380 call; and November 15, the day of expiration of the call, when you also liquidate the long futures position—the transactions will appear as shown in Table 28.

The point of maximum profit in this trade would have been at $380 an ounce. At that price the long futures contract would have an $80 profit and the December 380 call would expire worthless, enabling the writer to retain the $1,000 premium. By writing the call the investor was able to provide himself with a $1,000 cushion against lower prices.

WRITING PUTS AND SELLING SHORT FUTURES

Just as you can write calls in combination with having a long futures position, you can write puts in combination with having a short futures position. For investors who are new to the futures market, the first rule you must learn is that the price of any given commodity or financial instrument is no more likely to rally than to decline; fortunately, in trading the futures market, selling short is as readily accomplished as buying long. Unlike in the stock market, you don't need an uptick to go short, nor do you have to borrow anything. Nevertheless, the public is still overwhelmingly one-sided about futures prices, and most only think about being buyers. This bullish bias on the public's part is often greeted with enthusiasm by professional floor traders, who are apt to be short the contracts the public buys. Enormous amounts of money are often lost by futures traders who are unwilling to accept the idea of selling short. Don't let this be your shortcoming. If you've followed the futures market for any period of time, you'll find that prices are as apt to decline as rally—and, more importantly, that they tend to break much faster than they go up.

Assuming you've become bearish or even slightly bearish on a market, you can generate immediate income by writing a put and simultaneously selling short a futures contract. Let's say your commodity is heating oil traded on the New York Mercantile Exchange. The heating oil contract consists of 42,000 gallons and is quoted in cents per gallon. The minimum tick is $1/100$ of a cent, equal to $4.20. Because you are bearish on heating oil prices, you sell an August contract at 89.00 cents a gallon and you *write* an

August 87 put for a premium of 1 cent, or $420 for the option. Assuming you initiate the trade on May 15 and close it out two months later on July 15, you stand to profit on both the short futures position in August heating oil and the short put option. We'll assume the option expires on July 15, the month prior to the expiration of the futures contract. Let's say the price of heating oil falls to the strike price of the put, or 87.00 cents a gallon upon expiration. The transactions will appear as shown in Table 29.

Table 29

WRITES PUT–SELLS FUTURES

May 15

FUTURES	OPTIONS
Sells 1 August heating oil futures contract at 89.00 cents per gallon.	Writes 1 August 87 heating oil put option for 1 cent, or $420.

July 15

FUTURES	OPTIONS
Buys 1 August heating oil futures contract at 87.00 cents per gallon.	August 87 heating oil put expires worthless.
Gain: $840	Gain: $420

Net Gain/Loss: +$1,260

By writing an out-of-the-money option, the option strategist enabled his short futures position to gain additional profits prior to reaching the strike price, the point where additional profit is "locked out." The premium income from the put also provided a 1-cent cushion of profitability in the event of an adverse market rise.

Puts can also be used for the same play with short futures positions as calls provide with long futures positions. Let's say you've correctly predicted a 3-cent decline in October sugar, having sold October futures at 9 cents per pound, and the market is currently trading at, say, 6 cents. You have a $3,360 paper profit on the position, and you want to provide a little protection lest sugar futures rise suddenly and you lose money on your short position. Let's also assume that an October 6 sugar put is available for a ½-cent premium, or $560. Even if the October futures contract trades at 6½ cents upon expiration of the October 6 put, you'll still profit by the full 3 cents you initially earned by writing the October 6 put. We'll assume the initial short futures position was taken on July 15 and that the put was written on August 15 and held to expiration of the put on about September 15. The transactions would appear as shown in Table 30.

Table 30

SHORT FUTURES—WRITES PUT

July 15

FUTURES	OPTIONS
Sells 1 October sugar futures contract at 9.00 cents per pound.	No action taken.

August 15

FUTURES	OPTIONS
October sugar futures trade at 6.00 cents per pound, representing a 3-cent, or $3,360, profit.	Writes 1 October 6 sugar put for a premium of ½ cent, or $560.

September 15

FUTURES	OPTIONS
Buys 1 October sugar futures contract at 6.50 cents per pound.	October 6 sugar put expires worthless.
Gain: $2,800[15]	Gain: $560

Net Gain/Loss: +$3,360

The premium income generated by the October 6 put provided a cushion of profit. Had prices continued to decline below 6 cents per pound, the short futures contract would have continued to generate additional profits. But the gain would have been offset by the losses on the put option below the strike price of 6 cents.

WRITING NAKED OPTIONS

Just as the writer of a naked stock option expects the underlying security to remain in the same price range, the writer of a naked futures option expects the underlying futures price to re-

---

[15] The net gain on the futures contract is 2½ cents ($9¢ - 6½¢ = 2½¢$). Multiplied by the value of a 1-cent move—$1,120—this translates into a profit of $2,800.

main the same. The naked writer understands that if the option does not become exercisable and expires without value, the premium will be his to keep. On the simplest level, therefore, a futures speculator might write, let us say, a September 59 bond call for a premium of $^{27}\!/_{64}$, or about $422. If September bond futures are trading *below* the price of 59-00 upon expiration of the September 59 call in mid-August, the $422 call premium will be the writer's to keep. For the writer of a put, the same principle applies, only the put writer wants prices to stay *above* the strike price to remain out-of-the-money. A put writer might sell a March 60 bond put for a premium of one point, or $1,000. If March bond futures are trading above the strike of 60-00 upon expiration of the March call, the $1,000 premium money will be retained by the writer. Neither put nor call writer is required to own the underlying futures contract. But both must post sufficient margin to ensure the integrity of the option. This is the simplest explanation of naked put and call writing.

A naked writer might also use this strategy to acquire a long futures contract slightly below the current market price or to short a futures contract slightly above the market. If you write a Standard & Poor's (S&P) 160 put for a premium of $1,500 when the market is trading at 160.00, you'll be long one S&P futures contract at 160 if the market price falls below the strike. Because you have the $1,500 premium money in hand once you write the put, your actual purchase price on the S&P futures is 157.00 (S&P futures are worth $500 a point), or three points below the strike price. At 157, you may be bullish on S&P futures. But at 160, you may prefer to stand aside. By writing the at-the-money 160 put, you stand to gain $1,500 if prices stay above 160 at expiration. Above a price of 160, the 160-strike put will expire worthless and the premium will be yours to keep. If prices decline below 160, the put will be exercised and you (the seller) will be long one S&P futures contract at the strike. Since you received the premium, however, your effective price is 157.00. The only way you can lose on this strategy is if prices fall below 157.00. You'll then have a greater loss on the futures than you gained by writing the put.

For the call writer, the situation is reversed. The call writer must be willing to become a short seller of futures at the strike price, since the holder of the option who exercises will be the

buyer. If you write a U.S. Treasury bond 59 call for a premium of
$1,000, the option will be exercisable at any price above 59. But
since you received the $1,000 premium, your effective selling price
will be 60. At 60 you may be a willing seller, since you anticipate
higher interest rates to push bond prices down. Should bonds
never rally above the strike at 59, the $1,000 premium will be
your profit.

DAILY LIMITS

Unlike stocks and stock options, options on futures are limited
in how far they can move in one day's trading by what are known
as *daily price limits*. These are limits, above and below the previous day's settlement price, beyond which the underlying futures
(and hence the options) cannot trade. The purpose of the limits is
to establish a 24-hour "cooling-off" period before prices again
trade higher or lower. Of course, after a limit move, the price of
the futures can again move the limit on the following day. After a
number of limit moves, the daily limits are typically raised by 50
per cent. As an option writer you will want to apply the same
rules for writing naked stock options. Always limit your losses and
take quick defensive action.

SPREADS

If you can both buy and sell options on futures, it stands to
reason that you can likewise spread them in a variety of configura-
tions. The most popular spread among the new options promises
to be the *vertical* spread between higher- and lower-strike options
on the same futures with the same delivery month. For example,
when March bonds are trading at 62-00, you might purchase a
March 60 call for 2-49 ($2,766) and simultaneously write a
March 62 call for 1-42 ($1,656).[16] This would be a debit spread,
one in which you pay more than you receive initially. You will
profit if the long March 60 call rises faster than the short March
62 call. To make the example simple, we'll assume that bond

[16] You should remember that bond options are quoted in 64ths ($15.62½
per tick), while the bond futures themselves are quoted in 32nds ($31.25
per tick).

prices remain stable and at the expiration of the March calls, bonds are trading at 62-00. What will be the impact on the spread? The March 60 call will retain its cash value of two points (62 − 60 = 2), resulting in a cash value of $2,000 upon expiration. The March 62 call, however, will expire worthless. As a result, the option spreader will *lose* $766 on the March 60 call and *gain* the full $1,656 for writing the March 62 call. The net result (transaction costs aside) will be the difference, or $890. Assuming the spread was first placed on December 15 and held until expiration about February 15, the transactions will appear as shown in Table 31.

Table 31

BULL VERTICAL CALL SPREAD

December 15—March T-bond Futures at 62-00

OPTIONS	OPTIONS
Buys 1 T-bond 60 call for a premium of 2-49, or $2,766.	Sells 1 T-bond March 62 call for a premium of 1-42, or $1,656.
Cost: $2,766	Gain: $1,656

Net Cost: $1,110

February 15—March T-bond Futures at 62-00

OPTIONS	OPTIONS
Sells 1 T-bond 60 call for a premium of 2-00, or $2,000.	T-bond March 62 call expires worthless.
Loss: $766	Gain: $1,656

Net Gain/Loss: +$890

In the example given in Table 31, the spreader gains by selling time value. The March 62 call premium disappeared entirely as the option expired worthless. Had prices rallied above 62, the March 62 call would have retained value and perhaps—had the bond market moved up far enough—even have resulted in a loss. But the March 60 call would also gain on any rally. The risk in this spread is that the bond market might decline. Had both calls expired worthless, the call spreader would have sustained a net loss. The initial debit or $1,110, in that case, would have been the maximum loss.

To capitalize on a declining market, the positions might have been reversed. The bear vertical spread would have consisted of a long March 62 call and a short March 60 call. This spread could be accomplished at a credit, since you are selling a lower-strike option that already retains some cash value. For the spread to work, however, the market must decline. We'll assume bond prices are at 62-00 when the spread is first put on with the same premiums in the options and that the market retreats to 59-00 by February 15. (See Table 32.)

Table 32

BEAR VERTICAL CALL SPREAD

December 15—March T-bond Futures at 62-00

OPTIONS	OPTIONS
Sells 1 T-bond March 60 call for a premium of 2-49, or $2,766.	Buys 1 T-bond March 62 call for a premium of 1-42, or $1,656.
Gain: $2,766	Cost: $1,656

Net Gain: $1,110

February 15—March T-bond Futures at 59-00

OPTIONS	OPTIONS
T-bond March 60 call expires worthless.	T-bond March 62 call expires worthless.
Gain: $2,766	Loss: $1,656

Net Gain/Loss: +$1,110

A few words of caution are in order concerning spreads. Since the option on a futures contract concept is a new one, there's no guarantee sufficient liquidity will exist to make the new options good trading vehicles. For this, only time will tell if the options prove viable. From a strategy point of view, the trader new to options must have a plan for exiting the market when things go wrong. If you put on a bull spread and the market declines, you're going to be in trouble. If it is any consolation, the maximum loss is going to be the cost of the spread, the initial debit. But why sustain the maximum loss even if it is known and limited? When wrong, the best trading rule is always the same in any investment venture—get out! When you enter a spread position, you are anticipating a specific market action but you are hedging your bets. In the bull spread shown in Table 32, the spread returned a profit even though the market price of bonds did not rise. This would not have resulted if you'd simply purchased a March 60 call, since the diminishing time value would have eaten away at your premium cost. Spreads are valuable trading strategies when the price of the underlying security falls within certain specified limits. But they must be targeted toward a specific market situation, and then they must be monitored for profitability until closed out.

AN ABUNDANCE OF STRATEGIES

This brief introduction to the new options market on futures is by no means comprehensive. Virtually all the strategies discussed in the section on stock options apply to the new options on futures as well. Because it would be repetitive to cover each in detail, we'll simply refer back to the section on spreads, straddles, and combinations on stock options for the appropriate examples of the principles involved. Certainly, there will be a period of time when the participants in these new markets will be learning what works best. This should prove to be extremely profitable—at least temporarily—to those traders who are able to capitalize on the newness of the option concept. When listed stock options first started trading, option premiums were far, far higher than was justified considering the risks involved. As a result, the writers profited accordingly and the hapless buyers continued to sustain losses until they realized the premiums were too high. Today, the listed stock options market is considerably more competitive than it was back in 1973, and the writers have to settle for premiums that are much more realistic. Certainly, the same can be expected for the new options market on futures. At first, eager investors, happy to be able to gain the leverage of futures with limited risk, will no doubt *pay* handsome premiums. But once they realize the real money is being made *writing* options, the premium levels will fall and the writers will have to work for their money—just as they do in the listed stock options market today.

Looking ahead, the boom in options trading on futures should rival the boom in stock options trading. Already the number of proposed new options seems limited only by the ability of market professionals to come up with new ideas. To name just a handful of proposals, there have been suggestions to trade options on futures contracts, including financial instruments, precious metals, petroleum contracts, and agricultural products; options on stock index futures, the latest new entrant in the futures markets; options on stock group indexes, such as drug, computer, oil, and transportation averages; and options on foreign currencies. Because some of these option concepts are so new, there is a question whether they should be regulated by the CFTC as futures, or the SEC as securities. The jury is still out on which options will prove the most successful. But there's a pretty good chance the new options markets will revolutionize Wall Street as investors demand these more sophisticated trading vehicles, whose versatility promises to make them the most potentially rewarding new investments ever.

PART FOUR

Understanding the Basics
of Stock Index Futures

8

Stock Index Futures— The New High-risk/High-reward Investment Game

For years, stock market pundits spoke of stock market averages— the Dow, Standard & Poor's, Value Line, New York Stock Exchange composite—with a sort of reverence. The secrets of the stock market were often considered to be hidden within the gyrations of the oils or transportation indexes, as if the averages held the key to understanding the market. Among analysts the common refrain was, "But you can buy the averages." It was as if the ability to participate in a broad grouping of stocks would be the answer to the stock investor's quest. Well, we may be getting closer. Because today you *can* buy the averages; what's more, you can sell short the averages as well on at least three major indexes.[1]

THE NEW STOCK INDEX FUTURES

This new product in the stock investor's arsenal is known as the *stock index future*. It is neither a common stock nor an option, but akin to both. It is a *financial futures contract* that is based on

[1] While three major indexes are currently trading—Value Line, Standard & Poor's 500, and New York composite—several more are tied up in litigation or are awaiting approval.

one of a number of leading indexes. It most resembles a commodity futures contract—and indeed is traded on futures exchanges—but differs from a commodity futures contract in that the underlying "commodity" is not deliverable. Stock index futures are settled for cash on their expiration date. Apart from this feature, stock index futures work like any futures contract: an individual hands over margin money to his broker, who buys or sells a futures contract pegged to a market average. Since their inception, stock index futures have proven themselves as popular trading vehicles. The first sign of success when the exotic new "commodity" commenced trading in Kansas City in February 1982 was record-breaking volume for a new commodity contract. During the first month of trading, 44,000 contracts of the new Value Line stock index changed hands at the Kansas City exchange. Shortly thereafter, futures exchanges in New York and Chicago entered the stock index game—again to record-setting volume. With a potential bonanza in the offing for the exchange that gathers the major share of business, a number of exchanges rushed to introduce the new stock indexes.[2] Not surprisingly, with so much at stake (there are 32 million Americans who own stock versus just 150,000 to 300,000 who regularly trade futures), many of the initial attempts to trade the indexes were challenged in court. After a while it got so you needed a scorecard to keep track of the status of a proposed index. The Chicago Board of Trade, the nation's largest and oldest commodity exchange, wanted to trade a stock index based on the Dow Jones averages. But Dow Jones & Company, calling the Board of Trade's plans "an abuse of Dow Jones's name and property rights," didn't want its name associated with futures trading in which there are a large number of losing traders. The Chicago Board of Trade suggested using the index but dropping the Dow Jones name—a suggestion which prompted Dow Jones to take the Board of Trade to court. Dow Jones subsequently won its court case, and at this time the Chicago Board of Trade is without

[2] In the futures business, as in life itself, success begets success. At the time of this writing, the Chicago Mercantile Exchange's Standard & Poor's 500 index contract is leading in terms of volume and open interest. While not the first to introduce index futures, the Chicago Mercantile Exchange is perhaps the most innovative and aggressive commodity exchange in the country. Since speculators and hedgers alike want to trade the most liquid markets, you can expect the Standard & Poor's 500 contract to remain the most popular.

a stock index futures contract. A similar case occurred in New York when the Commodity Exchange, Inc., known as the Comex among commodity traders, was preparing to trade an index based on Standard & Poor's 500 stock index. The Comex wanted to call the index the Comex 500. But Standard & Poor's had already entered into an agreement with the Chicago Mercantile Exchange for use of its name. Standard & Poor's won its case. As a result, the three stock index futures trading today all have the blessing of the firms whose names appear in the index title. The three stock index contracts are listed below.

1. The Value Line Average Stock Index Futures Contract. The first stock index futures contract, which commenced trading February 24, 1982, at the Kansas City Board of Trade, the Value Line stock index is based on the Value Line composite average, which is a geometric index of approximately 1,700 actively traded stocks. Using a 1967 base period of 100, the index is computed every three minutes and widely distributed over the major wire services and ticker systems. Nearly 90 per cent of the issues comprising the index are traded on the New York Stock Exchange. The contract's size is always 500 times the quoted price. Thus, a quote of $100.00 corresponds to a contract value of $50,000; a quote of $150.00 corresponds to a contract value of $75,000; $200.00 to a $100,000 contract, and so on. As with all index futures, the settlement is in cash on the last day of trading, when the futures price becomes the actual cash settlement price of the index on that day. (Unlike agricultural commodities, in which the actual commodity is delivered upon expiration, it would be impractical to deliver a representative sample of a market average. For this reason settlement is in cash on the last day of trading. This feature ensures that any attempts to "squeeze," "corner," or otherwise manipulate a stock index will not work.)

2. The Standard & Poor's 500 Stock Index Futures Contract. The contract that has proven to be the most popular among the stock index futures to date, the S&P 500 stock index futures contract is traded on the new Index and Options Market division of the Chicago Mercantile Exchange. Like the Value Line index, the S&P index value is 500 times the quoted price and the minimum fluctuation is .05, which is equivalent to a $25 change in the value of the contract. The underlying Standard & Poor's index is one of the U.S. Commerce Department's 12 leading economic indicators. It is made up of 400 industrials, 40 public utilities, 20 transportation companies, and 40 financial companies and represents approximately 80 per cent of the value of all issues traded on the New York Stock Exchange. A "weighted" index that gives greater representation to companies with more stock outstanding, it is calculated by multiplying the shares outstanding of each of the 500 stocks by its market price. These amounts are then totaled and compared to a 1941-43 base period. The final settlement day occurs on the third Thursday of the contract month. At the close of trading on that day, all trades are marked to the market of the *actual* index and the settlement is made in cash.

3. The New York Stock Exchange Composite Index Futures Contract. This third entry into the stock index sweepstakes is traded on the New York Futures Exchange, a subsidiary of the New York Stock Exchange. The exchange's first primary contract, the stock index futures contract is almost singularly responsible for saving the NYFE (pronounced "knife") from extinction and raising its seat value over 200 per cent in a matter of months. The new contract resulted in record-setting volume on the NYFE when it first started trading and also set a record for the number of stock index futures contracts traded on opening day on any exchange. Based on a market-weighted average of the value of all the common shares listed on the NYSE, the closing index value is widely reported in major newspapers and other mass media. The size of the contract, like other index futures, is 500 times the value of the quoted price.

BUYING AND SELLING INDEX FUTURES—
THE SPECULATIVE APPROACH

Index futures enable you to speculate on the future direction of specific market averages without taking a position in the stock market. This speculative use of index futures is quite risky because of the high leverage involved when you bet on ups and downs in the stock market. The buyer or seller of the index futures deposits only a good-faith margin deposit with a commodity broker (or a stock broker who is licensed to deal in commodity futures) that usually amounts to about 10 per cent of the value of the underlying contract.[3] As a result, a modest 10 per cent adverse move in the underlying stock index will translate into a 100 per cent loss in margin. Prior to reaching the stage where one's equity is wiped out, however, the broker will contact you for additional margin. If you hesitate to supply additional funds, the position will be automatically liquidated and you will be out of the market—at a considerable loss.

Looking at the high-leverage situation in a more positive light, the same 10 per cent move in a favorable direction will translate into a 100 per cent profit on margin. Leverage is clearly a double-edged sword. But the stock index futures trader must also be aware that his loss is by no means limited. In fact, as long as he continues to hold a position, he is liable for the entire movement of the underlying contract.

Stock index futures can be very profitable for the stock investor who enjoys the action of the futures market. The simplest strategy is to buy a stock index futures contract if you are bullish on the underlying stock market average and sell such a contract if you are bearish. Selling short futures contracts involves none of the problems associated with selling short in the securities market. You don't need an uptick to sell short futures, nor do you have to borrow anything as you do in the security market.

We'll assume you are bullish on the stock market averages and that you wish to buy one contract of the Value Line stock index contract traded in Kansas City. Where do you begin? First, you'll want to acquire a basic understanding of what a stock index futures contract is and how to go about purchasing or selling the index futures. If you look on the commodities page of a major newspaper, you'll find the previous day's quotations listed according to the futures groups—metals, livestock, grains, foods, financials, stock indexes—or according to the exchange where the various futures contracts are traded. We'll reproduce in Table 33 the quotations for the Kansas City Value Line stock index contracts as they appeared in the New York *Times* on June 30, 1982. The quotations, of course, apply to the previous trading day, June 29, 1982.

[3] Margin in the futures market is merely a good-faith deposit. No money is borrowed and, hence, no interest paid on margin monies.

Table 33

VALUE LINE STOCK INDEX (KCBT)
$500 × Index Number

Season			High	Low	Close	Change	Open Interest
High	Low						
121.60	115.70	Jun	120.85	120.00	120.40	−.05	1,030
135.15	112.80	Sep	121.50	119.80	120.45	−.60	3,103
136.00	112.70	Dec	121.35	119.90	120.55	−.45	792
136.60	113.90	Mar	122.00	121.15	121.15	−.35	69
137.15	116.05	Jun	.....	.....	121.75	−.75	81
137.70	116.00	Sep	.....	.....	122.25	−.75	75

Previous sales: 2,156
Previous day's open interest: 5,153, up 319

The letters in parentheses next to the contract title identify the exchange on which the futures contract is traded, the Kansas City Board of Trade. Just below the title, the phrase, "$500 × Index Number" means the value of the contract is 500 times the index number. Therefore, on a day when the contract closes at 120.00, the value of the underlying contract will be 500 times as much, or $60,000. The season high and low represents the respective high and low prices at which a particular futures month traded during the life of the contract. Since contract months expire and others are introduced as time moves along, the months will repeat. The Kansas City Value Line contract trades in just four delivery months: June, September, December, and March. Six months are shown because six contract months are currently trading, but the distant June and September contracts are for June 1983 and September 1983. The first four contract months are for delivery in 1982.

The open interest measures how many contracts are currently outstanding—how many remain "open" in the sense that buyers have yet to sell and sellers have yet to buy. For instance, if you were to buy a stock index futures contract and held the contract, the open interest would increase by one. When you sell the futures contract, you decrease the open interest by one. Open interest is important, since it tells you which months enjoy the widest participation. In the Value Line example, the September 1982 contract clearly enjoys the greatest open interest. As a rule, you should always trade the contract month that has the largest open interest. Wide participation in a futures contract means there will be many traders to "take the other side"—to sell to when you are buying, and vice versa. The more traders competing for your purchase or sell order, the more favorable and equitable the fill price is apt to be. At the bottom of Table 33 is listed the previous day's sales and open interest and the change in the latter.

Looking at the quotations, you know that the September 1982 contract is probably the best to trade, since it enjoys the widest number of participants. When the September contract reaches maturity, all trading will cease and the settlement price of the *actual* Value Line index will determine whether all positions will be credited or debited that day. For instance, if you bought September futures at 115.00 and it settles at 120.00, the 500 points will be credited to your account. Since each point is valued at $5, your total profit will be $2,500. If, on the other hand, you had sold short September futures at 115.00 and the September contract expired at 120.00, the 500 points would be deducted from your account and you would have a loss equal to $2,500. Most traders do not hold futures contracts to expiration, although you can if you wish. Rather, you will offset by selling a previously acquired position or by selling or covering a previous short sale. The difference between where you buy and sell alone will determine your profit or loss.

According to the newspaper quote, the September 1982 Value Line stock index futures contract had a range from high to low of 170 points on the trading day, June 29, 1982. This represents five times as much in dollars, or $850 in value on the day. The "Change" column measures the difference between the previous close and today's close. For the day quoted, the market declined by 60 points or $300 from the previous day.

To participate in any price increase in a stock index futures contract, you'll have to deposit margin with your broker. This margin, however, is not the same as the margin you use when you purchase stock. When you purchase stock on margin, you actually borrow funds from your broker—funds on which you'll be expected to pay interest. This is money which you put up to show that you are good for any losses that occur. You don't borrow anything, and, of course, you are not expected to pay interest to anyone. You must always remember, however, that the margin merely shows you are good for any initial losses. If you continue to hold the position and there are losses beyond the initial margin, you'll be expected to post additional funds. Hopefully, you'll be smart enough to get out of any position in which you are losing money long before you lose all your initial margin.

The only real cost you have in purchasing a futures contract on a stock index will be a commission. (Margin isn't a real cost, since the money is returned to you if you earn a profit.) Unlike the stock market, in which you pay one commission for buying and another for selling, the futures market has just one *round-turn commission* which covers one buy and one sell in either order.[4] Commission fees in the futures market are unregulated and range from approximately $15 to $85 per round turn.

We'll assume you buy one September Kansas City Value Line stock index contract at 120.00 on July 1 and sell it a month later at 123.00. During that time, assuming the market made such a move, the value of the contract would have risen in value from $60,000 ($120.00 × 500 = $60,000) to $61,500 ($123.00 × 500 = $61,500). The difference, or profit, of $1,500 would be yours to keep, your only cost being that of a round-turn commission. The initial margin of $6,500 (about 11 per cent of the value of the underlying contract) would be returned to you in full. A record of the transactions is shown in Table 34.

Table 34
BUYING STOCK INDEX FUTURES
July 1
FUTURES
Buys 1 September Kansas City Value Line stock index futures contract at a price of 120.00. (Value: $60,000)

August 1
FUTURES
Sells 1 September Kansas City Value Line stock index futures contract at a price of 123.00. (Value: $61,500)

Net Gain: $1,500

[4] An added bonus in futures trading is that commissions are lower than in the stock market.

If you are bearish on stock market averages, you can easily speculate on an anticipated decline by *selling short* stock index futures. Assuming the same market action as in Table 34, the short seller would find himself in a loss position as prices rise (Table 35).

Table 35

SELLING SHORT STOCK INDEX FUTURES

July 1

FUTURES
Sells 1 September Kansas City Value Line stock index futures contract at a price of 120.00. (Value: $60,000)

August 1

FUTURES
Buys 1 September Kansas City Value Line stock index futures contract at a price of 123.00. (Value: $61,500)

Net Loss: $1,500

As you can see from the above example, the short seller's risk is that the market will rise. If the market price of September index futures had *fallen* 300 points to 117.00, the short seller would have earned a $1,500 profit. To prevent losses from getting out of hand, you should always place stop-loss orders when you buy or sell an index future. As a short seller, you'll want to buy on stop *above* your entry price; as a buyer, you'll want to sell on stop *below* your entry price. If you are new to futures trading, make sure you understand precisely what risk you are assuming when you take a position. Due to the high leverage involved, even a modest rise or fall in the underlying index can translate into considerable profits or losses in your account.

SPREAD STRATEGIES

The would-be speculator who's attracted to the opportunity for profit in stock index futures but is put off by the high risk might want to spread trade index futures. For the stock index trader, there are two key types of spreads—so-called *interdelivery spreads,* between contract months of the same index, or *intermarket spreads,* between stock index futures traded on different exchanges. Because a spreader is both long and short futures contracts, the risk is greatly diminished, since a rise in one month will probably be followed by a corresponding rise in another month of the same or related commodity. This tends to greatly decrease risk, since what you lose on one leg you gain on another. How, then, you might ask, do you profit? You profit because the legs might rise or fall at different rates. Thus, if you gain more on the leg you purchase than you lose on the leg you short, you have an overall net profit; conversely, if the market averages decline and you gain more on the leg you short than you lose on the leg you purchase, again the result is a profit. Thus, the spread trader attempts to make money on a *change in the differential between two contract months.*

Spread relationships tend to "get out of line" from time to time, presenting opportunities for profit. For instance, if December Value Line index futures tend to trade, say, 60 points *below* September, there is money to be made if the December contract is trading *over* the September futures. The spreader simply sells December and buys September and awaits the traditional normal pattern to return. Put another way, spreading involves selling overpriced contracts and buying undervalued contracts—and, hopefully, profiting from the difference. As a rule, the spreader is not so much interested in the direction of the overall market but in the changing differential between the contract months he spreads.

A simple interdelivery spread in index futures would involve simultaneously buying and selling two contract months of the same index. Let's assume that, for whatever reason, you think the June '83 Value Line stock index futures contract is *undervalued* in terms of the March '83 contract. That is, given a price rise, you think the distant June contract will rise faster than the nearer March contract. For that matter, in the event of a price *decline,* you suspect the June contract would show more strength and decline at a *slower rate* than the March contract. As a result of your thinking, you instruct your broker to spread the June and March Value Line average stock index futures. Specifically, you tell your broker to *buy* June '83 and *sell* March '83. Naturally, which contracts you buy and sell are vital to the success of the spread. You may or may not provide your broker with a price *limit* on the spread, specifying the *differential* you seek—say, June 50 points over March. You aren't particularly concerned about the absolute prices of the two contracts but the relative difference between the two months. Let's assume the spread order is filled at June 50 points over March (or March 50 under; it means the same thing), and you await price developments. Now, say in two months' time, by March 15, just prior to the expiration of the March contract, the June futures contract has actually risen 50 points, whereas the March contract has stayed the same. Obviously, the spread relationship has changed. The long June futures contract has gained 50 points, whereas the short March contract has neither gained nor lost. The result: a profit on the spread. We'll assume you purchased June at 112.50 and sold March at 112.00 on January 15. The spread was taken off on March 15 when June was trading at 113.00 and March was unchanged at 112.00. Table 36 shows the transactions.

Table 36

INTERDELIVERY STOCK INDEX SPREAD

January 15

June '83 VLA Stock Index	*March '83 VLA Stock Index*
Buys 1 June '83 Value Line stock index futures contract at 112.50. (Value: $56,250)	Sells 1 March '83 Value Line stock index futures contract at 112.00. (Value: $56,000)

March 15

Sells 1 June '83 Value Line stock index futures contract at 113.00. (Value: $56,500)	Buys 1 March '83 Value Line stock index futures contract at 112.00. (Value: $56,000)
Gain: $250	Gain: $0.00

Net Gain/Loss: +$250

As Table 36 shows, the spreader made a profit. In general, contract months tend to move together, although at not the same rate. This is why spreading can be profitable. It is also why the risk is so much lower than in an outright position. When you have a spread, the gain on one leg is often offset by a corresponding loss on another leg. When you have an outright position, you only have a long *or* short leg. As a result, when you are wrong you have no corresponding position to offset your losses. Interdelivery spreads are lower in risk than intermarket spreads. Understandably, since risk is always commensurate with reward, interdelivery spreads are not as apt to be as profitable as intermarket spreads.

When you trade intermarket spreads between contract months of different index futures on different exchanges, you have a slightly more sophisticated strategy. For one, the *value* of the underlying indexes may be different and you may have to *balance* the two legs of the spreads by buying or selling more contracts of one index and less of another. For instance, at recent trading levels, the nearby contract of the S&P 500 stock index future is valued at approximately $55,750. But the New York Stock Exchange composite index is valued at only $32,025, as compared to a value of $59,750 for the Value Line average traded in Kansas City. What are the implications for the spreader? You'll want to spread two New York stock index futures for every single contract you spread in the Chicago S&P or Kansas City Value Line indexes. The idea is to balance the *value* of the two legs as much as possible. For another, you'll usually spread the *same contract month* in two markets. Because the different indexes existed long before futures contracts were offered on them, there is a longstanding historical relationship between the various indexes. These can be used to devise spread strategies. Let's say that you think New York is undervalued in terms of Kansas City and that you decide to buy two New York September futures at 64.00 and sell one Kansas City September futures at 119.50 on July 1. By September 1, due to overall weakness in the stock market, let's say that *both* averages have declined, but that Kansas City, comprised of a larger number of so-called second-tier equities, has declined further. On September 1, let's assume that the New York Stock Exchange composite September index futures are trading at 58.50 and the Kansas City September index futures are at 108.00. The *gain* on the short Kansas City leg of the spread will be slightly more than the *loss* on the long New York leg of the spread. As a result, the spread will show a profit (see Table 37).

Stock index spreads, like commodity futures spreads in general, involve a trade-off between risk and opportunity. When you undertake a spread position, you are willing to give up a little profit in return for safety. Since this trade-off is an inherent part of

Table 37

INTERMARKET STOCK INDEX SPREAD— NEW YORK vs. KANSAS CITY

July 1

New York Stock Exchange Composite Stock Index Futures	*Kansas City Value Line Average Stock Index Futures*
Buys 2 September New York stock index futures contracts at 64.00. (Value: $64,000)	Sells 1 September Kansas City VLA stock index futures contract at 119.50. (Value: $59,750)

September 1

Sells 2 September New York stock index futures contracts at 58.50. (Value: $58,500)	Buys 1 September Kansas City VLA stock index futures contract at 108.00. (Value: $54,000)
Loss: $5,500	Gain: $5,750

Net Gain/Loss: +$250

spread trading, you shouldn't defeat the purpose of spreads—namely, safety—by misusing them and asking them to do a job for which they are not suited. This means you shouldn't use spreads to lock in a loss on outright positions. Let's say you buy September index futures in anticipation of a rise in the stock market averages. Instead of rising, the averages decline on you and you have a loss. The logical action is to take the loss. But some traders might decide to spread the loss by selling, say, a December index futures contract against the long September contract. The spread will only ensure that the paper loss stays locked in for the time being. Sooner or later the loss must be realized. So spreading a loss doesn't make sense.

Try to spread only liquid months. When you take a position in an illiquid contract—one with a small open interest—you are only asking for trouble. Every time you buy and sell a contract in an illiquid month, you have to give up a bigger share of your profits to obtain even a fill order. Remember, it is competition that keeps prices between buyers and sellers close together; in the absence of many buyers and sellers, you are at the mercy of the small group of floor traders who are willing to trade with you—to *their* benefit. So let the liquidity of a specific contract month be a guide to which months you spread.

Lastly, have a reason for taking a spread position. Unless there is a reason why one or more months seem "out of line," you may have to sit with a spread position for a long time without any profits to show for your risk and patience. Why have money tied up in margin unless it is working for you? Quite often, contract months do get out of line; but most of the time, there is little money to be made in a spread unless there is a good fundamental reason for the spread changing. Another rule for spreads is to watch the margin requirements and don't overtrade. Because spreads are less risky than outright positions, brokerage houses will provide you with special spread margins (typical spread margins are $1,500 versus $6,500 on outright long or short positions). This may cause you to overtrade. Just because spreads tend to be less risky than outright positions doesn't mean they are without risk. This is especially true of intermarket spreads, in which the long leg may decline in price and the short leg may increase. When this occurs, of course, you lose on both legs. Spreads can be very valuable trading tools for speculators in the new stock index futures markets. But they are not for everyone—especially the novice speculator who doesn't have a firm grasp on the technique and is unfamiliar with spread trading.

HOW TO HEDGE USING STOCK INDEX FUTURES

While speculative-minded investors will be content to buy and sell stock index futures purely for capital gains, another group of investors will look to the new futures contracts as a means of hedging their stock portfolios. To hedge means to take a comparable but opposite position in a related security to protect against loss. For the typical stock investor, who buys securities, the risk is that a market decline will cause the value of his shares to decrease in worth. Prior to the advent of stock index futures trading, an investor could hedge his portfolio by using the listed stock options market. But listed stock options only allowed him to hedge specific stocks; he couldn't hedge the averages. Now he can. Being long cash stock, the natural hedge would be to sell stock index futures. Although a given portfolio will not move point for point with an average, the chances are the average will help offset the bulk of any losses during a general market decline.

The one drawback with using stock index futures to hedge a portfolio is that not every investor's portfolio contains stock which is comparable in value to the value of the index futures. Thus, if you only have $5,000 or $6,000 in securities, you would probably do better by using listed stock options to hedge your position. But if your portfolio is in the $50,000 range or larger, the indexes should do just fine as a hedge.

THE SHORT HEDGE

Suppose, in general terms, that an investor owns a portfolio of stock valued at $200,000. His risk in owning that stock is that a market decline will cause his equity to decline. But if, in conjunction with owning the stock, he sells short stock index futures, a strategy known as a *short hedge,* then the decline in the stock portfolio should be offset, at least in part, by the gain on the stock index futures. Thus, the general rule is: *to protect a net long position in common stock, use a short hedge.*

To realize a meaningful amount of protection, the stock portfolio should be hedged by a number of futures contracts whose value is comparable. Let's look at a specific example. When the New York Stock Exchange composite index future changed hands recently at a price of 64.00, the underlying contract had a value of $32,000 ($64.00 × 500 = $32,000). To make the hedge comparable with the value of the stock portfolio, therefore, the investor would need to sell short six contracts on the New York Futures Exchange. We'll assume he sells those six contracts at a price of 64.00 on July 1. During the following two-month period, the stock market might have rallied, resulting in a rise in the index to, say, 70.00. For the short seller of futures contracts on a stock index, this rise will constitute a loss. His losses will amount to $18,000 plus commissions. (At $5 a point, the investor loses the difference between 64.00 and 70.00, or 600 points. This is $3,000 per contract. Since he is short a total of six contracts, the total loss is $18,000.) During the same period, the value of the stock portfolio will also increase along with the market averages. We'll assume the $200,000 stock portfolio gained 10 per cent in value during the same period, or $20,000. Although the investor was hedged against a decline in the market, he still made a modest $2,000 profit. In this instance the short hedge served as a sort of insurance. The loss on the futures position constituted the cost of the premium on the insurance. Fortunately, the gain on the stock portfolio offset the loss in futures (Table 38).

Table 38

SHORT HEDGE

July 1

STOCK PORTFOLIO	FUTURES
Owns stock valued at $200,000.	Sells 6 September New York stock index futures contracts at 64.00. (Value: $192,000)

September 1

STOCK PORTFOLIO	FUTURES
Owns stock valued at $220,000.	Buys 6 September New York stock index futures contracts at 70.00. (Value: $210,000)
Gain: $20,000	Loss: $18,000

Net Gain/Loss: +$2,000

In Table 38 the rise in the market averages (and hence the gain on the stock portfolio) resulted in the short hedge being counterproductive. But only because the market made a substantial rise. Had the market averages declined in value, the short hedge would have protected the value of the stock portfolio.

Hedging a stock portfolio is specifically designed for declining markets. Using the same example as in Table 38, let's assume the stock average declined to 63.00 by September 1 and that the value of the portfolio declined in value by $3,000 to $197,000. In this instance the decline in the portfolio would be exactly matched by the gain in the index futures (Table 39).

While the investor neither profited nor sustained a loss on the short hedge, he did prevent a loss of $3,000 in his stock portfolio. This is the job a short hedge is expected to perform. As you can see, the short hedge utilizing stock index futures makes owning securities a safer investment.

Stock index futures can also be used to lock in profits on a

Table 39

SHORT HEDGE

July 1

STOCK PORTFOLIO	FUTURES
Owns stock valued at $200,000.	Sells 6 September New York stock index futures contracts at 64.00. (Value: $192,000)

September 1

STOCK PORTFOLIO	FUTURES
Owns stock valued at $197,000.	Buys 6 September New York stock index futures contracts at 63.00. (Value: $189,000)
Loss: $3,000	Gain: $3,000

Net Gain/Loss: $0.00

stock position when an investor is reluctant to sell his stock. There are a number of reasons why you might be reluctant to sell a stock position. You may not have held the stock long enough to qualify for a long-term capital gain; you may wish to continue receiving the dividends; you may want to save money on the commissions involved—and, most importantly, you may consider an anticipated market decline only temporary. You may anticipate a significant market rise in the months ahead and not want to sell the stock. At the same time, you aren't willing to let the profit you've already earned on the stock slip away. How can the short hedge help? By selling stock index futures, you may also earn a profit as the market declines, thus locking in profits without selling the stock. Thus, the short hedge can help you maintain your profit level despite a downturn in the price of the stock you own.

Suppose that some time ago you purchased 2,000 common shares of Johnson & Johnson at an average price of 23. Your cost was $46,000 plus commissions. Now let's say Johnson & Johnson is trading at 39½ and your shares are worth $79,000. For tax reasons you'd prefer not to sell the stock at this time, although you have reason to believe the shares are overbought and ready for a decline. To preserve your paper profits, you might put on a short hedge by selling two March New York Stock Exchange composite index futures on the New York Futures Exchange.

We'll assume the March contract is trading at 64.00 (value: $32,000). Because the stock is valued at $79,000, you'll sell two stock index futures valued at $64,000. (Note: it will not always be possible to match exactly each leg of a hedge.) We'll assume it is July 1 and that you hold the short hedge until the following March 1 when Johnson & Johnson shares are trading at 30, following a 9½ point decline. The total paper loss on the shares will now be $19,000, since they are valued at only $60,000. This $19,000 represents your paper loss on the shares you still own.

At the same time, we'll assume the market averages likewise made a broad decline. The New York composite averages for March delivery have declined to 50.00 from 64.00, a 14-point decline. Since you sold the index futures at 64.00 and are now able to buy them back at 50.00, your profit is $14,000 on the two contracts ($14.00 × 500 = $7,000; $7,000 × 2 = $14,000). This profit offsets more than 70 per cent of the loss. The net loss is $5,000, as compared to a loss of $19,000 in an unhedged position (see Table 40).

Table 40

SHORT HEDGING A STOCK PROFIT

July 1

STOCK PORTFOLIO	FUTURES
Owns 2,000 shares of Johnson & Johnson valued at $79,000 with stock at 39½. (Shares originally purchased at 23 for $46,000.)	Sells 2 New York stock index futures contracts at 64.00. (Value: $64,000)

March 1

STOCK PORTFOLIO	FUTURES
Owns 2,000 shares of Johnson & Johnson valued at $60,000 with stock at 30.	Buys 2 New York stock index futures contracts at 50.00. (Value: $50,000)
Paper Loss: $19,000	Gain: $14,000

Net Gain/Loss: −$5,000

Now that we've looked at how investors who *own* stock can use short hedges in the stock index markets, let's consider the reverse situation. An investor who is *short stock* would use a *long hedge* in index futures. The short seller's risk is that the market will rise.

The long hedge, which is accomplished by buying stock index futures, is designed to offset that risk. We'll take an example in which an investor is short shares valued at $70,000. He anticipates lower share prices which will enable him to buy back, or cover, his short position at a profit. During the time he is short stock, however, his position is at risk from a market rise. To hedge his position, therefore, he buys stock index futures. We'll assume the hedge is placed on July 1 when Kansas City Value Line stock index futures are trading at 120.00 (value: $60,000) and the hedge is lifted on September 1 when the index is at 115.00 (value: $57,500). During the July–September time period, the price of the short seller's stock declines from $70,000 to $65,000 (Table 41).

Table 41

LONG HEDGE

July 1

STOCK PORTFOLIO	FUTURES
Sells short stock valued at $70,000 in anticipation of lower prices.	Buys 1 Kansas City Value Line stock index futures contract at 120.00. (Value: $60,000)

September 1

STOCK PORTFOLIO	FUTURES
Buys back stock position for $65,000.	Sells 1 Kansas City Value Line stock index futures contract at 115.00. (Value: $57,500)
Gain: $5,000	Loss: $2,500

Net Gain/Loss: +$2,500

Since the stock and market averages declined in the above example, it is clear that the long hedge wasn't really required. But knowing the market to be uncertain, the investor used the long hedge to protect himself in case of a market rally. The primary economic justification for stock index futures is to provide a price or value protection mechanism for portfolio holdings. With a hedge, long or short, you won't always make as much money on your stock holdings, but you won't lose as much either. Thus, the stock indexes help to moderate losses—and occasionally gains—

when used as hedging instruments by transferring the risk to those who are willing to undertake it—namely, the speculators.

Returning to the example above, let's say the market rose after the stock trader shorted shares valued at $70,000. The hedge would help him recoup funds he would lose on the short stock position. We'll assume the short stock position *increased* in value (thereby creating a loss in the stock position) by $9,000 to $79,000. And the Value Line stock index futures rose in price from 120.00 to 130.00. In this instance the gain on the stock index futures would not be sufficient to offset the loss on the stock. But it would offset a portion of the stock loss (see Table 42).

Table 42

LONG HEDGE

July 1

STOCK PORTFOLIO	FUTURES
Sells short stock valued at $70,000 in anticipation of lower prices.	Buys 1 Kansas City Value Line stock index futures contract at 120.00. (Value: $60,000)

September 1

STOCK PORTFOLIO	FUTURES
Buys back stock for $79,000.	Sells 1 Kansas City Value Line stock index futures contract at 130.00. (Value: $65,000)
Loss: $9,000	Gain: $5,000

Net Gain/Loss: −$4,000

The relationship between any given stock position and an average cannot be considered comparable on a one-to-one basis. In general, however, the averages serve as a barometer of stock prices and can be used for hedging purposes. In the example above, the position still lost money despite being hedged. The point is, the hedge helped recoup over half the funds lost on the short position.

Hedging is designed to reduce what is called *systematic risk* in the securities market. Systematic risk is the correspondence of a security's price movement with that of the general stock market. To the degree that hedging is effective, it will reduce systematic risk. What it cannot protect against is *unsystematic risk*—that risk pertaining to the business risk aspects of individual stocks. When used as a hedge, stock index futures are intended to be used purely as a supplement to stock ownership. Those who attempt to use the indexes as a substitute for stock ownership will find that they are engaged in a far different course of investment action— one that requires the knowledge and capabilities of the commodity futures trader. There is nothing wrong with being a speculator in stock index futures as long as you are aware that it is not a security you are trading but rather a highly leveraged futures contract with all the attendant risks.

A host of institutional investors will find the new stock index futures contracts ideal for hedging. As a general rule, hedging generally involves *smaller losses* and *smaller profits* than those of an unhedged position. Investment bankers, executors of estates, market makers and stock specialists, underwriters, and portfolio managers—all can profit from the effective use of stock index futures hedging techniques. To illustrate one of the most useful and common examples of using futures hedging techniques, let's take the case of a corporation seeking to raise capital in the equities markets. Typically, when new stock is offered to the public, it is done by an investment banker who agrees to either guarantee the issuing company a "net" price or who sells the shares on a "best efforts" basis. In the former case the investment banker assumes the market risk; in the latter case the corporation assumes the risk. In either case the inherent risk in offering stock to the public over a period of several months can be offset by using stock index futures.

The risk depends on the state of the stock market at the time the shares are offered for sale. If the market is weak, the share price may have to be lowered in order to attract buyers. As a result, it is difficult for an investment banker to guarantee a price when he isn't certain the market will take the shares at the agreed-upon price. Suppose a company intends to raise $4.95 million by selling 90,000 shares at $55 each on August 26. At the same time, the underwriter, who wishes to hedge the stock offering, sells Value Line stock index futures at the Kansas City Board of Trade. We'll assume that September index futures are trading at 154.00

(value: $77,000). Because the underwriter wishes to raise $4.95 million, he'll want to hedge a comparable amount of stock, so he sells 64 contracts at 154.00 (value: $4.928 million). Assuming that the stock market does indeed decline between August 26 and September 20, the day the last of the stock is sold, the actual capital raised may fall short of the desired $4.95 million. But because the underwriter sold Value Line index futures contracts, the gain in the futures market may well offset the loss in the cash market. If we assume the actual net received on the 90,000 shares amounted to $53 per share, the actual capital raised will be only $4.77 million. But if the stock index futures market falls during the underwriting to, let us say, 149.00, the 500-point gain on 64 contracts will amount to $160,000 (Table 43).

Table 43

STOCK OFFERING—A SHORT HEDGE

August 26

CASH	FUTURES
XYZ Corp. plans to offer 90,000 shares at $55 each. (Planned Proceeds: $4.95 million)	Sells 64 Value Line stock index futures contracts at 154.00. (Value: $4.928 million)

September 20

CASH	FUTURES
XYZ Corp. completes sale of 90,000 shares at average price of $53 each. (Actual Proceeds: $4.77 million)	Buys 64 Value Line stock index futures contracts at 149.00. (Value: $4.768 million)
Loss of Planned Proceeds: $180,000	Gain: $160,000

Net Gain/Loss from Hedging Stock Offering: —$20,000

The short hedge helped minimize the loss resulting from a declining market at a time when the underwriters had to offer down the price of shares in order to raise capital. Since the short futures position gained $160,000 during the period of time when the planned stock offering fell $180,000 short of anticipated revenues, the net result was only $20,000 shy of the intended goal. Compared with the short fall of $180,000 on the unhedged stock position, this represents a considerable difference.

ANTICIPATORY LONG HEDGE

Another hedging technique involves the use of futures as a temporary substitute for a cash position in the stock market. Let's say on July 1 a fund manager decides U.S. Steel is a good buy at 18½. He wants to buy about 3,000 shares having a value of $55,500, but is awaiting a quarterly influx of cash which he won't have available until September 1. In this case he might use what is known as an *anticipatory long hedge* by buying futures contracts in lieu of stock for cash. If the market does indeed rise during the time he holds the long futures contract, the profit on the futures position will offset the foregone loss on the cash stock position. We'll assume the fund manager purchases one September Standard & Poor's 500 stock index futures contract at a price of 120.00 on July 1 and offsets the long futures contract at a price of 127.00 on September 1. During the same time period, we'll assume U.S. Steel gains 1½ points and is trading at 20 on September 1. The transactions of the anticipatory long hedge are shown in Table 44.

Table 44
ANTICIPATORY LONG HEDGE
July 1

CASH	FUTURES
Would have purchased 3,000 shares of U.S. Steel at 18½. (Value: $55,500)	Buys 1 September Standard & Poor's 500 stock index futures contract at 120.00. (Value: $60,000)

September 1

CASH	FUTURES
Would have held 3,000 shares of U.S. Steel at 20. (Value: $60,000)	Sells 1 September Standard & Poor's 500 stock index futures contract at 127.00. (Value: $63,500)
Foregone Profit: $4,500	Gain: $3,500

Net Results from Anticipatory Hedge:
+$3,500 Gain in futures market
−$4,500 Foregone appreciation in cash market
−$1,000 Net opportunity loss

Since a broad market index cannot be a perfect hedge for an individual stock, the fund manager would still sustain an opportunity loss on this transaction. However, the long hedge did return a portion of the opportunity loss. As the funds for the purchase of the U.S. Steel shares became available on September 1, the fund manager would have purchased the $60,000 worth of U.S. Steel stock, now selling at 20, for a net price of $56,500, since he now has $3,500 in profits from the futures market to augment his cash purchasing power.

The primary purpose of hedging is management of risk. The simple short hedge serves to minimize the risk of owning securities that may decline in value during the period held (a very real risk, you'll agree, when you consider, for example, that almost 90 per cent of the issues traded on the New York and American stock exchanges and on the over-the-counter market decreased in price during a single quarter of 1981); the simple long hedge, on the other hand, protects those who have to guard against a price rise during the time the hedge is in place. Put simply, you sell index futures (short hedge) to hedge a long stock position; you purchase index futures (long hedge) to hedge a short stock position. All hedging is based on this simple notion that you want to take a comparable and opposite position in the futures market to that of your actual cash position in securities. As an offsetting mechanism, hedging should ease your losses in the stock market, although it will somewhat lessen your stock market gains. Used in this manner, stock index futures provide protection. Overall, it should improve your long-term trading record.

HEDGING LISTED STOCK OPTION POSITIONS

Just as stock index futures can be used as protective hedges against market rallies or rallies in stocks, they are likewise effective hedges against positions you might hold in the listed stock options market. When the indexes are used in this manner they are said to be performing a *cross hedge*. It must be stressed, however, that there is no guarantee that any one stock or stock option will move in tandem with the market averages. But to the degree that this systematic risk exists, the stock index futures will provide hedging protection. Moreover, before you decide to hedge a stock option position, you should think through your position. Does it make sense as a hedge? Is the size of the contract you are using to hedge comparable with the size of the options position? If it is not, you may be in for a surprise. What you thought was a hedge may, in reality, not be a hedge at all but rather two speculative positions—on which you may stand to lose on both sides.

Since call buying is a favorite practice of some speculators, let's examine a call purchase which is hedged by a comparable yet opposite position in stock index futures. Suppose you buy calls on Polaroid stock and want to hedge the position in the stock index futures market. We'll assume that on July 1, in anticipation of Polaroid common rising, you purchase 30 Polaroid October 15 calls at $3¾ when Polaroid common is at $17⅞. Since the 30 calls give you the right to purchase 3,000 shares of Polaroid, the potential value of the stock you control is $53,625 ($17⅞ × 3,000 = $53,625). You next check the index futures markets to decide on which contract to hedge. To provide the necessary amount of protection, you want the total contract value of the index you select to be in the range of $50,000 to $60,000. Moreover, you want to use an index contract month that will still be trading at the expiration of the October 15 calls—to provide downside protection in the event the call loses value. We'll assume you decide to *sell* one contract of December Value Line stock index futures for a price of 119.00.

We'll assume that on October 15, the price of Polaroid has declined slightly to $17 and the in-the-money October 15 call has a value of only 2. Having purchased the calls for 3¾ points, you are going to sustain a loss on the calls. But during the same period of time, we'll assume the market average likewise declined and you *gained* on your short futures position as it fell from 119.00 to 111.00. Thus, the *gain* on the short futures hedge would offset, in part, the *loss* on the long calls. The transactions are in Table 45.

Although the hedge didn't completely recoup the loss on the calls, it did earn more than 75 per cent of the loss. As a result, the net loss amounted to just $1,250, a considerable improvement on the $5,250 loss on the calls alone.

Turning the situation around, index futures can also be used to hedge option *writers*. Suppose that you write calls and, fearful of a *rise* in prices, you buy a stock index futures contract. Any rise in

Table 45

SHORT CROSS HEDGE

July 1

OPTIONS	FUTURES
Buys 30 Polaroid October 15 calls at 3¾ when Polaroid is trading at 17⅞. (Cost: $11,250)	Sells 1 December Kansas City Value Line stock index futures contract at 119.00. (Value: $59,500)

October 15

OPTIONS	FUTURES
Sells 30 Polaroid October 15 calls at 2 when Polaroid is trading at 17 for $6,000.	Buys 1 December Kansas City Value Line stock index futures contract at 111.00. (Value: $55,500)
Loss: $5,250	Gain: $4,000

Net Gain/Loss: −$1,250

prices would be offset by a corresponding gain in futures. A decline in prices, however, would provide you with a profit on your short call option position and a loss on the futures position. Let's take an example. Let's say you write 20 Pitney Bowes 30 calls when Pitney is trading at 31¾ on July 1 for a premium of 3¼ each. The net writing income will be $6,500 ($325 × 20 = $6,500). Since you don't own the shares, the potential exposure on the 2,000 shares covered by the calls is $63,500 ($31.75 × 2,000 = $63,500). To hedge this risk, we'll assume you *purchase* one December S&P 500 stock index futures contract at a price of 124.00 (value: $62,000). By October 15 the Pitney shares have declined ¾ point to 31 and the time value of the calls has disappeared. As a result, the Pitney October 30 calls are trading for a premium of 1 point. The naked writer, therefore, buys back his short calls and takes his 2¼-per-share profit on the 2,000 shares. At the same time, the S&P index has declined to a price of 118.00, resulting in a $3,000 loss in futures. Happily, the gain on the calls was larger than the loss on the futures. The result: a net gain of $1,500 (see Table 46).

In Table 46 the long cross hedge was not needed, since the calls lost value as the naked writer anticipated. Had the calls risen in

Table 46

LONG CROSS HEDGE

July 1

OPTIONS	FUTURES
Sells 20 Pitney Bowes October 30 calls for 3¼ each when Pitney common trades at 31¾. (Receives: $6,500)	Buys 1 December Standard & Poor's 500 stock index futures contract at a price of 124.00. (Value: $62,000)

October 1

OPTIONS	FUTURES
Buys 20 Pitney Bowes October 30 calls for 1 each when Pitney common trades at 31. (Pays: $2,000)	Sells 1 December Standard & Poor's 500 stock index futures contract at a price of 118.00. (Value: $59,000)
Gain: $4,500	Loss: $3,000

Net Gain/Loss: +$1,500

value, however, the naked writer would have found himself in rather serious trouble, since he didn't have the shares to deliver. The long hedge would have protected him in that instance by providing the profits to pay for the shares or the higher cost of buying back his short call options.

It is not necessary to run through an example using puts. The principles are the same. A put buyer's risk is that the stock rallies against him; he would use a long futures hedge to protect his upside risk. Conversely, a put writer's risk is that the stock declines; the put writer, therefore, would employ a short hedge in index futures. Since it is virtually impossible to find a stock that will move exactly with the market averages, you'll have to be prepared for a greater profit or loss on one leg or the other. But if the hedge is properly balanced in the sense that both legs represent stock valued at approximately the same amount of money, the hedge should work most of the time.

STOCK INDEX OPTIONS

Of the eight futures exchanges that submitted proposals for the new commodity options three-year pilot program that was approved by the Commodity Futures Trading Commission in September 1981, three requested approval to trade options on the new stock indexes. Actually, all three exchanges changed their proposals *after* the CFTC deadline. As a result, options on Treasury bonds, gold, and sugar began trading before options on stock index futures.

Options on stock index futures work in the same manner as do options on Treasury bonds, gold, and sugar. An investor will be able to choose between puts and calls at varying strike prices. There will be two sides to every option, with the buyer of a *call* having the right to *purchase* the underlying stock index futures contract, and the buyer of a *put* having the right to *sell* such a contract. The writer or seller of an option on an index futures contract will have his position marked to the market daily, much in the same manner of a speculator in the futures market. To take profits or minimize losses, either buyer or seller of an option will be able to offset his position prior to expiration, or either can wait until the option expires. Upon expiration the buyer of a call is given a long futures position in the stock index at the strike price; the buyer of a put, conversely, is given a short futures position at the strike. Call writers are, in effect, going short futures at the strike price; and put writers have agreed to take a long position at the strike price. The only difference between an option on a stock index futures contract and an option on a deliverable commodity such as gold, sugar, or heating oil is that the settlement is in cash. Thus, if you buy an option on a stock index futures contract and hold the option until maturity, you will be granted a long or short futures position, depending on whether you bought a call or a put. If you then hold the futures to maturity, the settlement will be in cash. On deliverable commodities, of course, when you hold the long or short position to maturity, you will be expected to take or give delivery.

While the introduction of options on stock index futures creates a host of new trading strategies for the speculator and hedger alike, the simplest strategy is to buy a call in anticipation of a rise in the underlying stock market average or buy a put in anticipation of a decline in the underlying average. Why not simply take a futures position in the underlying index? Simple. Limited risk. When you purchase a call option on an index, your risk is limited to the premium cost. When you take a long futures position on the index, your risk is unlimited—and exists as long as you hold the position. Knowing the precise amount of liability one is subject to in undertaking an option position is important. Let's say you purchase a call on December Kansas City Value Line stock index futures at a strike of 120.00. Your premium cost is $1,000. If the price of the underlying December stock index futures moves up to 127.00 during the time you hold the call, you'll have 700 points in intrinsic or cash value in the option. The call's premium will rise to at least $3,500 ($7.00 × 500 = $3,500). Because you paid $1,000 for the right to purchase the call, your net profit will be $2,500. Your risk is that the index doesn't move above the strike when you hold the call. At a price of 120.00 or lower, the call would expire worthless and you would lose your entire $1,000 premium—but no more. The put buyer, on the other hand, would be looking for lower prices in order to return a profit on his investment.

WHEN TO BUY STOCK INDEX CALLS

Stock index calls can be used in conjunction with stock index futures, common stock, or both. This complicates call-buying strategies somewhat but also means additional opportunity. The most basic strategy, discussed above, involves purchasing one or more call options on stock index futures in order to benefit from a price rise. What if you already have a nice profit in a stock index futures position? Does it pay to buy additional futures positions? It depends.

To arrive at a definite answer, ask yourself what you will do if the index future declines. Will you be willing to cut your losses? And if so, where? Remember, you are responsible for the full, highly leveraged adverse move of any futures contract you hold. With an option on a futures position, your downside risk is strictly limited to the premium cost. As a rule, use calls to *add* to profitable positions in the stock index futures market. Then, if your market judgment is found wanting, you can simply abandon the call and take profits on the long futures position that you acquired at a lower price. In the futures market the strategy which uses paper profits to take on additional positions is known as *pyramid-*

ing. While pyramiding can result in spectacular profits, it does have the impact of raising your overall cost. As a result, any decline in prices can easily fall below the new "average" cost of assuming the position, and you can have a net overall loss. Pyramiding is extremely risky. In the event of a price turnaround, you can find yourself drawing from profits in a few contracts to finance the margin on many contracts. To avoid this situation, use calls to add to your position. The cost is known and you maintain the original purchase price on your futures. And if the market rallies, you participate in the full move above the strike on the calls as well as maintaining your normal futures position. One other point: do *not* buy calls to recoup losses on a long futures position. While this may occasionally work in the stock market using listed stock options, in the futures market you want to take losses quickly. Buying a call on an index futures position that already has a loss only compounds the problem. If you have a loss on a futures position, take the loss. Do *not* engage in sophisticated options strategies hoping to come out of such a futures position profitably—especially if you are merely speculating in futures and not hedging a common stock position.

Let's look at an example in which you purchase a call to *add* to a profitable futures position. We'll suppose you purchase four Kansas City Value Line stock index futures contracts at a price of 114.00 on June 15 in anticipation of higher stock market averages. A month later, on July 15, following a rise to 118.00, you have a profit of $4.00 on each of the four positions. This amounts to a total of $8,000 in profit ($4.00 × 500 = $2,000; $2,000 × 4 = $8,000). Rather than purchase additional futures contracts, we'll assume you buy an at-the-money September 118 stock index call for a premium of $750. We'll also assume the call has one month to run prior to expiration. On August 15, September index futures are at 119.00, a modest rise. With a 118.00 strike price, the call you purchased for $750 has a cash value of only $500. As a result, you will take a small loss in the call but will realize an overall gain in the futures position. The transactions are in Table 47.

In Table 47 the upward move was almost exhausted when the single call was acquired. As a result, the call never proved profitable, since the price of the underlying futures contract did not rise the required $1.50 to reach the break-even on the call. With the

Table 47

PURCHASING A CALL TO ADD TO A FUTURES POSITION

June 15

FUTURES	OPTIONS
Buys 4 Kansas City Value Line September stock index futures contracts at 114.00. (Value: $228,000)	No action.

July 15

FUTURES	OPTIONS
September stock index futures trade at 118.00. (Value: $236,000)	Buys 1 September 118 Kansas City Value Line stock index call option for $750.

August 15

FUTURES	OPTIONS
Sells 4 Kansas City Value Line September stock index futures contracts at 119.00. (Value: $238,000)	Sells 1 September 118 Kansas City Value Line stock index call option for $500.
Gain: $10,000	Loss: $250

Net Gain/Loss: +$9,750

strike at 118.00, the break-even on the $750 call was $119.50. Had the prices of the underlying September futures risen above 119.50, the call would have returned more than its cost and it would have continued to add profits as the price rose. Whenever you use a strategy involving options on futures, you must remember that the expiration date on the option is *approximately one month prior* to the expiration date on the futures contract.[5] Thus, September *options* will expire in August, but September *futures* will expire in September. The options market has been set up this way so that you'll have time to exercise the option and hold the underlying futures contract if you wish. It is assumed that

[5] All options should be readily identifiable by their terms. For Value Line stock index options, a September 118 call would be an option to purchase a September futures contract at a price of 118.00. A September 118 put would be an option to sell a September futures contract at 118.00.

most options traders, however, will simply liquidate their options without acquiring the futures contract, just as most stock options traders never acquire the underlying security but rather offset their option positions.

In Table 47, rather than *buying* a call to *add* to a position, you might have *written* a call to guarantee a price of $118.00 on at least one contract. The income of the call would supplement the profit on the futures position and it would provide a cushion of profit if the price of the underlying futures contract had declined in price. Specifically, having written a September 118 Value Line stock index call for a premium of $750, the investor would have gained an additional $250 if the call expired when the price of the September futures was 119.00. The first $500 in profit would go to the buyer of the call; as the seller, the investor would still get to keep the additional $250 of the $750 premium.

ARBITRAGE

The new options on index futures creates an opportunity for sophisticated arbitrage possibilities which should keep computers working overtime. Among the more popular riskless arbitrage possibilities are those involving trading both puts and calls in conjunction with futures positions. One popular strategy is known as a *conversion*. In a conversion, a trader seeks out an underpriced put to buy and immediately writes a call option. At the same time, he purchases a long futures contract in the underlying index. If the market rises and the short call proves profitable, the trader has a long futures position to deliver at the call's strike price. If, on the other hand, the market price plummets, he has a put option to earn him profits below the strike. The key to making this strategy work is to find a situation in which a put is priced low relative to the corresponding call. The *reverse conversion,* understandably, works in reverse fashion. In a reverse conversion, you look for a call that is cheap relative to a put. You then purchase the call and write the put while selling short index futures. If the market declines you'll have the short futures to deliver against the put; if it rallies you'll have a call option to earn profits above the strike—at least sufficient to offset the loss on the short futures—*plus* you'll have the writing income on the put option. It's a heads-you-win, tails-you-win situation—*if* it's done right.

HOW TO HEDGE WITH STOCK INDEX PUTS AND CALLS

Portfolio managers and other large institutional investors will find the stock index options valuable tools in hedging their holdings. Rather than rely on stock index futures for placing the hedge, the institutional investor will pay a fixed premium for a number of put or call options on the index futures and avoid concerns about fluctuating margin requirements in the futures hedge. Instead, the investor will know his hedge commitment at the outset.

The index option hedge works in the same manner as the short or long futures hedge except that the hedger will substitute puts or calls for short or long stock index futures positions.

Let's look at an example in which a fund manager has a portfolio of $400,000 in common stock that he wishes to hedge for about five months. He anticipates short-term weakness in the stock market, and he wants to protect the value of his portfolio without having to sell stock. He decides to *buy stock index puts* to hedge his stock portfolio. On June 15, being long $400,000 worth of common stock, the portfolio manager buys 12 December 66 puts on New York stock index futures for $750 each, or a total of $9,000. The puts are trading at-the-money, since the December stock index futures are at 66.00, representing a value of $33,000 per contract ($66.00 × 500 = $33,000). He buys 12 puts because he wants the hedge to balance out on both legs. Since he has $400,000 in stock, he reasons that puts potentially valued at $396,000 (12 × $33,000 = $396,000) should serve as a good hedge.

Five months later, on November 15, the stock in his portfolio is valued at $390,000, or $10,000 less than its market price five months earlier. As a result, the fund manager has a $10,000 paper loss. During the same period, however, the price of December stock index futures declined from a price of 66.00 to 63.00, a $3 decline. Because the index put options had a strike of 66, however, the put now has $3 in cash value. Assuming that on the day that the December index options expire, the December stock index futures are at 63.00, the puts will be valued at $1,500 each ($3.00 × 500 = $1,500). Since the fund manager has 12 puts, the total value is $18,000 ($1,500 × 12 = $18,000), or a 100 per cent profit on the original $9,000 put investment. Since the paper loss in stock amounted to $10,000 and the realized gain in put options amounted to $9,000, the fund manager will have a $1,000 net loss on the hedge—a far better situation than if he remained unhedged (see Table 48).

Table 48

STOCK INDEX PUT OPTION HEDGE

June 15

STOCK PORTFOLIO	OPTIONS
Owns stock valued at $400,000.	Buys 12 December New York stock index puts for $750 each (cost: $9,000) when December futures are at 66.00. (Value: $33,000)

November 15

STOCK PORTFOLIO	OPTIONS
Owns stock valued at $390,000.	Sells 12 December New York stock index puts for $1,500 each (receives: $18,000) when December futures are at 63.00. (Value: $31,500)
Paper Loss: $10,000	Realized Gain: $9,000

Net Gain/Loss: −$1,000[6]

Turning the situation around, let's say the same fund manager decides to sell short common stock in anticipation of lower prices, but he wishes to protect himself by purchasing stock index call op-

---

[6] Since the fund manager still holds the stock, there is a chance the stock market will rally and the temporary paper loss will later result in a realized net gain in addition to the profits on the hedge.

tiõns. We'll assume that on October 15 he sells short shares valued at $86,000 in anticipation of lower prices. At the same time, he purchases three at-the-money December 64 New York stock index calls for $1,000 each (total cost: $3,000) when December futures are trading at 64.00 (value: $32,000). Now, if the stock declines in value, he'll have a profit on his short stock position; rising market averages, however, will make his calls valuable. His risk is limited to the $3,000 premium cost.

One month later, on November 15, the fund manager realizes his judgment about the direction of the stock market was wrong. The shares he sold that were valued at $86,000 have now risen in value to $102,000. He buys back the shares—covers his short position—and realizes a loss of $16,000. The three 64-strike calls, however, have also risen, since the market has made a broad upward move. December index futures are now trading at 76.00. Thus, the calls, which give the holder the right to purchase the underlying December futures contract at 64.00, will have at least $12.00 in value, or $6,000 per contract, since the index is valued at 500 times the quoted price. Since the fund manager has three calls, their total value is $18,000, resulting in a net profit of $15,000, since his initial premium was $3,000 for the three calls. The result: a $16,000 loss on the stock position, a $15,000 gain on the call option position, or a net loss of $1,000. Considering the alternative to hedging—losing $16,000 in an unhedged short stock position—the mere $1,000 loss is welcomed by the fund manager. The transactions are in Table 49.

The rules for hedging using stock index options should now be pretty clear. If you are long stock, you want to buy puts to guard against a price decline in the shares you hold. If you are short stock, you want to buy calls to hedge against a rise in the price of the shares you are short. Try to balance the hedge by having the underlying value of options comparable to the value of the shares you are long or short. You can use in- or out-of-the-money options, depending on your own attitude toward risk. There are many modifications you can make that will help you "individualize" your own hedge to meet your specialized needs. Those suggested here are only a few of the many trading strategies available to the investor of the eighties.

Table 49

STOCK INDEX CALL OPTION HEDGE

October 15

STOCK PORTFOLIO
Sells short stock valued at
$86,000.

OPTIONS
Buys 3 December 64 New York
stock index calls for $1,000 each
(cost: $3,000) when December
futures are at 64.00. (Value:
$32,000)

November 15

STOCK PORTFOLIO
Buys back stock valued at
$102,000.

OPTIONS
Sells 3 December 64 New York
stock index calls for $6,000 each
(total value: $18,000) when
December futures are at 76.00.
(Value: $38,000)

Loss: $16,000   Gain: $15,000

Net Gain/Loss: −$1,000

THE FUTURE OF STOCK INDEX FUTURES AND OPTIONS

Already, stock index futures and options are being called *the*
market of the eighties. This brief introduction to these new markets should acquaint you with just some of the *possibilities* of this
important and innovative investment vehicle. Not only can the
new markets improve investment performance, but they help to
expand an investor's strategies and provide greater adaptability
and versatility—the precise tools needed to cope with the changing
investment climate. Significantly, and often contrary to popular
belief, the new index and options markets make the ownership of
common stock *safer* than ever before. This has at least two important implications. From an economic standpoint these new investment vehicles will enhance the ability of the equity markets to
raise much needed capital in the years ahead. There is a very important economic justification for their existence. From an investment standpoint the versatility provided by the new markets will
result in a proliferation of trading strategies—all designed to reap

profits for the investor who understands that *flexibility* and *timing* will be the key to success in the stock market of the eighties. In the years ahead, more and more of the 32 million institutional and small investors who currently trade stocks will turn toward these innovative markets. The ranks of the index and option traders will increase as investors come to appreciate that, while risk will never disappear in an uncertain world, the ability to manage investment risks *has* changed. This should work to everyone's advantage, the conservative-minded and speculative-minded alike. Thanks to these exciting new markets, you can now take a more active role in your investment future.

Glossary

ASKED   The price at which a potential seller is willing to sell. Also known as the offer.

AWAY FROM THE MARKET   A stock option for which the strike price is a substantial distance from the current price of the stock.

BEARISH   The investment attitude of an investor who believes a stock or stocks will decline.

BEAR SPREAD   Selling the lower strike call and buying the higher strike call. The reverse of the bull spread. Also called a *bear horizontal spread*.

BETA   A figure which measures the amount by which a particular stock is likely to change price relative to a given move in the stock market as a whole. A measurement of 1 suggests the stock is likely to move in tandem with the market as a whole. Higher-volatility stocks will have a Beta in excess of 1 and lower-volatility stocks will have a Beta less than 1.

BID   A proposal to *buy* a definite option or commodity futures contract at a specified price which is made on an exchange floor and is subject to immediate acceptance.

BULLISH   The investment attitude of an investor who believes a stock or stocks will rise.

BULLISH CALENDAR SPREAD   Selling the near-term call and buying a longer-term call when the stock is some distance below the striking price of the calls.

BULL SPREAD   Selling the higher-strike call and buying the lower-strike call. Also called a *bull vertical spread*.

BUTTERFLY SPREAD   A bull spread and a bear spread together, in which two options share a common strike price with a single option one strike higher and lower. Sometimes called a *sandwich spread*.

CBOE   Chicago Board Options Exchange. The largest organized options exchange in the world. The CBOE first opened its doors on April 26, 1973, and promptly revolutionized options trading. By standardizing expiration dates and exercise prices, the CBOE provided liquidity to options trading and greatly enhanced its popularity.

CALENDAR SPREAD   The spread between two options with the same underlying stock and exercise price but different expirations. Also known as a *time spread* or *horizontal spread*.

CALL   An option giving the buyer the right to purchase 100 shares of the stock for a given price within a given period of time.

CHARTING   The use of graphs and charts to analyze market performance.

CLASS   The group that encompasses all the call or put options offered on a particular underlying security.

CLEARING CORPORATION   A nonprofit organization that handles the accounting of the option trades between members of the exchange. It also supervises the capital requirements of its members and issues exercise notices when options are exercised.

CLOSING PURCHASE TRANSACTION   A transaction in which an investor who is obligated as a writer of an option intends to terminate his obligation as a writer.

CLOSING SALE TRANSACTION   A transaction in which an investor who is the holder of an unexpired option intends to liquidate his position as a holder. This is accomplished by selling in a closing transaction an option of the same series as the option previously purchased. Such a transaction has the effect of liquidating the investor's pre-existing position as a holder of the option instead of resulting in the investor's assuming the obligation of the writer.

COMBINATION   Buying or selling a put and a call with different strike prices and sometimes different expiration months.

COMBINATION SPREAD   Long options at one exercise price and expiration date and short options at a different exercise price and expiration date.

COMBINATION WRITE   Selling an out-of-the-money put and an out-of-the-money call with the stock approximately centered between the two striking prices. The most money that the combination writer can take in is the amount he receives when he writes the combination.

CONSOLIDATION   A pause in a market trend, with the expectation that the trend will be resumed in the same direction.

CONTINUOUS AUCTION MARKET   A marketplace which provides a continuous process for holders and writers of options to liquidate their positions.

COVER   The purchase of stock, or an option on it, in order to fulfill a naked commitment. If you have sold a naked call option and then purchase it in the secondary market as a closing transaction, you are said to have covered your position.

COVERED WRITING   Selling (writing) an option contract involving a number of shares covered by an equal number of shares owned.

CREDIT   A positive balance resulting from an opening transaction.

CYCLE   The months in which options expire.

DEEP-IN-THE-MONEY   An option which has a large value because the stock is substantially beyond the strike price.

DELTA   The amount by which the option will increase or decrease in price if the underlying stock moves by 1 point. The delta of a call option is close to 1 when the underlying stock is well above the striking price of the call.

DIAGONAL SPREAD   A spread between options of the same class that have different exercise prices and different expiration dates. Generally, the long side of the spread would expire later than the short side of the spread.

DISCOUNT OPTION   An option on which the premium plus the exercise price is less than the current market price of the underlying security.

DIVIDEND   The payment by a corporation of its profits to the owners of the stock. A dividend may be either of cash or stock.

EX-DIVIDEND   The process in which a stock's price is reduced when a dividend is paid. The ex-dividend date is the date on which the price reduction takes place. Stock owners receive the dividend if they own the stock on the ex-dividend date. Short sellers of the stock on that date must pay the dividend.

EXERCISE NOTICE   Written statement of an option holder's intention to exercise the option.

EXERCISE PRICE   The price at which the call buyer may purchase shares from the call writer. Or in the case of a put, the price at which the put buyer may sell shares to the put writer. Same as *striking price*.

EXPIRATION DATE   The date the option expires. Also known as the *maturity date*.

FILL-OR-KILL ORDER   An order that must be filled immediately or canceled.

FLOATING SUPPLY   The number of common shares available for trading that are not closely held.

FUNGIBILITY   The characteristic of total interchangeability.

FUTURES CONTRACT   A firm commitment to make or accept delivery of a specified quantity and quality of a commodity during a specific month in the future at a price agreed upon at the time the commitment was made.

FUTURE TIME VALUE   That part of an option's price that is greater than its intrinsic, or cash, value.

GOOD TILL CANCELED   An order to buy or sell an option that remains in effect until it is executed or is canceled by its originator. For example, a GTC order would be to buy one Burroughs April 30, now trading at 4, when it reaches 3.

HEDGE   An offsetting position which will limit or minimize the effect of an otherwise adverse price movement.

HORIZONTAL SPREAD   A spread involving simultaneous buying and selling of options having the same strike price but different expiration months. A horizontal spread is also known as a *time* or *calendar spread*.

INITIAL MARGIN   The minimum margin required when an option transaction is initiated.

INSTITUTION   A large investment firm engaged in investing in securities. Typically, the large institutions consist of insurance companies, mutual funds, and banks.

IN-THE-MONEY   When an option has intrinsic value. A call option is in-the-money if the underlying stock is higher than the striking price of the call. A put option is in-the-money if the stock is below the striking price.

IN-THE-MONEY BULL SPREAD   When the stock is at or above the higher strike price of the spread.

INTRINSIC VALUE   The portion of an option price that represents the cash value of the option. In a call this represents the amount above the striking price for which the stock is currently selling. For example, if the stock is currently trading at 85 and there is an 80-strike call available, the intrinsic value is $5. For a put the intrinsic value is that amount of the stock's price *below* the striking price. The same as *cash value*.

LEVERAGE   The profit potential per investment dollar.

LIMITED RISK   When applied to options trading, it means that the option holder can lose only the amount of his investment and no more.

LIMIT ORDER An order to buy or sell at a specified price or better.

LIQUIDITY Conversion of a noncash asset to cash and back again.

LISTED STOCK OPTION A put or call option that is traded on a national options exchange.

MARKED-TO-THE-MARKET The debit or credit of a brokerage account by the sum of the dollar change in value of open contracts resulting from daily price movements. Performed on a daily basis.

MARKET ORDER An order to buy or sell an option at the best possible price as soon as the order gets to the exchange floor.

NAKED WRITER OR SELLER One who sells (writes) an option without owning the underlying stock, in contrast to a covered writer.

NONVOLATILITY SPREAD A spread that makes money when the stock stays at the same price.

OFFER Indicates a desire to sell at a given price.

OFFSETTING TRANSACTION To take an equal and opposite position in the market.

ON-THE-MONEY An option for which the exercise price is equal to the market price of the underlying stock. Also known as *at-the-money*.

OPENING PURCHASE TRANSACTION A transaction in which an investor intends to become the holder of an option.

OPENING SALE TRANSACTION A transaction in which the investor intends to become the writer of an option.

OPEN INTEREST The amount of opening and closing transactions in each option series. Each opening transaction adds to the open interest and each closing transaction decreases the open interest.

OPTION A legal document allowing the owner to buy or sell a share of stock at a specified price during a specific period of time.

OPTION PERIOD The time period during which the option buyer must exercise or lose his right to buy according to the terms of the option contract.

OUT-OF-THE-MONEY When the option has no intrinsic value.

OUT-OF-THE-MONEY BULL SPREAD When the price of the stock is below the strike price of the option you are buying.

PARTIAL COVERED WRITING Selling (writing) an option contract involving a number of shares that exceeds the number of shares owned.

PREMIUM The amount of money that a buyer pays to a seller for the right to buy (in the case of a call) 100 shares of a given stock within a certain time. The premium is payable at purchase of the option and is not applicable to the purchase price of the stock at exercise of the option.

PRICE SPREAD A spread involving the purchase and sale of options of the same class having common expiration dates but different exercise prices. Also known as a *money* or *vertical spread*.

PUT BEAR SPREAD   Selling the lower-strike put and buying the higher-strike put.

PUT OPTION   Gives the holder the right to *sell* the underlying security at the striking price at any time prior to the expiration date of the option. A put option is just the opposite of a call. The purchaser of a put expects the stock to go down.

PUT SPREAD   Long and short positions in puts.

RANGE   The difference between the high and low price of an option, futures contract, or stock during a given period.

RATIO CALENDAR SPREAD   Done with either puts or calls, selling more near-term options than longer-term ones purchased, all with the same strike.

RATIO CALL SPREAD   A neutral strategy in which one buys a number of calls at a lower strike and sells more calls at a higher strike.

RATIO CALL WRITING   A strategy in which one owns a certain number of shares of the underlying stock and sells calls against more shares than he owns.

RATIO SPREADING   An option strategy whereby a spreader may choose to construct his spreading position by varying the ratio of his long and short options.

RATIO STRATEGY   A strategy in which one has an unequal number of long securities and short securities.

RATIO WRITE   Buying stock and selling a number of calls representing a greater number of shares against the position. (Occasionally constructed as shorting stock and selling puts.)

REGULATION T   The Federal Reserve Board rule governing, among other things, the amount of credit (if any) that initially may be extended by a broker to his customer.

RESTRICTED OPTION   An option that one cannot enter an order to sell (uncovered) or to buy as an initial (opening) transaction.

RETURN IF EXERCISED   The return that a covered call writer would make if the underlying stock were called away.

RETURN (ON INVESTMENT)   The percentage profit that one makes, or might make, on his investment.

REVERSE HEDGE   A strategy in which you purchase calls on more shares than you have sold short. Also known as a *simulated straddle*.

REVERSE HORIZONTAL SPREAD   A type of ratio spreading in which the spreader buys two near-term options and sells one longer-duration option having the same striking price.

REVERSE STRATEGY Strategies which are the reverse of better known strategies. For example, a ratio spread consists of buying calls at a lower strike and selling more calls at a higher strike. A reverse ratio spread consists of selling the calls at the lower strike and buying more calls at the higher strike.

ROLLING DOWN Buying in your existing option and selling one with the same expiration at a lower strike price.

ROLLING OUT A strategy in which you buy in the option you previously sold and sell another option at the same strike price with a longer duration. Also known as *rolling over*.

ROLLING UP Buying in an option you previously sold and selling one with the same expiration date but a higher strike price. This is typically done when the stock has gone up in price.

SELLING A SPREAD A spread transaction that begins with a net receipt of money by the spreader.

SERIES Options of the same class having the same exercise price and expiration month.

SHORT The selling side of an open option or futures contract. To be short an option, futures contract, or stock means to owe it to someone else. Whereas the investor who is long buys a security and then sells it, hopefully for a higher price, the short seller sells the security first, and then buys it back later, hopefully for a lower price.

SPECIAL PUTS AND CALLS Unlisted options traded in the OTC market that dealers have in their inventory. These unlisted options are not traded on the listed options exchanges.

SPECULATOR One who is willing to assume greater than normal risks in pursuit of a rapid capital gain.

SPREAD Being long one or more options of a stock and short one or more options on the same stock, but of a different series, a different strike price, or a different expiration date.

STOCK INDEX FUTURE A futures contract pegged to a stock market average.

STOP POINT The stock price that triggers investor action should the shares of the stock reach that price.

STRADDLE Buying or selling both a put and a call at the same strike price.

STRADDLE BUYING A straddle purchase consists of buying a put and a call with the same terms.

STRIKE OR STRIKING PRICE The price at which an option may be exercised. Also known as the *exercise price*.

SYNTHETIC SHORT SALE A position that is equivalent to the short sale of the underlying stock. It is created by selling a call and simultaneously buying a put.

TECHNICAL INDICATORS Tools used by analysts to predict futures price trends.

TECHNICAL REBOUND A short, reflex rally in a downtrend, sometimes also referred to as a *bounce*.

THEORETICAL VALUE The price of an option, or a spread, as computed by a mathematical model.

TOTAL RETURN CONCEPT A covered call-writing strategy in which one views the potential profit of the strategy as the sum of capital gains, dividends, and option premium income rather than viewing each one of the three separately.

TRADER'S INDEX A market indicator based on a ratio of advancing issues/declining issues divided by advancing volume/declining volume.

UNCOVERED WRITING Selling an option without owning the underlying stock or any equivalent security. Also called *naked writing*.

UNDERLYING SECURITY The security which one has the right to buy or sell according to the terms of a listed option contract.

VALUE LINE STOCK INDEX FUTURES The new stock index futures traded at the Kansas City Board of Trade. The Value Line stock index was the first such stock index futures contract to be traded.

VERTICAL SPREAD A spread between options with different strikes but the same maturity dates. The vertical spread can be a bullish or bearish spread depending upon which strike-priced option is purchased and which is sold.

VOLATILITY SPREAD A spread position in which one will make money if the stock moves in either direction, provided only that it moves far enough and soon enough.

WARRANT A certificate which gives the holder the right to buy a specific number of shares of a company's stock at a stipulated price within a certain time limit.

WRITER The granter or seller of an option contract.

Index